THE
POWER OF
EMPATHY

London: Piatkus, 2000   0749921021

THE
POWER OF
EMPATHY

**A Practical Guide to Creating Intimacy,
Self-Understanding and Lasting Love**

ARTHUR CIARAMICOLI
AND KATHERINE KETCHAM

PIATKUS

First published in the USA in 2000 by
Dutton, a member of Penguin Putnam Inc.

Published in the UK in 2000 by
Judy Piatkus (Publishers) Limited
5 Windmill Street
London W1P 1HF
e-mail: *info@piatkus.co.uk*

For the latest news and information on all our titles,
visit our website at www.piatkus.co.uk

The moral right of the author has been asserted

*A catalogue record for this book is available
from the British Library*

ISBN 0 7499 2102 1

Printed and bound in Great Britain by
Butler & Tanner Ltd, Frome and London

To David

CONTENTS

INTRODUCTION

I would not exchange the sorrows of my heart for the joys of the multitude. And I would not have the tears that sadness make to flow from my every part turn into laughter. I would that my life remain a tear and a smile. . . . A tear to unite me with those of broken heart: a smile to be a sign of my joy in existence.

—Kahlil Gibran, *Tear and a Smile*

This is a personal book. In these pages I tell many stories about my own life, the people I have loved, and those I have lost. I also relate the details of my relationships with patients, professors, students, and colleagues. In these stories I reveal my joys and my sorrows, my fears, hopes, dreams, and moments of despair.

I decided to disclose these personal details only after many, many weeks of agonized reflection. Even after making the decision, I woke up countless times in the middle of the night, tortured by questions. Who would want to know these intimate truths about my life, facts that I have revealed to only a few of my closest friends? Why, I asked myself, do I feel the need to communicate these private experiences to strangers? What lessons do I hope to impart?

These questions reveal the struggle between my professional and personal identities. My training and experience as a clinical psychologist have taught me to maintain tight control over my emotions. I've learned over the years to keep my feelings closely guarded and my personal life to myself, honoring the boundaries that necessarily exist between patient and therapist. Yet from a personal point of view I know that trust is established in relationships when we are willing to reveal our innermost thoughts and feelings. Only when we find the courage to open ourselves up to others, giving up our own perspective in order to enter another person's world, can we hope to create intimate, enduring relationships. If we hold back and "play it safe," we diminish the power of empathy to bring us closer together.

As I struggled with the decision, I tried to put myself into the reader's mind, seeking to understand how I could best communicate what I have learned about empathy through my life and my work. I eventually decided to take that leap of faith and tell my story. Empathy has changed me from the inside out; if I wanted to communicate its potential, I had to be willing to honor its profound effect on my own life.

So I have decided to open up my life to the reader, knowing that my experiences have led me to understand the power and the promise of empathy. I am a clinician who works with men and women, both young and old, who are suffering and struggling to find a way out of their despair, but my primary qualification for writing about empathy is the fact that I am a human being who searches, struggles, and suffers—just like every other human being.

The most meaningful way I can connect with others is to tell my stories. For that's what we do in life when we engage in heartfelt relationships—we tell stories and we listen to stories, and then we take the time to search for meaning in those narratives, hoping to find a common thread, a theme that will point us in a certain direction, a goal to move toward, a light that will shine through the darkness and reveal the pathway before us.

In my work and in my life I have discovered one absolute truth—empathy is the light that shines through the darkness of our pain and our fear to reveal what we have in common as human beings.

It is a flash: a breakdown of the reality of this life that lives in us. At such moments, you realize that you and the other are, in fact, one.

—JOSEPH CAMPBELL

PART ONE

Chapter 1

Empathy's Paradox

Empathy is the capacity to understand and respond to the unique experiences of another. Empathy's paradox is that this innate ability can be used for both helpful and hurtful purposes.

I look at the ocean, and I think about empathy. Sitting on the beach watching the breakers crash against the rocky shore, I know that from one moment to the next this massive body of water is reshaping and transforming itself. As the tides change and the currents shift, everything is in flux, moving, tumbling, rearranging itself. The waves break and recede, eroding the high cliffs, smoothing the sharp edges of 350-million-year-old rocks. Clouds create their shadow places on the water's surface, while the sun's bright shafts create turquoise patches of shifting light. At night, from a distance, the water looks like glass on which the moon etches a silver pathway.

Looking at the ocean from my place on the beach, I can be lulled into thinking that I know and understand its depths. Yet the truth is that for every bit of knowledge I have acquired there remain manifold mysteries to be explored. And so it is with human beings. Looking at the exterior we can convince ourselves that we understand the depths. How often do we observe the people in our world and imagine that we know them from the inside out? How often are we surprised by a shifting current of opinion or a tidal wave of emotion that brings new insight and understanding?

As the tides direct the ebb and flow of the ocean, so does the power of empathy surge within us. Empathy is an innate force, part of our biological inheritance, giving us energy, direction, and purpose in life. Empathy is not a feeling or sensation that suddenly washes over and engulfs us, but an intelligent, deeply respectful exploration of what lies beneath the surface of our world. Helping us maintain a sense of balance and perspective in an ever-changing landscape, empathy teaches us how to flex and bend, letting go of our preconceptions and entering into our relationships with open hearts and open minds.

I define empathy as the capacity to understand and respond to the unique experiences of another. Empathy's paradox is that this innate ability can be used for both helpful and hurtful purposes. Like the ocean's currents, empathy can be gently soothing at one moment and fiercely destructive in the next. I always think of Lisa's story when I am trying to convey the healing, nurturing power of empathy.

A tall, attractive woman in her mid-thirties, Lisa was clearly in a hurry the first time I met her. She shook my hand and introduced herself, then sat down, placing her large leather briefcase on the floor next to the chair. Her movements were crisp and efficient. Every few minutes she would glance at her watch.

"In a first meeting I usually take a few notes," I said. "Is that okay with you?"

She frowned slightly. "I'm not sure you need to do that," she said. "I know you're a psychologist, but I'm not looking for long-term therapy. I heard you have an expertise in alternative medicine, and I need something like a vitamin or herb to calm me down and help me sleep. Maybe when I'm not so busy, I can think about a stress reduction course, but right now I just need something to help me get through the day."

Lisa's desire for a quick solution and her obvious discomfort with the idea of exploring anything deeper than her surface symptoms led me to slow things down a bit. Something was driving her, and if I was going to help her, I needed to understand what it was. "I would be happy to answer your questions about vitamins and herbs and their potential to reduce stress," I said. "But first I need to understand more about you. I can hear that you want something right now, but I don't think it would be very responsible of me to give you advice without understanding more about your situation. Do you mind if I ask you a few questions?"

Lisa's frown lines deepened and her mouth tightened in a *This is not what I expected* expression. "Well, okay, if you think it's absolutely necessary," she said, pointedly gazing out the window and shifting uncomfortably in her chair.

I thanked her for her patience and began to ask her the standard questions. Was she married? Yes. Children? Two young daughters, six and eight years old. Occupation? A mid-level executive with a Boston technology firm, just received a big promotion, travels frequently, works ten-hour days. Parents' ages?

"My mother is 65," she said. "I have two sisters and a brother, all older. I'm the baby of the family."

"You didn't mention your father," I said.

"My father is deceased," she said. I noticed that the skin around Lisa's eyes was suddenly soft and moist.

"I'm sorry," I said. "Would you mind telling me when he died?"

"Three years ago," she said, biting her lip. "He died in April."

"He died three years ago this month," I said.

Lisa nodded her head and then abruptly leaned down to look for something in her purse. That quick, involuntary action told me that we had arrived at a place of deep emotional importance. I watched as she continued to rummage around in her purse, keeping her eyes downcast; all I could see was the top of her head. After a moment, she straightened up and offered me a weak smile. "Sorry," she said, holding a wad of Kleenex in her hand.

"That's okay," I said. "I think I understand."

"You do?" she asked, dabbing at the corners of her eyes with the tissue.

"You only get one," I said.

"One? One what?"

"One father," I said.

She looked at me for a moment, and it was as if something inside her suddenly gave way. She sighed deeply, and her eyes filled with tears. "I start crying whenever I talk about him," she said apologetically. "My sisters tell me I should get over it. They say I'm acting like a baby."

"I may not fully understand your situation," I said, "but I have a hard time thinking that because you have tears for your father, you're a baby."

The tears began to fall down her cheeks, and she made only a half-hearted attempt to stop them.

"Your tears tell me that you have very deep, very powerful feelings about your father," I continued.

"Yes," she said. "I loved him very much. I miss him terribly."

"I think your reaction to his death is very understandable," I said.

"Even after three years?"

"Definitely," I said.

"So you understand what I'm going through?" she said, her eyes searching mine.

"I think I do," I said, "but I'm sure there is much more to learn."

A moment passed and then Lisa eased back in her chair and gave me a very sad, very weary smile. She began to talk about her husband, who had been laid off from his job a year earlier and was suffering from a serious depression. She said she didn't know how they would be able to make the mortgage payments for their expensive home, and she expressed concern about how her young children were coping with her long workdays and her husband's depression.

"I feel like the dam burst," she said at the end of the session. "I've been putting all this energy into pretending that everything is okay. Admitting that it's not okay is a huge relief."

This was a moment of empathic understanding, in which Lisa's self-awareness suddenly broadened and deepened. With empathy directing the interaction, her world gradually expanded, and she could see what she had not been able to see before. With new insight into her grief and her fears, she had a better understanding of herself and her sometimes difficult relationships with her sisters, her husband, and her children. With this expanded perspective, she resolved to take the time to explore her emotions and work on strengthening her relationships with her family members. Empathy, which always involves honest self-appraisal, offered her a new direction and revealed the possibilities for self-transformation.

It would have been so easy at the beginning of that session to comply with Lisa's wishes, talking about the stress in her life and offering her some helpful advice on herbs and vitamins. She would have taken the herbs and perhaps, in the short run, they would have made a difference. But her pain would not have gone away.

With empathy guiding my way, I knew that giving Lisa what she wanted was not necessarily the same as giving her what she needed. Looking beneath the surface led me to a deeper respect for her struggles and her pain. Together we slowed things down, a process that was calming to both of us because we were able to enter into a meaningful relationship, talking about the issues that really mattered to her and committing ourselves to a deeper, broader understanding of her unique experiences and the depth of the emotions connected to them.

Lisa's story reveals the constructive, beneficial aspects of empathy, a driving force within us that seeks to understand others, not in a superficial way but in depth. But empathy also has a dark side that can be used for destructive purposes. Kindhearted people do not have an exclusive right to empathy. I will never forget the moment, twenty years ago, when I first began to understand empathy's dark side. I was sitting in my home office reading a collection of scholarly articles titled *Advances in Self Psychology*. Skimming through the chapters, slightly bored by all the theoretical jargon, I started reading an article by the psychoanalyst Heinz Kohut.

Empathy, Kohut was saying, can be used not only for benevolent, constructive purposes but also for destructive ends. When the Nazis attached loud sirens to their dive-bombers, for example, they knew that this strange noise coming from the sky would create panic in people on the ground below. Using empathy—the ability to look into other people's hearts and souls, knowing their thoughts and feeling their emotions—the Nazis could play on their victims' fears in a calculated attempt to destroy them.

Reading Kohut's analysis of the Nazis' sadistic empathy, I was suddenly, passionately excited, for at that moment I understood that empathy is much more powerful than I ever imagined. Kohut's insights into the dark side of empathy revealed both the paradox and the unrealized potential of this innate human capacity. An experience I practiced every day in my interactions with troubled men and women was suddenly revealed as a mystery, with a depth and breadth I could only begin to comprehend. Here was an enigma to be teased apart, for at one moment empathy can guide us to the most noble and uplifting experiences of life—altruism, mercy, self-sacrifice, love—and in the next instant the same capacity reveals the deceptions and betrayals lurking in the darkest recesses of the human soul.

Sadists are not the only people who use empathy to manipulate others. Salespeople use empathy, Kohut continued, when they alternate between a stern, authoritarian voice and a soft, coaxing strategy designed to break down the customer's resistance. This is akin to the way many parents discipline their children, alternating between a commanding "you will do this or else" approach and a tender, loving appeal to the child's emotions. The salesperson, as Kohut put it, "is in the empathic contact with the child in the customer who was once made to obey by similar means, i.e., through near-simultaneous command and seduction."

I had watched salespeople at work, and I knew how the most deceitful among them corner their prey, quietly assessing the most vulnerable targets and moving in quickly and decisively for "the kill." "Look, ma'am," I once heard a car salesman say to an elderly woman, "you *need* a car, you can't keep driving that old thing around, it's not safe!"

In the next moment his stern, parental tone shifted to a warm, coaxing inflection. "Isn't this the softest leather you've ever touched, and the ride is so smooth, you don't even feel the bumps." Then, just a moment later, "I have an appointment in"—looking at his watch—"fifteen minutes, but I can reach my manager right now and get you the best deal you could get anywhere, okay?"

Growing up I was always getting advice from my father, who owned a furniture store and was a gifted salesman himself, about how to deal with con men. My father sold only high-quality furniture, and he knew how to convince customers to choose his superior, if slightly more expensive, products rather than some cheaper imitation. He truly believed in his products, and he was an ethical man, so customers grew to trust him. But my father knew better than most how easy it is to manipulate people's emotions and thoughts. Over the years he learned how to determine if others were truly interested in your welfare or if their primary motive was to win you over in order to get something they wanted.

Of all the skills he taught me, my father placed the highest value on this ability to assess other people's characters and motives. After returning home from a twelve-hour workday, my father would sit down with a cup of coffee and a cigarette, and ask me about my day. I would tell him my stories, and he would offer me his counsel, teaching me in his incomparable way how to look into other people's hearts and souls to discern their intentions. "Always remember, Arthur," he would tell me, holding on to my wrist for emphasis, "that someone who seems like a friend may be using you, and someone who seems like an enemy may only be afraid of you. Look into the other person's eyes. Does he look right at you, or does he avoid looking at you? What is he doing with his hands? Does he shift his weight from one foot to the other? Does he put his arm around your shoulder to convince you that you're his best friend? Always ask yourself, 'What is this guy trying to sell me?' And always, always"—and here he would squeeze my wrist harder—"consider the source."

My father taught me how to calmly and thoughtfully assess other people's character in order to align myself with those who truly cared about my welfare and protect myself against those who wanted only to take advantage of me. I will never forget the time he visited me at work one day and I introduced him to a colleague I admired. Later my father said, "Arthur, Arthur, this is the man you look up to? Have you lost your self? I watched this man when you were talking, and he wouldn't look into your eyes! He didn't listen when you talked, he just waited until you were done so he could get his words in. Then he talked as if he were preaching to the masses." My father raised the pitch of his voice to emphasize his last point. "And did you look at his pants? Arthur, they were three inches too short!"

I burst out laughing, but my father was dead serious. "His pants are three inches too short, Arthur," he said, emphasizing each word, "because he never looks down. He's too high up there, he doesn't care about you or me or anyone else, he only cares about himself and maintaining his lofty position."

My father used empathy as a sort of X-ray vision to size up people, and he passed that wisdom on, hoping to teach me how to see into other people's minds and hearts in order to discern their intentions. Like the psychoanalyst Heinz Kohut, my father understood the power—both constructive and destructive—of empathy. I never associated my father's careful analysis of facial expressions and body movements with empathy, but after reading Kohut's analysis of the ways the Nazis and salespeople used empathy to manipulate their intended victims, the connection suddenly seemed strong and valid.

I was hooked. I wanted to know more about empathy, how it works, how it can be used to influence others, and how people can use it to protect themselves. For it seemed to me that if empathy can be used to manipulate others for destructive purposes—as a would-be rapist might target a vulnerable young woman, gently coaxing her into his car—it can also be used by the potential victim to discern malicious intent. If empathy can be used to exploit people's emotions and direct their behavior in order to take advantage of them, it can also be used to protect and defend oneself. Empathy's sword is also its shield.

As the years have passed I have become even more passionate about empathy. I am not a research scientist, so if you are looking for a scholarly treatise on empathy, this is not the book for you. I'm a clinician—I work with people who are hurting and need help—and my interest lies in the connections between empathy and intimacy. I want to know how empathy can be used to strengthen the bonds between us, offering hope and solace when someone is in despair, stitching together a relationship that has been torn apart by misunderstanding, building confidence, trust, and faith in those who have lost their sense of self. I teach women and men of all ages how to use empathy as an assessment tool, helping them recognize when people are well intentioned and good-hearted and when others may be using empathy in an attempt to deceive or inflict harm.

Although I am not a researcher myself, I will describe the work of various researchers and their fascinating laboratory analyses of empathy. In the last decade empathy has come into its own as a legitimate subject of scientific inquiry. Research psychologists are exploring the different ways men and women express empathy in their relationships, distinctions between automatic (spontaneous) and controlled (intentional) empathy, how our emotions influence our behavior, and, even more fascinating, how facial expressions or body movements can involuntarily elicit specific emotions, like anger, fear, or joy.

Scientists are careful to remain objective, but they can also be passionate about empathy. The University of Texas psychologist William Ickes, one of the most prolific and respected researchers in the field of empathy, makes this astonishing statement in his book *Empathic Accuracy*:

> Empathic inference is everyday mind reading. . . . It may be the second greatest achievement of which the mind is capable, consciousness itself being the first.

First, we are conscious—awake and aware of ourselves as thinking, feeling beings. Then we are empathic, meaning that we are capable of understanding each other on a deep level, actually feeling the emotions and understanding the thoughts, ideas, motives, and judgments of others. Empathy is the bond that connects us, helping us to think before we act, motivating us to reach out to someone in pain, teaching us to use our reasoning powers to balance our emotions, and inspiring us to the most lofty ideals to which human beings can aspire. Without empathy we would roam this planet like so many disconnected bits of protoplasm, bumping into each other and bouncing off without so much as a how-do-you-do, awake but unfeeling, aware but uncaring, filled with emotions but having no means of understanding or influencing them.

By increasing our awareness of other people's thoughts and feelings, empathy shows us how to live life fully and wholeheartedly. Empathy is primarily interested in that process of becoming, enlarging, and expanding, for in truth that's what empathy is—an expansion of your life into the lives of others, the act of putting your ear to another person's soul and listening intently to its urgent whisperings. *Who are you? What do you feel? What do you think? What means the most to you?* These are the questions empathy seeks to explore. Playful and curious, always interested in the moment-to-moment interaction, empathy has the soul of a poet, the heart of a child, and the wisdom of a seer.

At least when it is used constructively, for friendly purposes. For empathy's dark side is an equally important part of the story I will tell. Every day people use empathy to influence you. Your boss convinces you to work overtime by appealing to your work ethic or playing on your fears of losing your job. Your lover coaxes and flatters you, hoping to make you forget an insensitive remark. A child's eyes fill with tears when she does not get her way, in part from frustration but also in an undisguised attempt to change your mind. "Daddy, you work so hard, I feel like I never get to spend time alone with you anymore," my sixteen-year-old daughter Alaina says, her voice filled with compassion. Then she flashes me a winning smile. "So, do you think you could take me and Erica to the mall this afternoon?"

I find my daughter's enticements endearing, even though I know I am being manipulated. That's the point—as long as you know what is happening, you can decide whether or not you want to be a willing participant. Empathy teaches you when it is safe to say yes and when it is better, in the short or the long run, to say no. Empathy knows how to set limits and draw boundaries. Empathy protects you at the same time it teaches you how to open up to life's experiences.

When empathy is used constructively for benevolent purposes, it can mend relationships and heal deep, long-standing rifts between people. In interactions with hundreds of patients I have witnessed the power of empathy to build bridges of understanding. I have watched empathy in action, marveling at the way it can soothe tensions and, at the same time, lead to a deeper understanding of the self. I have come to believe that empathy, more than any other human faculty, is the key to loving relationships and the antidote to the loneliness, fear, anxiety, and despair that affect the lives of so many of us.

Empathy is the bridge spanning the chasm that separates us from each other. With empathy as our guide we can extend our boundaries, reaching into unexplored territory to create deep, heartfelt relationships. Through extending the self, we give our inner lives a dynamic energy and sense of purpose. Reaching out to others, we participate in the most meaningful experiences of life—gratitude, humility, tolerance, forgiveness, mercy, and love.

I believe that empathy can make this world a kinder, safer place to live. When people lose touch with each other, when they focus only on their needs and are quick to judge or slow to forgive, life becomes more difficult for everyone. When relationships with others and with oneself are strengthened with empathy, the sorrows and pains of life are easier to bear. Empathy doesn't cost anything, and it isn't just for the rich, the highly educated, or the well-read—it is for everyone. And empathy is contagious—if you give it away, it comes back to you tenfold.

My fascination with empathy is rooted in the way I was raised. I grew up in a world where people looked out for each other. Neighbor watched out for neighbor. Aunts, uncles, and cousins dropped by for Saturday afternoon visits. Families sat on their porches or front steps after dinner and chatted with passersby. The funeral director knew the furniture store owner, who knew the bank officer, who knew the daughters and sons of the high school football coach. Words like *tolerance, forgiveness, faith*, and *hope* were not just ideals but real experiences, put into practice every day.

In this book I will tell you many stories about the people I have known and the experiences I have had. I will tell you about a conversation my father had with my high school guidance counselor, who suggested I join the Army because my only talent was playing football. I will tell you about a German spy who betrayed my father in World War II and the lessons my father learned from that experience about friendship and deception. I will tell you about my final conversations with my mother in the hospital, when she was dying of breast cancer. And I will relate many stories about my interactions with professors, colleagues, and patients. I believe these personal stories show how empathy works in real life.

Before we begin, however, I need to tell you the story of how this book came to be. A few years ago I wrote a scholarly book about the process of therapy and my philosophy of human relationships. Like most academic books, it didn't reach a large audience. "I found it very interesting," one of my patients told me, "but I'm not sure I understood what you were talking about."

I knew I needed to write a book to reach a wider audience. I also knew that I'd have to include some very personal stories to do this honestly and effectively. I was not sure I wanted to do that. I drove to my best friend Richard Tessissini's house. Richard grew up with me in Milford, Massachusetts, and over the years he has participated in all the joys and sorrows of my life. He loved my parents as if they were his own, and years later he continues to grieve their deaths.

"So what do you think, Richard?" I asked. "Should I write about David?"

Richard was silent for a moment, watching me. Then he smiled, and in that smile I felt all the sorrow and joy that we had shared. "It all begins with David," he said. "He is the heart of it all."

I nodded my head, knowing he was right. David, my greatest teacher, showed me that empathy is more than a philosophical construct or psychological theory. David taught me about the power of empathy to lead us through the darkness back into the light.

Chapter 2

David

Empathy understands the resilience of the human spirit.

D avid was a healthy, handsome young man who lived in a blue-collar town where families had known each other for generations and neighbor looked out for neighbor. A talented athlete with a quick wit and sensitive nature, David had a gentle, open way that made people feel good just to be in the same room with him. Adored by his parents, respected by his teachers, admired by his friends, David felt confident in his abilities and secure in his sense of self.

When David went off to college in 1970, he dreamed of doing something meaningful with his life; he hoped to give something back to the world that had been so good to him. He had never been very interested in academic life, however, and he quickly became bored with his classes. After just a few months he dropped out of school. Hanging around the streets of his hometown, looking for something to do with his life, he became depressed and unsure of himself. He feared that he was making a mockery of everything he had been taught. Seeing the concern in his parents' faces, he felt ashamed of himself.

What could he do without a college degree? His father didn't have a college degree, but he had made a good life for himself. He had been a World War II hero, part of an elite group of soldiers who parachuted behind enemy lines and organized the partisan forces, eventually helping to overthrow Mussolini, the Italian Fascist dictator. Hoping the Army might prove to be his salvation, too, David volunteered to go to Vietnam. At least it was something to do, he figured, a way to prove to his family—and perhaps, more important, to himself—that he was not lacking in courage or motivation.

David never got his chance to go to Vietnam. As college students protested the war and members of Congress began to call back the troops, David spent two years at Fort Dix, New Jersey, and another year in an Army laboratory in Massachusetts, where he volunteered for various pharmaceutical experiments. After his discharge David returned to his hometown and once again joined up with a group of hard-drinking, drug-taking high school and college dropouts. He started drinking too much. He smoked marijuana and experimented with LSD. Eventually he got hooked on heroin.

His parents were frantic to help him. His father offered him a job and spent hours lifting weights with him in a makeshift gym in their cellar. His mother had long talks with him, holding his hand, promising that she would do anything within her power to ease his pain. Admitting that he was in trouble with drugs, David agreed to see a doctor, who diagnosed him as chronically depressed and prescribed both sedatives and antidepressants. David visited his parish priest, who advised him to go to church and pray every day. He took megadoses of vitamins and minerals and spent hours reading self-help books. Then he got high and mocked the simplistic advice.

His family pleaded with him to go into a drug treatment program, but David insisted he could kick the habit himself. During one attempt to get sober, his mother nursed him at home for three days as he shook and sweated through heroin withdrawal. That time he was straight for two months before he started using again.

Early one afternoon in October 1974, David was drinking beer in a neighborhood bar; he was also high on heroin. Some acquaintances sat down next to him and talked him into driving the getaway car for a robbery that night. "It's easy money," they said, "no weapons, nobody's going to get hurt, all you have to do is drive the car." It seemed simple, so David agreed. Everything went according to plan except for one disastrous event—after the robbery the store owner had a fatal heart attack.

One of the men involved in the robbery was picked up by the police that night and jailed without bond. The word was that he would get life. Terrified of being sent to prison, David fled the country, ending up with other American dropouts in a seedy hotel in Amsterdam.

One day David got a phone call from his older brother, who begged him to come home. His brother told him that his parents had hired a criminal lawyer, who assured them that, since David was not involved in planning or committing the robbery, he would spend no more than five to seven years in prison.

"I'll wire you the money for the plane fare today," his brother said.

"I will kill myself if I have to go to prison," David said.

"David, please, think about this," his brother pleaded. "You can't hole up in Europe for the rest of your life. You need to come home. Mom and Dad miss you, David; they can't live without you. They asked me to tell you that no matter what happens when you come back, they will stand by you. We will all stand by you."

"Let me think about it," David said, crying softly. There was a long silence, after which he said, "I love you. Tell Mom and Dad I love them, too."

"We'll work this out," his brother promised. "I'll call you tomorrow to firm up the plans."

After the phone call David walked to the Chinese district of Amsterdam, where he purchased a bag of pure heroin. Back at the hotel he talked for a while with his friends, said good-bye, and returned to his room, where he locked the door and injected himself with a lethal dose. When his body was discovered hours later, the needle was still in his arm.

David was my brother; he was my only sibling. When he died twenty-five years ago, I was twenty-seven years old. I had my master's degree in counseling psychology and was finishing up my coursework for a doctoral degree at the University of Massachusetts.

When I look back on that day and the days that came after, the pain is still with me. The memories are engraved in my mind. I remember the day after I talked to David, begging him to come home. My father and I went out to dinner and then stopped at my grandmother's house, where I called David in Amsterdam to arrange for his trip home. When I asked for him, the woman at the desk told me to hold on for a moment, and then the hotel manager came on the line. She told me that David was dead; he had died, she said, of a heroin overdose. I looked at my father, who was sitting on my grandmother's sofa, gazing up at me with a mixture of hope and fear. Our eyes met and in that instant, he knew. He didn't cry that day; he seemed resigned, defeated. We drove home and found my mother sitting in the dark in the living room. "Ma," was all I said. She stood up, grabbed David's high school picture from its place on the fireplace mantel, hugging it to her chest, and cried out, "He's gone, isn't he?"

I remember asking the funeral director to call me when the plane carrying David's body arrived. I did not want my parents to see him—I did not want them to know that he had killed himself, because I believed that would be too much for them to bear. The funeral director called late one night and told me he was picking up the body at 2:00 A.M. at Logan Airport. I sneaked out of my parents' house at 4:30, walked the eight blocks to the funeral home, and banged on the front door, waking up the poor man and his wife. Still half-asleep he led me past the caskets in the upstairs room, down the stairs to a small, windowless room in the back corner of the basement. The smell of embalming fluid made me sick to my stomach.

I looked at the body, dressed only in underwear, the face severely swollen, and I did not recognize my brother. "That's not David," I said.

The funeral director, who knew and loved my family, gently touched my arm. "Arthur, you must be very sure," he said. "You must not make a mistake. When you are ready, look again." I saw, then, the tattoo on David's arm. I looked at the hair, cropped just above his ears. *"Dad thinks you should get a haircut before you come home; he thinks it will look better in court."* Those were some of the last words I said to David on the phone, just hours before he killed himself.

I never told my parents that David's death was a suicide. I never told them that I read the Amsterdam police report, which reviewed the evidence in painstaking detail, and the official coroner's summary, which unequivocally concluded that David killed himself. I convinced the funeral director to change the cause of death from a heroin overdose to heart failure. The local newspaper editor was suspicious but eventually agreed to print the facts as I presented them.

At David's funeral I watched my father walk around in a daze, smiling absently at the mourners, standing for long moments in front of the floral arrangements with an intent expression on his face. I remember thinking, What is he looking for? At the burial service I was holding my mother's hand when suddenly she pulled away from me, threw herself on top of the casket, and sobbed uncontrollably. I tried to comfort her, but she was beyond reach. I had to pry her fingers off the casket and half-carry her back to where my father stood, his arms hanging helplessly at his sides, his face twisted with grief.

I didn't cry during the funeral. I wondered what that meant. Why couldn't I cry? I stopped eating, thinking that if I felt hunger, I would feel emotion, too, but still I could not cry. I wondered if what I was feeling was relief, and then I wondered what kind of person could feel relief when his brother was dead. Or was I angry with David, knowing that he had ruined my parents' lives, understanding that they would be in mourning for the rest of their days and none of us would ever again be able to recapture what we had lost?

I don't know even today why I didn't cry. I have often wondered if I was too scared to cry—too scared to look at death face to face, too scared to watch my strong father crumble, too scared to know that my mother wanted to die with David.

I returned to school to finish my fieldwork for my dissertation, but I couldn't focus on anything. I couldn't think, I couldn't react, I couldn't feel. I remember my friends asking me to join them for a beer. I looked at them, bewildered. Go out? Drink a beer? Why would I want to do that? It made no sense to me.

I lost faith. My days and nights were haunted by one question: What could I have done to save him? I went over and over my last conversation with David. Remembering every word, I could hear his voice as if a tape were playing inside my head. "I love you," David told me. David rarely told me that he loved me—was that a clue I should have picked up on? Instead, when my brother needed me the most, when he needed to hear the words, "I love you, too," I froze. David was pleading with me for a lifeline, and I left him alone without the words that might have saved him. He wanted to know that he was loved, and in my anger and distrust, having heard his false promises so many times before, frustrated by the way David's addiction had turned his life inside out, and mine with it, feeling sick and tired of the constant heartache, I could not give him the words he needed. I could not bring myself to say, "I love you, too."

When David said, "I will kill myself if I have to go to prison," I remember thinking that he was being selfish and immature. I was impatient with him; I thought he should take responsibility for his actions. Did he hear the irritation in my voice? Did he feel that even I, his only brother and his best friend, had turned against him? He said he would kill himself, and I passed right over it, telling him he had to think about Mom and Dad, letting him know that the family would stand by him, reassuring him that everything would work out. I offered him a Band-Aid, when he was bleeding to death. I negated his emotions and left him alone with his pain because I was unable to cope with my own conflicted emotions. Why didn't I address the threat of suicide, as any good clinician would do? I was angry with him. I didn't want to be manipulated by him anymore and because of that fear, I misinterpreted his talk of suicide. What if I had listened, really deeply listened to him, hearing more than the words themselves, going beyond my own anger and fear to reach into the depths of his despair? What would have happened then? Could I have saved him?

In every book I read, every paper I wrote, and every conversation I had, I searched for ways to understand what had happened to my brother. I hungered to know what had destroyed his spirit and will to live. I retreated into a world of books and papers, filling up my tiny apartment with texts and scribbled notes. I talked to my books, asking them the questions I could not ask human beings. Why did David turn to drugs, and why was he unable to stop? Why did he sever every meaningful relationship in his life? What words would have consoled him, what advice would have gotten through to him, what could I have said or done that might have made him feel understood, accepted, loved?

All the psychological theories about loss and grief, all the tools and techniques I had been accumulating in graduate school could not make my pain go away. Frustrated with superficial explanations, I forced myself to ask the truly difficult questions: Why do people self-destruct? How did David, who had so much, lose everything? What kind of a person was I to respond to him the way I did? Why did I want to be a psychologist anyway? Is it really possible to help other human beings change the direction of their lives? How do you break down the barriers between people and communicate heart to heart?

My questions brought forth one immediate answer—I knew that I didn't want to practice traditional psychoanalysis, transactional analysis, Gestalt therapy, or any of the other standard psychotherapeutic methods. I didn't want to follow a fixed plan of action, reducing my understanding of human nature to one theoretical model. For I realized in the months after David died that I knew nothing. *Nothing.* In my classes and interactions with professors and students, I was constantly amazed by the fact that so few people talked about caring, understanding, the art of listening, or even simple human kindness. Most of my professors and fellow graduate students endlessly discussed concepts like psychic structures, cognitive styles, and counteractive defenses. The emphasis then—and it is even more pronounced today—was on cataloging the patient's symptoms, determining a diagnosis, and attaching a label. The label ("paranoid," "borderline," "manic-depressive," "obsessive-compulsive") automatically determined the therapeutic techniques or drugs that would be used to eliminate the symptoms and, whenever possible, restore normality.

Normality. The word haunted me. What, I wondered, is normal? In his youth David was "normal" by anyone's standards. Handsome, charming, well-mannered, a gifted athlete, loving son, loyal brother, caring friend, David was the model of a healthy, wholesome young man. When he dropped out of school and started drinking too much, he became increasingly despondent. When he got hooked on heroin, he became depressed, anxious, and fearful. When he became involved with other young people who were addicted to drugs, he made bad decisions. When he broke the law and moved to another country, he lost hope. What label, what diagnostic category could contain the whole of my brother?

I heard them all. According to the most popular psychological theories of the time, David was suffering from "depressive illness," "personality disorder," "addictive personality," "narcissistic crises," or an "unresolved Oedipal complex." "He was a lost soul," an elderly relative suggested. "A product of the seventies," offered another. "A victim of drug abuse," a friend decided. "A college dropout with no place to go and nothing to do," offered a neighbor. "A risk taker and pleasure seeker," pronounced a fellow graduate student. "I think the Army did him in," one of David's friends told me.

Each of those theories may have contained part of the truth, but, even when taken all together, they could not explain what happened to crush David's spirit, extinguishing his will to live. The efforts to explain him, to capture him as an entomologist pins a dead butterfly to a screen, diminished the truth of who he was. The theories pulled him apart, piece by piece, until he was merely a collection of disconnected parts waiting to be analyzed and studied, then boxed, cataloged, and stored away.

I vowed then that I would never again reduce individuals to abstractions by attaching labels to their behaviors. Theories and labels may make it easier for psychologists and philosophers to homogenize human behavior, but they get nowhere near the truth of what motivates one person to move in a certain direction while another person chooses a different route. The theories cannot penetrate beneath the surface to expose the heart and soul of the unique individuals who are suffering and searching for a way to end their torment. They cannot speak to the despair that people feel when they are cut off from those they love the most in the world.

What happened to David that made him give up hope? What could have been done to save him? Those were the questions that guided me in my life and my work. I wanted to understand suffering, and I hoped to learn how to alleviate it. I turned to the Bible for solace and wisdom. I read books about Hinduism, Buddhism, Sufism, and Taoism. I studied text-books by famous scholars, obscure papers by clinicians, and self-help books by popular writers. I thought about my mother and my father and the lessons they taught me about empathy as the pathway to love and forgive-ness. "Never give up," my father would say. "Never give up hope," my mother would add.

Why did David give up? I am convinced that David lost hope because he felt disconnected from the people he loved. Isolated by drugs, cut off from his family, believing that his relationships were irrevocably severed, he was like a man deprived of oxygen, gasping for breath. David was dying long before he killed himself. All the turns he made led to dead-end streets; all his cries for help went unheard and unanswered. Backed into a corner by his addiction, overpowered by shame, fear, guilt, and grief, he came to be-lieve that there was no way out.

David's death, ironically, deepened my faith in human relationships. Looking back on his life, I can see all the missed opportunities, the critical junctures where a gentle word or a helping hand would have made a differ-ence. All the wrong turns that marked my brother's final years have guided me to an understanding of how to help people make the right turns, how to listen and respond with compassion, how to reach into the heart and soul of another human being and offer words of comfort and solace, and how to never, ever give up hope. I learned to focus more on the questions than the answers, and I came to believe, with all my heart and soul, in the endless possibilities of growth, change, and self-transformation.

This is the way of empathy. Empathy never gives up. Empathy understands the resilience of the human spirit. Empathy, when used in benevolent, constructive ways, refuses to use the words *lost cause* or *hopeless*.

I am driven to empathy, of course, because I want to save my brother. I want to believe that, if I could talk to David today, I might be able to bring him back to life. During those long months when we all agonized over what to do as David's despair deepened and his addiction to drugs severed every important relationship in his life, I would have acted. I would have called him every day and traveled thousands of miles to tell him, over and over again, that I believed in him, that I loved him, and that nothing would ever stop me from doing everything in my power to help him.

I am driven to empathy, too, because I want to guide others to avoid the mistakes I made and save other families from the torment my family endured.

And, finally, I am driven to empathy to save myself. Empathy healed me, teaching me about forgiveness and helping me create and maintain the relationships that have brought hope back into my life. Every day empathy reminds me that life has meaning, purpose, and direction.

Sometimes patients ask me, "Do you really think I can change? Is there truly hope for me?" At those moments I affirm what I have come to know about them. I point out the specific ways they can grow and the unique aspects of their history that they can understand and overcome. I tell them that I will be there to listen to them, and I will try to respond with respect for their unique thoughts and feelings. I will never lose hope, I tell them, and at those times when they feel as if they cannot take another step, I will lend them my hope and my faith until their strength returns.

With these words I see the transformation in their eyes, the spark of hope, the rekindled spirit. I look in their eyes, and I see my brother staring back at me.

Chapter 3

Wired for Empathy

Empathy is part of our genetic endowment, a gift bestowed by nature to ensure the survival of all living things.

Living through and beyond my brother's death, I learned about the power of empathy to heal even the deepest wounds. Empathy gave me the insights that eventually allowed me to begin the process of forgiving myself. Empathy guided me in my interactions with my parents as they struggled to deal with their endless grief. And empathy led me to a deeper understanding of the creative possibilities for growth and change that exist within all individuals, no matter how troubled or despairing they might be.

I believe that David would be alive today if empathy had guided the actions of those who were trying to help him. I often think about my own reactions to my brother's despair and even now, twenty-five years later, I wish I could go back and change what I said and did. I wish I knew then what I know now. I wish, with all my heart and soul, that I had a second chance to save him.

Patients often ask me, "How do I learn to forgive myself for actions that I deeply regret?" My answer varies only in the wording. "You forgive yourself by not repeating those actions in the present," I tell them. "You prove to yourself, through your relationships, that you can expand and increase your tolerance for others. With each interaction you commit yourself to the process of becoming a more tolerant, forgiving, loving human being."

That is the way of empathy, and it is the only way I know that will take us from despair to hope, from resentment to forgiveness, from fear of our weaknesses to faith in our potential. Human beings are evolving creatures, and empathy is the inner force that allows us to adapt and change in response to our experiences. I imagine empathy as a river that carries us along in its currents, gently guiding us into new territory and revealing the world itself as an unfolding mystery. Without the powerful current of empathy, we would swirl around in the eddies of our own rigid perceptions, caught up in our fears, captured by our past, unwilling or unable to break away. Life without empathy would be stagnant and circular, repeating itself endlessly in predictable patterns with few surprises or mysteries to break the monotony.

Without empathy we would not be able to connect to each other in any meaningful way, nor would we have the desire or inclination to care for each other. We would lead solitary lives, our thoughts disconnected from our emotions, each of us an island with no bridges of understanding to connect one to another.

Empathy is part of our genetic endowment, a gift bestowed by nature to ensure the survival of all living things. If we cannot connect to each other, we will not survive—that is the underlying biological law of empathy, and it is the reason why empathy is not only coiled up in the ropes and twists of our DNA but also tightly woven into the genetic material of elephants, chimpanzees, caterpillars, ants, and even, most incredibly, single-celled organisms. When scientists discuss the evolution of empathy, they don't trace it back to monkeys, birds, or even tiny insects like fleas or mayflies. They start talking about the amazing life cycle of the cellular slime mold.

When I first heard about the slime mold (there are millions of them in a teaspoon of garden soil), I wasn't particularly impressed. I would much rather talk about human relationships and the connection between empathy, intimacy, and self-awareness. I soon became intrigued, however, for, in spite of its lowly origins, the slime mold has many surprising truths to reveal about empathy's life-giving powers and such lofty "human" ideals as altruism and self-sacrifice.

The slime mold begins life as a single-celled organism that is content to sit tight and gobble up bacteria for food. When the food supply is low, slime mold cells find themselves in a precarious position because they are incapable of setting off on their own in search of food. This is where a primitive form of empathy steps in. Responding to a chemical signal called a pheromone—human beings have this same chemical messenger (cyclic adenosine monophosphate) circulating in their systems—the individual cells gather together, metaphorically joining hands to march off in search of dinner. The slime mold cells are able to move en masse through the soil like a tiny tank composed of living, moving parts. When the mass of cells finds a secure resting place and sufficient food, the individuals at the front of the colony die, giving up their reproductive possibilities so that those at the back can feast and prosper.

Researchers who study the slime mold—and many do because the individual cells' ability to communicate and congregate with each other models the way the human fetus develops in the womb—believe that the merging of the cells is governed by "communicative" or "social" genes. These genes encourage the cells to establish relationships with each other and form communities that increase the species' chances of survival. Each cell is able to understand the needs of the other cells and respond in ways that benefit not just the self-centered needs of the individual but the community as a whole.

If a single-celled organism can communicate with others of its kind with such dazzling efficiency, what feats of understanding and insight are available to higher life-forms? Moving up the evolutionary ladder, we find an unusual but definitely empathic relationship developing between ants and myrmecophilous (ant-loving) caterpillars. These caterpillars have "ant organs," specifically designed to attract and communicate with ants. One of these organs is located on the caterpillar's posterior; when stroked by ants this gland secretes a clear fluid rich in amino acids. The ants lap it up, getting a healthy, nutritious snack for a minimum amount of effort.

With a free meal provided whenever they want it, the ants tend to stick around. That's precisely what the caterpillar wants, because in times of trouble you can't find a more loyal or tenacious friend than an ant. When the caterpillar is threatened by a predatory insect like a wasp, it enlists the ants' help by calling on a second "ant organ." A pair of tentacles behind the caterpillar's head emits a chemical signal, which alerts the ants to move into a defensive position, ready to attack any offending creature. If the wasp tries to sting the caterpillar, the ants are prepared to fight the enemy to the death.

Ant-loving caterpillars provide a fascinating look at the precursors of "negative" empathy. The caterpillar dupes the ants into thinking that

their survival depends on the caterpillar's destiny when, in truth, the caterpillar needs the ants much more than the ants need the caterpillar. The
wasp, after all, could care less about the tiny ants—it wants to feast on the
plump, fleshy caterpillar. But the ants have been won over by the free
twenty-four-hour buffet and the caterpillar's ability to communicate with
them in language they understand. With these enticements the ants align
themselves with the caterpillar, willing to fight to the death to protect it.

As animals evolve and develop the ability to think and reason, their capacity for empathy (both beneficial and destructive) progresses by leaps
and bounds. The ability to communicate with others is enhanced by the
capacity to "read" the other's emotions and thoughts. While most people
consider a talent for mind reading to be a thoroughly human trait, more
primitive (or, to be more accurate, differently adapted) species also appear
to be able to infer the feelings and motivations of others.

In *The Beak of the Finch* the science writer Jonathan Weiner interviewed a woman who described a surprising encounter with one of the
birds she feeds every day.

> This one day, I was inside the house, sitting on the bed reading . . . and a
> finch landed on a pillow right next to my head. And I could see that he had
> something wrong with his beak. It was pox. Pox shows normally on feet, but
> sometimes you get a nasty growth on the beak, inside.
>
> I managed to scrape it off. Then I painted the spot with gentian violet. I
> tried to help him out.
>
> I never had a finch do that before—fly right up and look in my face.
> They cock their heads and look at you when you are feeding them, but this
> was something very different. It felt—to get thoroughly anthropomorphic—
> like a tiny cry for help. Of course you'll never know. It could have been that
> he could not eat, was basically starving, and I was the source—the one who
> put out the rice. Who knows? To me, it felt like a "help me."

Although we will never know what that particular bird was thinking, it
does not seem too much of a stretch to imagine that the finch knew it was
starving to death and as a last resort turned to a kindly human being for
help. Whether it was a calculated move or a serendipitous encounter, the
finch's unusual behavior may have saved its life.

Attributing human feelings to animals—the so-called error of anthropo-
morphism—is not considered great science. Scientists require proof, and

there is no way to determine accurately what animals are feeling or think-ing since they don't have the language skills to express themselves. Still, many wise and intelligent human beings believe that animals of other species experience joy, sadness, and even such "higher" emotions as guilt, shame, grief, and envy. Furthermore, in an undeniable expression of empa-thy, the animals pick up on these emotions in other animals (including hu-mans) and respond to them.

In his book *When Elephants Weep* Jeffrey Masson, who was originally trained as a psychoanalyst, tells the story of an empathic encounter be-tween two natural enemies—the elephant and the rhinoceros.

A rhinoceros mother and her calf came to a salt lick, and the rhino calf got stuck in the mud. The mother sniffed at the calf, making sure it was uninjured and then moved off to forage in the woods. When a group of elephants arrived at the salt lick, the mother rhino returned to attack the lead elephant. The elephants retreated, and the rhino wandered off again to forage in the woods. Masson describes what happened next:

> An adult elephant with large tusks approached the rhino calf and ran its trunk over it. Then the elephant knelt, put its tusks under the calf, and began to lift. As it did so, the mother rhino came charging out of the woods, and so the elephant dodged away and went back to the other salt lick. Over several hours, whenever the mother rhino returned to the forest, the ele-phant tried to lift the young rhino out of the mud, but each time the mother rushed out protectively and the elephant retreated. Finally the ele-phants all moved on, leaving the rhino still mired. The next morning, as hu-mans prepared to pry it loose, the young rhino managed to pull free from the drying mud on its own and join its waiting mother.

Why did the elephant risk the mother rhino's fury? Once again, while most scientists are wary of attributing human emotions to animal behav-ior, I find it difficult to come up with a logical alternative explanation. The elephant obviously recognized the baby rhino's distress and repeatedly tried to help—an act of benevolent selflessness by anyone's definition. If empathy is understood as the ability to accurately understand and sensi-tively respond to the experience of another living being, can there be any doubt that the elephant felt and expressed empathy?

One day not so very long ago, a zookeeper happened to be watching when a wounded baby sparrow crash-landed in the chimpanzee cage. One

of the chimps immediately grabbed the tiny bird. Rather than dismember-
ing the bird or swallowing it for an afternoon snack, as the zookeeper expected, the chimp held it tenderly in its cupped hand, gazing at it with
what appeared to be fascination. The other chimps gathered round, and
the baby bird was passed with great care from one to the next. After the last
chimp had its turn, it walked over to the bars of the cage and handed the
bird to the astounded zookeeper.

Did the chimpanzees recognize that the baby bird was in trouble, and
did that understanding lead to an empathic response, which in turn generated a desire to help? Nothing pulls our human heartstrings quite as effectively as witnessing the distress of others. We can walk by hundreds of
people every day without even thinking about their states of mind, but as
soon as we notice that someone—friend or stranger—is visibly distressed,
we feel a strong desire to respond.

The same basic empathic instinct may be operating in other species. If
the sparrow had been active and healthy, the chimp might have gobbled it
up without a second thought, delighted perhaps at its ability to scoop the
bird out of the air and celebrating its unexpected competency with a
mouthful of feathers and flesh. A wounded bird, however, created a momentary confusion. Automatic reactions gave way to thoughtful consideration as empathy began to wield its influence. What's wrong here? the
chimp may have been thinking. Why is this bird sitting on the floor of the
cage rather than flying around like the other birds? How am I supposed to
react to this strange creature?

Pondering those questions slowed things down a bit, giving the chimp a
few moments to observe the baby bird. Perhaps the chimp looked into the
bird's eyes and recognized its fear. Perhaps it felt the bird's heart beating
fast or noticed its frantic attempts to escape. Although we will never know
with any certainty what the chimp was thinking and feeling, we do know
this much—in that space carved out of normal life by pain, fear, and unusual circumstance, an empathic encounter occurred.

Here is another story about "cross-species" empathy, this time between
chimpanzees and humans. Seventy-five years ago a young man working in
Africa fell ill with malaria. His name was Cherry Kearton, and he shared his
home with a chimpanzee named Toto. All day, day after day, Toto sat by his
sick friend. When Kearton asked for medicine, Toto brought him the bottle of quinine. When he asked for a book, Toto would point to different

volumes until Kearton nodded his head. Toto would then pull out the desired book and carry it to his bedridden friend. During his long recovery Kearton would sometimes fall asleep, fully dressed, on his bed. When he woke up, he discovered that Toto had removed his boots.

Kearton was convinced that Toto's actions were motivated by the affection between them and the chimp's extraordinary ability to understand what he was thinking and feeling. In his account of these events, written in 1925, Kearton acknowledged the skepticism some might feel on hearing this story. "It may be that some who read this book will say that friendship between an ape and a man is absurd, and that Toto, being 'only an animal,' cannot really have felt the feelings that I attribute to him," Kearton wrote. "They would not say it if they had felt his tenderness and seen his care as I felt and saw it at that time."

Because monkeys and other nonhumans are unable to express themselves verbally, we cannot know with any certainty what they are thinking or feeling. We can, however, make assumptions about their emotions and thoughts based on their behaviors, facial expressions, and body movements. Of course that's exactly what we do with other human beings, for we are constantly, if subconsciously, reading other people's emotions and thoughts by watching their facial expressions for subtle changes, noting the way they purse their lips, raise their eyebrows, or grit their teeth; observing the way their muscles shift to express tension, fear, or disgust; registering how they stand relaxed, hands in pockets, or nervously shift from one foot to the other. Through careful observation of other people's nonverbal behavior, we can infer, often with surprising accuracy, what they are thinking and feeling.

This ability to decipher the unspoken thoughts and feelings of others is part of the genetic endowment of empathy, something we carry over from the self-sacrificing slime mold, ant-loving caterpillar, rhino-saving elephant, and human-loving chimp. All living beings need empathy; without it we would have no means of understanding each other or reaching out to each other for support, encouragement, tenderness, or affection. Without the ability to understand each other's thoughts and feelings, we would not be able to read their intentions. All strangers would be construed as enemies or regarded with indifference; even friends and family would be treated with disinterest. We would turn and walk away from others' pain or distress, incapable of understanding that their feelings affect our emotions and thoughts, unwilling to offer help because we would have no way of knowing that their fate is intimately tied up with our own.

EMPATHY IN THE BRAIN

Empathy is so critical to our development and ultimately to our survival that it is wired directly into our brains, specifically into two distinct but interconnected regions of the brain—the amygdala and the neocortex. The amygdala (there are actually two of these almond-shaped structures, located on either side of the brain) is part of the primitive brain known as the limbic system. This is the emotional brain—the instantaneous generator of lust, fury, frenzy, and bliss, the place where tears take shape and our most meaningful personal memories are stored.

With every person we meet and every new situation we find ourselves in, the amygdala's most forceful question is: Am I in danger of being hurt or harmed? If the answer is yes, the amygdala sends out an immediate alarm that triggers hormones, mobilizes the muscles into action, forces blood to the heart, and creates a general state of readiness to run away from the danger or to stay and fight. This automatic reaction to real or perceived danger is called the fight or flight phenomenon, and anyone who has ever had an anxiety or panic attack can attest to the amygdala's power to generate intense emotional reactions.

In the far distant past the amygdala ruled all the brain's circuits, acting as a master switchboard to create automatic responses to various physical threats. Then, somewhere around 100 million years ago, mammals began to evolve a new layer of brain cells dedicated to more "cerebral" pursuits. The neocortex or thinking brain, which wraps over the primitive limbic system like a thin blanket, allowed our mammalian ancestors to think about their feelings and adjust their behaviors according to these thoughtful reflections. For example, whereas amygdala-driven snakes and frogs will eat their newborns if they're hungry (and, even more significant, never suffer a moment of guilt or grief), neocortically controlled mammals willingly sacrifice their own lives to protect their young.

Over millions of years the thinking brain developed an interactive relationship with the emotional brain, interjecting cool reason into hot emotion and allowing moments of thoughtful reflection to slow down automatic responses. The basic emotions of fear, anger, sadness, and joy gradually expanded into subtler, more complicated expressions. Anger branched out into such complex emotions as annoyance, resentment, and indignation. Sensations of contentment and satisfaction evolved into feelings of delight, amusement, ecstasy, and bliss. Devotion matured into affection. Emotions like self-pity, despair, embarrassment, and humiliation became part of the human repertoire. As we developed the capacity to put another person's needs above our own, altruism and self-sacrifice became part of our vocabulary.

In a fascinating, if cruel, experiment with monkeys raised in the wild, researchers severed the connections between the amygdala and the neocortex and then returned the monkeys to their natural habitat. Without the neural wiring that supports empathy, the monkeys could no longer arrive at reasonable conclusions about other animals' friendly or hostile intentions. While a normal monkey might think along the lines of *This big ape looks like a brute, but I'm not worried because his eyes are gentle and he's not baring his teeth at me*, or *This female doesn't want to hurt me, she's hanging all over me because she's attracted to me*, the surgically altered monkeys retreated from all contact with their former friends and family members. They lived as virtual isolates, ruled by the amygdala-generated emotions of anger and fear and uninspired by neocortically inspired emotions like kindness, loyalty, devotion, and love. Deprived of empathy the animals were denied any hope of intimacy.

If we could return to our first months of life, we would better understand the thoughts and feelings of those empathically impaired monkeys. For in human infants the amygdala, which is almost fully formed at birth, reigns supreme, while the slow-to-develop neocortex earns its dominance over a period of years, even decades. Our brain development actually mirrors the evolution of the brain through time; just like our ancient mammalian ancestors, we begin life as amygdala-driven organisms.

From the first breath we take, we are able to express our emotions—crying out in pain, pulling back in fear, widening our eyes in surprise. Newborn infants often begin to cry or whimper when they hear other babies wailing, sharing each other's feelings even though they have no way of cognitively understanding what those feelings mean. Developmental psychologists call this emotional contagion sympathetic distress. At two months infants will cry when they see another person's tears. Once again this is an automatic, amygdala-driven response, in which the other's misery is perceived to be one's own. In responding to their mothers' happy, sad, or angry faces, ten-week-old infants change their own facial expressions. Four-month-old infants happily smile at smiling faces.

By the time children are eight months to one year old, they begin to understand that they are separate and distinct from others. With the emotional brain still in control, however, they can't quite figure out what to do about the other's distress. In their first attempts to soothe and comfort someone who is visibly distressed, children "mirror" the other person's behavior. Thus, when a child sees another child crying, he may wipe his own eyes, even though he has no tears to dry.

In the next few years, as the neocortex develops and interacts in increasingly sophisticated ways with the amygdala, children further recognize themselves as separate beings and recognize that they have thoughts and emotions all their own. Gradually they expand their repertoire of comforting behaviors. By the first year children are able to adjust their behaviors based on the information they see in an adult's facial expressions. Responding to a smile or a nod of the head, a one-year-old is more likely to pick up an unfamiliar toy or happily play with a stranger, while a frown or a troubled expression from the parent instructs the child to be more cautious.

Happiness is the easiest expression for young children to recognize, followed by sadness, anger, and fear. By four or five years of age children can accurately label these basic emotions, although many researchers believe children's understanding of them exists long before they develop the language skills needed to express it. More complex emotions, like shame, contempt, and disgust, are more difficult to decode, as researchers put it, and require several more years of brain development and relationship experiences.

By age six children understand that there can be a difference between the emotions people feel and those they exhibit. Around age seven children are able to understand situations involving emotions like jealousy, worry, pride, humility, and guilt. When children and young adults learn to consider both nonverbal cues, such as facial expressions and body movements, and verbal cues, such as tone of voice, they become increasingly skilled at discerning motivation and intent. By the time children are nine to eleven years old, they are able to recognize through nonverbal communication when people are trying to deceive or manipulate them.

Children of all ages who cry and are comforted or giggle and hear laughter in return learn that the world responds in comforting, reassuring ways to their emotional displays. If their tears are repeatedly greeted with indifference or their fears are ignored, however, they learn that the world is often unresponsive and uncaring. With continued neglect their emotional responses begin to narrow, and fear takes precedence over all other emotions.

The neural wiring that underlies empathy, in other words, can be tenderly wrapped and reinforced by our early experiences with loving, attentive human beings, thereby protecting us from emotional jolts. Repeated interactions with angry, violent, or neglectful caretakers, by contrast, may short-circuit the wires responsible for sending or receiving empathy. When we travel along a particular emotional pathway to discover over and over again that the world mistreats us or pays no attention to our feelings, we eventually learn that there is little incentive to keep trying, and we begin to shut down emotionally.

MIRRORING

We mirror what we see in life, and our empathy expands or contracts in response to our early encounters. If we don't receive empathy from others—if, as children, we speak and are ignored, if we laugh and no one joins in our laughter, if we cry in pain or fear and people tell us our tears are inappropriate or a sign of weakness—we begin to avoid expressing those emotions. When our caretakers are inattentive, depressed, or filled with anger and resentment, the mirror they hold up for us offers a distorted vision of reality. Looking in the mirror of their confused thoughts and feelings, we see a distorted, unrealistic image of ourselves. As children we have no way of knowing that the image we see is warped, and so we come to believe that the reflection is real, and our self-image conforms to the cracks we see in the mirror.

If, by contrast, our parents or guardians are genuinely concerned when we are hurt, thoughtfully tend our wounds, speak to us in a loving tone of voice, and let us know through their words and actions that they understand what we are experiencing (thus providing an accurate mirror), we feel accepted and understood and gradually gain confidence in our ever-increasing repertoire of emotional displays. When the mirror we gaze in is clear and undistorted, we see ourselves as we truly are.

If we look in a cracked mirror, we see a confusing image and have a difficult time making sense of our feelings. If the reflection that gazes back at us is clear and genuine, we come to see ourselves as we truly are and our emotions feel reasonable and valid. Mirroring is a difficult concept to explain, but I often find that this real-life example helps people understand the process. My daughter Erica was very sick as a young child, requiring several surgeries and more than a dozen hospitalizations for what her doctors believed was an intestinal problem. Frail, physically weak, and often suffering from intense pain, Erica could not run or play with her friends and was frequently left out of other children's games. When she was five years old, a team of specialists discovered that Erica had a third kidney, which they removed in an eight-hour operation.

A few weeks after Erica returned home from the hospital, I stopped by her room to check on her. Peeking in her door, I saw her sitting on the bed, patting herself on the back. "Shhh, it's okay honey," she was saying to herself in a soothing, reassuring voice. "Everything is going to be all right, Mommy will take care of you."

Listening to my five-year-old calm herself, using her mother's gentle tone of voice and loving assurances, taught me more about the power of mirroring than any textbook I ever read on the subject. Knowing that she was loved and believing she was worthy of that love, Erica could care for herself by repeating the words her mother had spoken to her on many occasions. Her mother's loving voice had become her own internal voice.

When we are treated with empathy—when people accurately understand and sensitively respond to our thoughts and feelings—we learn that we are worthy of such tender care. Our empathy for ourselves grows by leaps and bounds as we mirror inside what the outside world has revealed to us about our self-worth. As we mature and the thinking brain gains control over the emotional brain, we begin to push ourselves in the direction of growth and self-discovery. We feel the need to give back what we have been given, mirroring to the world the trust, faith, and love that we have taken into ourselves.

If we don't feel loved and if our feelings are continually discounted, we don't know how to soothe ourselves. Because we haven't learned how to take care of ourselves, we find it difficult to care for others when they are hurt or distressed. We mirror back the neglect and inattention we were given, and our focus remains riveted on our own unmet needs and desires.

Human beings are incredibly resilient, however, and we never stop learning, from the day we are born until the day we die. Given empathy and appropriate guidance, people with emotionally impoverished childhoods can learn how to express their emotions and expand their empathy. This is where we differ, of course, from the slime molds, caterpillars, birds, elephants, and apes. All living beings are wired for empathy, but humans alone have the ability to express our feelings through spoken language, to tell people what we are thinking, and to reach out for help when we feel sad or lost.

Through empathy we can overcome our fears and learn how to reconnect to each other. This is what happens in therapy. People come into my office convinced that there is no hope left and no reason to keep trying. They tell me they do not know how to express their thoughts and feelings; sometimes they tell me they have lost the ability to feel. They talk about the world as a cold and uncaring place. Hoping against hope, they open their hearts and their souls to reveal their despair.

Guided by their unique experiences, motivated by my belief that an empathic relationship can heal even the most desperately wounded spirit, I work to strengthen the connections between the thinking and feeling brain. Gently and with great care, I search through the maze of wires for the broken and severed places. Together we wrap and reconnect the frayed wires to let empathy flow freely, often for the first time.

Many years ago I worked with a sixteen-year-old boy who had lost his way and was struggling to find his place in the world. Tommy was the son of the cleaning woman in the hospital where I worked. Although I didn't know her personally, we would always say hello and exchange pleasantries when we passed in the hallway. When her husband died suddenly of a heart attack, she was left to care for five children by herself. Tommy, her eldest child, began to drink heavily, failed several high school courses, and seemed to be deeply depressed. Several times he had threatened suicide. One day when we passed in the hallway, Tommy's mother asked me if I would be willing to talk to her son.

In our first meeting Tommy was withdrawn and uncommunicative; over a period of several weeks, he began to open up and talk about his father. I listened, following his lead, letting him guide me to where he needed to go. "I don't want to live like this anymore," he told me one day. A moment passed before he added, "I want to make my father proud of me."

That day marked a turning point in Tommy's life. He stopped drinking and joined the baseball team, devoting himself heart and soul to his father's favorite sport. A natural athlete, Tommy quickly became an invaluable member of the team, but every game was torture for him because his father, always his greatest fan, was not in the stands to cheer him on. Tommy approached each game as if it were the World Series; hoping for perfection, he would inevitably end up disappointed in his performance.

Tommy had created a myth in his mind, believing that if he could become a great baseball player, he would please his father and relieve his guilt for not being the son he thought he should have been. "I was so self-centered," he told me once. "I never thanked my father for coming to my games, helping me with my homework, or taking the time to talk to me when I was upset about something."

"Every adolescent goes through a period of being self-absorbed," I said, explaining that being preoccupied with your own thoughts and feelings is a natural developmental stage during adolescence. "In adolescence you are developing your sense of self and that will preoccupy you until you begin to feel more stable about who you are."

"But still, I don't think I was a good son to him," Tommy said.

"You were a loving son, Tommy, as affectionate and respectful as you could be at that age."

"How do you know that?" he asked me, with more hope than suspicion.

"By the way you talk about your father," I said. "By the way you passionately describe him, telling me what a great man he was. By the way you mourn him and long for his company."

Over time, with empathy guiding our interactions, Tommy came to understand that no matter what he did or did not achieve, his father would still have loved him. As his understanding of himself and others expanded, Tommy learned how to realistically assess his strengths and his weaknesses, accepting what he could and could not do. Through honest interactions and a commitment to the process of change and growth, Tommy discovered that when he was more accepting of himself, even with all his faults and flaws, he was released into himself and into the process of becoming the person he was meant to be. Empathy saved his life by guiding him to the understanding that his life was worth saving.

I know from my experience with hundreds of patients that empathy is a teachable skill that can be developed and nurtured in our relationships with each other. In therapy, in strong marriages, in loving friendships, we gradually work out our early disappointments, discovering the power of empathy to strengthen our sense of self and our connections to each other. Learning how to express empathy—how to be honest, open, and forgiving toward ourselves and others—is a central part of the process. For feeling empathy is not enough. If we are to change, grow, and become the people we are meant to be, we must learn how to express empathy in our relationships. Expressing empathy is, in truth, the key to experiencing it, for empathy is one of those realities, like love, forgiveness, or truth, that we "get" only when we are willing, first, to give it away.

Chapter 4

Expressing Empathy

Being empathic is much more important than having empathy.

As weeping parents comforted terrified students in the aftermath of the high school shootings in Littleton, Colorado, on April 20, 1999, news reporters discussed the amazing displays of empathy they were witnessing. One reporter choked back tears as he looked over the crowd and in a hushed, reverent voice said, "Empathy is everywhere you look in Littleton, Colorado."

He was mistaken. The truth is that sympathy and compassion were alive and well that day, but empathy was having a harder time expressing itself. Whereas sympathy seeks to console, empathy works to understand. Empathy requires a certain emotional distance—you have to step away from the grief, fear, and anger to create a space in which your thoughts can exert a calming influence on your feelings. Biases need to be set aside. The automatic impulse to judge and censure must be countered. The desire for revenge is stilled and silenced by the more compelling need to understand and ultimately, perhaps, to forgive.

Empathy eventually found its voice in the aftermath of the Colorado tragedy. People began to reflect on the *how* and *why* of the murders, asking difficult, perhaps unanswerable questions. Why didn't we reach out to the students before they turned to violence? How could we have recognized their feelings of isolation and alienation? What could we have done to help them and, in the process, saved the lives of thirteen innocent people?

In those questions—and in the refusal to come up with ready-made answers—empathy began to make itself heard. Several days after the shootings I was watching a television talk show focusing on the question of who should take responsibility for the tragedy. Everyone seemed to be searching for someone to blame, and the focus gradually narrowed down to the killers' parents. Someone mentioned a rumor that was circulating about one of the killers' mothers; apparently she had visited a local beauty salon two days after the shootings. What kind of mother, people wondered, would get her hair done just days after her son had gone on a killing spree and then shot himself dead?

As harsh judgments began to fill the airwaves, a local newscaster interviewed Reverend Joel Miller of Littleton's Unitarian Church. Would he mind responding to rumors that the killers' parents were cold and unfeeling? The minister's answer was brief but to the point. "We don't know enough about what happened in these two families to make judgments," he said.

We don't know enough to make judgments. That statement embodies the heart and soul of empathy. The core of empathy is understanding, and understanding always precedes explanation. In the effort to understand, empathy asks questions and refuses quick answers. "I don't know" is one of empathy's most powerful statements. From that admission of not having all the answers, empathy starts searching for ways to expand the picture in order to develop a broader understanding.

Empathy begins with understanding, but, contrary to what so many people think, it does not end there. Empathy does not say, simply, "I understand what you are feeling or thinking." That is only the first step in a long and effortful process. For once you have enough knowledge and understanding, empathy asks that you put your ideas into action. *Being* empathic is much more important than *having* empathy, because it is what we do with empathy that counts. Moving our understanding from the inside to the outside, we can learn how to express empathy in constructive ways, always with the intent to help, not harm.

Expressing empathy is not a simple step-by-step process of "say this" or "do that." In fact, psychologists who study empathy emphasize the hard work involved in accurately understanding other people's emotions and then responding in ways that honor the uniqueness of the individual and the situation. In a recent scholarly article, the psychologists Sara Hodges and Daniel Wegner describe empathy as a process akin to climbing a mountain:

> Climbing mountains and pursuing empathy are both hard and effortful tasks ... Our success at reaching a mountain peak depends on having enough handholds and trail markers to allow us to proceed, and expending the effort to keep climbing.

The "handholds and trail markers" that allow us to proceed along the pathway of empathy are many and varied, but they all center on how we communicate our thoughts and feelings to each other. Every one of us has the innate capacity for empathy—as I emphasized in Chapter 3, the ability to understand other people's thoughts and feelings is wired into specific parts of our brains. The difficult part is transforming our understanding into thoughtful actions.

Most people imagine empathy as an automatic emotional response to another person's feelings or thoughts. The word *automatic* is important, for we visualize empathy as an immediate, spontaneous reaction to another's pain, joy, grief, or fear. Considered in this way empathy is a submissive emotion, a giving in and letting go, a sort of virtual reality—we put ourselves in the other person's shoes, passively absorbing his experience, vicariously observing the world through his eyes, feeling her emotions, even thinking her thoughts.

The ability to read another person's mind is powerful stuff, no doubt about it, but if empathy ends there it doesn't do much of anything, does it? While we can use empathy to reach a better understanding of each other, that increased sensitivity does not necessarily lead us to action. This was Hillary Rodham's complaint about empathy when she delivered the 1969 student commencement speech at Wellesley College, twenty-four years before she became the country's first lady. "Part of the problem with empathy ... is that empathy doesn't do us anything. We've had lots of empathy," she said, and then she went on to discuss the grave problems facing our nation that empathy was unable to solve.

In the end most of us would agree with Hillary Rodham Clinton that empathy seems to be curiously devoid of action or movement—it doesn't appear to go anywhere, do anything, change anyone. Empathy is one of those emotional experiences that seem to take more out of us than they put back in. We *feel* it, no doubt about that, but what can we *do* with it?

Yet here is a basic, irrevocable truth about empathy: If we don't do anything about our insights into other people's thoughts and feelings, then we're not being empathic. If we just sit there, saturated with shared emotion but unwilling or unable to make the transition from feeling to action, we are denying empathy its natural progression. For empathy is always, without fail, action-oriented. Empathy asks, with a real desire to understand: *What can I learn?* Empathy says, with deep feeling and an open mind: *Teach me.* Empathy wonders, at every twist and turn in the relationship: *How can I help, what can I do, where do I go next?*

Knowing how to put empathy into action is an art that takes practice, and, like all arts, the empathic response requires patience, determination, and flexibility. I recently had an intense encounter with a patient—I'll call him Gordon—whose anger and frustration challenged me to draw on my full repertoire of empathic expressions. Gordon, thirty-three, is a Yale graduate and works as an investment counselor at a large Boston bank. Married with two adolescent children, he is intelligent, articulate, and extremely intense. His boss, who was concerned about Gordon's contentious (and often intimidating) behavior with his co-workers, strongly encouraged him to enter therapy.

It was Wednesday at 7:00 P.M., Gordon's regular weekly session. He strode into my home office, handsomely dressed in a classic blue suit, white shirt, and newly shined shoes, sat down in the chair, and glared at me. "So, tell me, Dr. C," he said, sarcastically emphasizing the word *doctor*, "do you really think this is working?"

"I'm not sure what you mean," I said in a calm voice.

"You don't know what I mean?" He leaned forward, his hands gripping the sides of his chair. "I've been coming here for almost a year, and you don't know what I mean?"

"That's right, I don't understand what you mean right at this moment," I said. "Would you mind explaining it to me?"

"You wrote the book, Doc, you figure it out." And with that statement, Gordon sat back, arms folded over his chest, and stared out the window, studiously avoiding my gaze.

"I can see you are upset," I said. "I can also see that you are reluctant to tell me what is bothering you."

The look on Gordon's face said it all: *You think you're so bright, don't you?*

"In the past when you have been hurt or offended," I continued, "you've approached me in this indirect way. I think we could save some time if you would tell me directly what is bothering you."

"I don't know what's bothering me," he said, backing down a little. "You're the doctor, you figure it out."

"It seems like you're irritated with me," I said.

"Yeah? So? So what?"

"Could you tell me how you became irritated with me rather than being evasive?" I said.

"This isn't working," he said.

"What's not working, Gordon?"

"Us. You and me. This relationship isn't working. When we meet together, I tell you all these private truths about myself, and you don't reveal anything meaningful about yourself. You always act so perfect"—here he almost sneered—"like you know everything. I don't feel like I can trust somebody who acts so perfect."

"I need to understand this, Gordon," I said. By my tone I hoped to convey that I was genuinely interested in his answers to my questions. "Where did this perception of perfection come from?"

"I don't know where it came from," Gordon said. "Maybe it came from you. All I know is that I want to defeat you because you always seem so in control, as if you have it all together."

"I think your feelings go even deeper than that."

"You're right," Gordon said, leaning forward, his facial muscles drawn tight, eyes narrowed. "I want to pound you into submission. I want to stand over your broken body. I want to end it."

At that point I had many choices. I could have told Gordon his anger was inappropriate or misdirected. I could have diverted his attention to other subjects, hoping to dilute his anger, or I could have intimidated him by matching his anger with my own irritation. But empathy led me down a different pathway. I wanted to understand what Gordon was feeling and thinking, and I wanted him to know that I would go with him even into this place of anger and fury, even as he questioned our relationship and its value, even as he tried to intimidate me physically. I needed to let him know that I would follow his lead, and I would not be scared off by his intensity.

I knew by the words Gordon was using and the emotions he was expressing that we were approaching a place of extreme importance. I sensed the importance of the moment, as Gordon was revealing aspects of himself that he had never disclosed before. His anger was covering over deep hurts that I knew we needed to explore. Hoping to express my deep interest and at the same time convey the fact that I was not frightened off by the intensity of his emotions, I decided to meet him head-on.

"I can hear that you are furious with me," I said.

"I *am* furious with you—I'm angry because you're not helping me." Gordon was silent for a moment, struggling with his thoughts. He took a deep breath. "I've been gone on a business trip, you know. I missed two sessions with you."

"I know," I said.

"All kinds of things happen on these trips. I make mistakes, I lose my temper, I get disappointed with myself. And then I wonder if this is working."

"And that's when you get angry with me," I said.

"That's when I want to beat you into submission, to prove I am as good as you, even better than you," he said.

"What will beating me into submission do in regard to the disappointment you feel in yourself?" I asked.

"I want to get back at you for not helping me. I'm tired of not getting what I want from life." Gordon's anger seemed to leave him, as he sighed deeply and slumped in his chair. "I'm tired of struggling so hard. I've been working hard all my life, never living up to what I think I should do or what others think I should do."

"Who has told you that you do not live up to their standards?" I asked.

"You know, my father, all his big successes, thinking I could be just like him, I go to the same Ivy League school he went to, work for the same company, everyone thinks I'm just like him. But I'm not like him. Sure I try to compete with him, I'm just as competitive as he is, but I can't live the way he lives, always trying to get the edge on other people, I don't want to compete with everyone like that, but in some ways I can't stop . . ." Gordon's voice trailed off.

"I know how deeply you have been hurt by that way of life and how hard you are trying to change it," I said.

"You say you understand, but you don't seem to care, you don't even think about me when I'm gone," Gordon said, exposing the vulnerability that lay beneath his anger. "I feel like I'm trying to climb this mountain all by myself."

"Actually, I have been thinking about you," I said, hoping through my tone of voice and facial expression to convey that I understood how much he was suffering. "I have thought often about how deeply distressed you were the last time we met, and it bothered me that you were so tormented. I believe you have the capacity, with help, to work yourself out of this state, but I have to be honest—you are not always easy to help."

Gordon seemed to be listening carefully, so I decided to take that opportunity to continue explaining what I had come to know about him that I believed interfered with his progress. "Sometimes I think you are so preoccupied with defeating me that you can't learn from our interactions," I said. "You seem to have this sense that you are somehow below me, or that I feel superior to you, so you come out fighting. Together we have discovered where some of that comes from, but I think it's hard for you, particularly when you are under great stress, to believe we're on the same team and that we need each other's help to scale that mountain."

"I could beat you," he said weakly.

"I believe you could," I said, acknowledging the truth that human beings can hurt one another if that is what they choose to do. I wanted Gordon to know that I was not invulnerable to his anger. "But tell me—after you beat me, and you're standing over my defeated body, where is the victory? Can you tell me how you would feel after you beat me into submission?"

Gordon looked at me for a moment, searching for words to describe his feelings, and then I noticed tears in his eyes. He took a moment to collect himself. "I want you to help me get over the mountain," he said finally.

"That would mean a lot to me," I said.

This conversation reveals the convoluted pathways empathy has to travel in real life and some of the surprising twists and turns that need to be negotiated with great care. In this very intense interaction I was more forthcoming with my feelings about Gordon than I had been in the past. In previous sessions empathy had guided me to hold back a bit, allowing Gordon to experience the depth of his anger and seeing where it would take us.

On this occasion, however, I felt that I needed to step in and help him differentiate between the past and the present. He seemed to be stuck in the mud of the past, sinking ever deeper; understanding the intensity of his struggle, I was guided by empathy to offer him a lifeline before he disappeared out of reach.

When empathy guides a relationship, offering the "handholds and trail markers" that keep us from losing our way, we can see more clearly where we need to go and trust our ability to keep our footing even when the path is steep and narrow. Empathy helps us maintain a position of heightened awareness and patient attentiveness—an attitude that the psychologist William James called "the strenuous mood."

James believed that, by adopting a posture of caring deeply about life in general as well as our own moment-to-moment experiences, we can learn how to negotiate our way through and around even the most treacherous situations. He drew on his own experience as a mountain climber to emphasize the need to believe in yourself and others. James wrote:

> [Faith] creates its own verification. . . .
>
> Suppose, for example, that I am climbing in the Alps, and have had the ill-luck to work myself into a position from which the only escape is by a terrible leap. Being without similar experience, I have no evidence of my ability to perform it successfully; but hope and confidence in myself make me sure I shall not miss my aim, and nerve my feet to execute what without those subjective emotions would perhaps have been impossible.
>
> But suppose that, on the contrary . . . I feel it would be sinful to act upon an assumption unverified by previous experience—why, then I shall hesitate so long that at last, exhausted and trembling, and launching myself in a moment of despair, I miss my foothold and roll into the abyss.
>
> In this case (and it is one of an immense class) the part of wisdom clearly is to believe what one desires; for the belief is one of the indispensable preliminary conditions of the realization of its object. There are then cases where faith creates its own verification. Believe, and you shall be right, for you shall save yourself; doubt, and you shall again be right, for you shall perish. The only difference is that to believe is greatly to your advantage.

Empathy is synonymous with James's "faith," that inner sense of calm certainty that generates belief in ourselves and others. Without empathy we stand alone, trembling before the abyss. With empathy we are able to say to ourselves and others: You can do it. I will stand with you, I won't let you fall. If you stumble, I will help you regain your balance and together we will climb the mountain.

While the mountain-climbing metaphor fits in this context, I need to emphasize a critically important point: Empathy is not a tool or a technique that can be easily mastered. Empathy is, instead, an innate capacity that requires careful nurturing and constant attention. Empathy offers us "handholds" and "trail markers," but these are merely guides on the way up and over the mountain. They do not ensure that we will keep our balance, nor do they guarantee our success.

Because every individual and every situation is unique, empathy always has to be on its toes, attentive, aware, curious, watchful. If empathy gets lackadaisical, it ceases to be empathy, for empathy's most enduring characteristic is that quality of focused attention. Shift your focus, avert your eyes, adapt an attitude of "I don't care," and empathy quickly loses its footing. Empathy must always be willing to move, even if that means backtracking or sidestepping.

Learning how to express empathy—putting your thoughts and feelings into words that will find their way into another person's heart and soul— requires self-awareness, careful reflection, and a considerable amount of practice. To help people learn how to express their insights in ways that help rather than hurt, I have devised the following guidelines.

Seven Essential Steps for Expressing Empathy

1. Ask open-ended questions
2. Slow down
3. Avoid snap judgments
4. Pay attention to your body
5. Learn from the past
6. Let the story unfold
7. Set limits

Step 1: Ask Open-ended Questions

When Gordon said to me, "You always act so perfect," I could have reacted defensively and thrown the problem back on him ("This is not about me, Gordon"), or I could have repeated his statement to him, using a closed (already answered) question. "So, Gordon, you think I act as if I'm perfect?" With that defensive question I would have been saying, "Do you honestly think this is my problem?" which of course would have implied that it wasn't my problem at all, it was Gordon's problem. The question would have subtly assigned blame ("It's really your problem") and been intended to lead Gordon to accept my interpretation of his thoughts and feelings.

Closed-ended questions automatically introduce a power play in which the respondent is left to wonder whether to disagree with the answer contained in the question. The choice is between a submissive response like, "OK, you're right, I see where I've gone wrong," a combative reaction like, "You're wrong, and I'm sick to death of your high-and-mighty attitude," or a sullen refusal to communicate. Whatever the choice, one person wins while the other loses. In terms of empathy, of course, everyone loses, because communication has stalled out, understanding can't progress, and all parties involved in the discussion find it difficult to respond with sensitivity.

Suppose Joel comes late to a session. "We had a little disagreement last week," I say. "Do you think you might be angry with me and arrived late for our session as a way of letting me know how you felt?" That's a closed question because I have already reached a conclusion (Joel is angry with me). I'm using the question to lead the patient to agree with my interpretation.

Here's an example of an open-ended question I might have asked instead. "I notice that you have been late for the last two sessions, Joel— might this have some meaning we haven't discussed?" That question leaves the answer in the air, unformed. I am truly seeking information and asking the patient to tell me more.

"You know, I've been doing this a lot lately," Joel might respond, "cutting everything too close, showing up late for appointments, disappointing my wife and kids, upsetting my boss." Or Joel might say, "I had a terrible fight with my wife when I was leaving the house, she said I'm spending too much money in therapy, and she's furious with me for telling you all these details about our relationship." These answers convey important information about Joel's state of mind and point the way to a potentially productive discussion. Or the answer might be as simple as, "I can't believe my luck, two weeks in a row there's been a major traffic accident on the Mass

Pike," in which case we can put the matter behind us and discuss what really matters to the patient.

Here's another example of a closed-ended question. A mother and her teenage daughter are talking after the daughter returns from a date. "So, honey, do you really think he's cute?" the mother asks. With her question the mother is leading her daughter to agree with her interpretation (i.e., he's not cute). The question presents the daughter with a dilemma. She can submit to her mother's opinion, allowing her mother to direct her thoughts and feelings, or she can disagree with her and create a moment of confusion and even, perhaps, contention.

Or suppose you just had your hair cut. The stylist hands you a mirror and, before you have the time to look at yourself, says, "Isn't that cut flattering on you? Don't you think it's just perfect for your face?" Those questions don't require answers. The automatic response is agreement. "Sure, yeah, it looks good," you may say, even as you're thinking, I paid twenty-five dollars to look like a lawn mower ran over my head?

Open-ended questions express empathy because they convey respect for the individual's unique reactions and responses. When you ask an open-ended question, you communicate the fact that you want to learn from the other person, and you are truly interested in his perspective. You give over control, allowing the other person to lead you where she wants or needs you to go rather than trying to move the conversation in specific directions. Closed-ended questions slam the door in people's faces, while open-ended questions reveal the unlimited possibilities that exist when we push our prejudices and preconceptions aside, swinging the doors wide to new experiences.

Step 2: Slow Down

Empathy always makes an effort to slow things down so that emotions can be tempered with thoughtful reflection. Full-boiled emotions are not conducive to the expression of empathy. In an intense encounter, like the conversation with Gordon, it is critically important to go slow in order to avoid getting caught up in the emotions. In this sense empathy is like the bit in the horse's mouth that allows you to pull in the reins. When emotions are running away, empathy steps in to slow the wild gallop to a manageable trot.

To calm things down you sometimes need to back up a little, as in this discussion I had with Mike, a thirty-six-year-old recovering alcoholic who told me he had decided "out of the blue" to get married.

"I just walked into Dunkin' Donuts, I saw Nancy standing there, and boom—that was it," Mike said, smiling broadly. Normally calm and even-tempered, he appeared unusually revved up. "I knew right then and there that I wanted to marry her, no question in my mind."

Mike had been a patient for six months, and this was the first time he had ever mentioned Nancy. "That's a big decision," I said. "How did it come about?"

"Well, I was in an AA meeting, then I went to Dunkin' Donuts, I saw her, she was smiling at me, and I decided I wanted to marry her. It happened just like that."

When I asked Mike to backtrack and tell me about the meeting, he frowned. "I thought you might want to hear about the woman I intend to marry."

"Mike, it's not that I don't want to hear about Nancy, but I don't think I can fully understand your situation without knowing how the circumstances evolved. Let's just go back and retrace your steps before you walked into Dunkin' Donuts for coffee. What happened at the meeting?"

"It was just a regular meeting." Mike shifted in his chair, his energy suddenly drained, frown lines appearing in his forehead. "You know, all the regular stories, lots of tears, plenty of emotion."

"Just a regular meeting, then," I said.

"Yeah. Well, not really, I guess," Mike said, his frown lines deepening. "I got in an argument with an old-timer after the meeting, and then my sponsor got upset with me."

"Do you know why he was upset with you?"

"Because he's a jerk," Mike said with a dismissive wave. "So I got mad. I swear, I was so mad I could have killed him."

"You know, Mike, I don't quite understand that second part."

"What second part?"

"What made you so mad?"

"I'm just so sick and tired of the way everyone treats me in these stupid meetings. I don't feel like I belong."

"So you felt out of place and the meeting became very difficult for you."

"Yeah. I couldn't wait to leave."

"What were you experiencing when you left?"

"I was angry. I felt like I didn't fit in."

"And not very long after the meeting you walked into Dunkin' Donuts and saw Nancy?"

"Yeah, that's pretty much how it happened."

We talked for another ten or fifteen minutes, and Mike became increasingly reflective. "I guess it was a pretty emotional day," he said. "So you're thinking maybe I was looking to run away from my anger?"

"It sounds to me—and help me out here if I'm misinterpreting this—like you were affected by the emotions at the meeting and may have been looking for someone to settle you down or take your conflict away."

Mike leaned forward, put his hands together, and sighed. "I don't know, I'm pretty confused now that you slow it down like this."

"Maybe that's the way to proceed," I said. "To accept the fact that you're confused and uncertain about how to handle this particular situation, that you're learning right now, and you will continue to learn and grow as you think about this and other major life decisions."

At the end of the session Mike said, "I guess that was pretty stupid, deciding to get married to someone I hardly know. I can be so damned impulsive. Sometimes I don't know what's wrong with me."

"I think when you're hurt or offended, you're used to taking action quickly," I said. "As you learn to tolerate your emotions, you will act less impulsively. You have displayed that ability in the short time you have been here today."

"I have?" he said.

"Yes, you have," I answered.

When our emotions are at full boil, it helps to take a moment to think and reflect. Slowing things down allows our thoughts to catch up with our feelings, inserting some calm and reason into an emotional situation. When we consciously try to slow things down, we let empathy express itself, for empathy, as psychological researchers have discovered, cannot survive in an overheated (or frigid) environment. Like a plant that requires a balance of shade and sunlight, empathy wilts when it is exposed to extremes.

Negative emotions like fear or anger make high metabolic demands on our bodies, creating a state of intense physiological arousal. "It is generally thought that during situations in which levels of physiological arousal are high, there is an accompanying narrowing of perceptual focus," write the psychologists Robert W. Levenson and Anna M. Ruef. When our hormones are flowing and our muscles are tensing, our perceptual focus is narrowing. In a very real sense, we can see only our own anger and fear; other emotional subtleties fade away. We are literally "blinded" by emotion, concentrating only on surviving the situation by fighting or fleeing.

When the full boil of emotions is reduced to a gentle simmer, empathy begins to expand. We can see the whole picture again, not just the narrow focus. Helping others to slow things down and put their emotions in perspective is a powerful way to express your empathy for them. For as empathy works to cool and soothe, we are able to regain our balance and reach a more accurate understanding of our thoughts and feelings. My empathy for Mike allowed him to slow down and reach a clearer understanding of his actions. As our relationship continued, his empathy for himself expanded, and he learned how to slow things down without outside help.

Step 3: Avoid Snap Judgments

Quick decisions and snap judgments are not part of empathy's repertoire of expressions. With Gordon, for example, I had enough knowledge about his thoughts, emotions, and past history that I could have offered him a two- or three-sentence summary of his emotional state and then spent the rest of the session discussing my theories about his thoughts and feelings.

I know from past experience that Gordon has a quick temper and often uses anger to keep a safe distance from others. This is a general theory of his behavior supported by many experiences in the year we had been working together. So, I could have said: "Gordon, I believe you are angry with me because you are feeling intimidated by me." Or, "You want to beat me into submission because I remind you of your father, who was always belittling you and putting you down."

These are essentially "grow up and get over it" statements, slightly more elaborative versions of pejorative comments like "You're insecure," "You're threatened," or "You're envious." Such comments put labels on our behaviors, in contrast to empathic expressions, which seek to provide a deeper understanding of behavior.

"Grow up and get over it" statements also tend to characterize behavior as fixed and unchanging, while empathy always seeks to link thoughts and feelings to specific events. "I noticed that when you talked about your business meetings, you seemed quite affected—what were you experiencing at that moment?" I said to Gordon at one point. That question helped to focus his attention on the specific events that triggered his emotions, offering an opportunity to expand his self-awareness by tracing the origin of his reactions rather than letting self-loathing statements ("I'm stupid," "I'm incompetent," "I'll never be as successful as my father") take over. In moments of frustration people often lose sight of the specifics and fall back on generalities, which invariably lead to intolerant or punitive judgments.

The power of empathy is contained in its focus on the moment-to-moment experience. Empathy avoids at every turn the natural human tendency to summarize or categorize behaviors based on past experience. No matter what I know about Gordon's past, I can't know with certainty what he is thinking and feeling *at this moment*. He is a changing, evolving person, as we all are, and empathy always expresses itself in ways that respect and honor the transformative nature of the human being.

When the Greek philosopher Heraclitus said, "You can never step twice into the same river," he was expressing empathy, acknowledging the fact that the person you are today is different from the person you were yesterday. One of the greatest disservices we can perform for others is to assume that their personalities are fixed or rigid. In this way we imagine the river of life as a shallow pool cut off from other sources of water and gradually becoming stagnant. When we say to another person, "You always react that way," "That's the way I am, I'm never going to change," or "I can read you like a book," we toss obstacles into the river and dam up the free flow of empathy. In this way we not only deny the possibility of change but also prevent personal transformations from happening.

I shudder inwardly whenever I hear one person say to another, "I know how you're going to respond, I've seen it happen a thousand times" or "I don't even have to ask what you're thinking, I know you better than you know yourself." In those statements I can almost see the trees falling into the river of empathy, creating barriers to its circulation. For while the past can be a good predictor of the future, empathy reminds us that real life is fluid and human beings are ever-adaptable, capable of yielding and bending with changing circumstances.

If we assume that we are forever fixed in our ways of being, our personalities set in stone, then our interactions with each other become predictable, an endless repetition of old patterns and rote responses, with little possibility for expanding our perspectives or enlarging our view. Such a constricted world—ruled by theories, characterized by labels, governed by preconceptions—is like a dry riverbed, hard, parched, separated from other streams and tributaries, bearing little resemblance to its original, powerful self.

Step 4: Pay Attention to Your Body

When Gordon raised his voice and told me that he wanted to defeat me, his eyes narrowed, his face red with fury, looking for all the world as if he wanted to pounce on me, I could feel my heartbeat speed up. I could literally feel Gordon's anger in my body as my autonomic nervous system began to mirror his.

Researchers call this phenomenon *physiological synchrony*, and it is a powerful reminder of the fact that our minds (emotions) and bodies (physical reactions) are intimately intertwined and interdependent. Empathy has a definite physical component; in fact, one psychological researcher defines empathy as "an autonomic nervous system state which tends to stimulate that of another person." Our nervous systems, in other words, "talk" to each other. When a mother plays with her infant, their hearts begin to beat in time. When you pet your dog, your heartbeat slows down—and so does your dog's. When you interact with people who are angry and hostile, your physical reactions match theirs—the blood flow to your muscles increases, your blood pressure rises, stress hormones (adrenaline, noradrenaline, and cortisol) begin to pump through your system, and you start to feel the effects of anger and stress in your body.

The autonomic nervous system branches out from the central nervous system (the brain and spinal cord) to convey sensory signals to the body's glands and visceral muscles (blood vessels, heart, intestines). Two separate but interrelated systems control the body's reactions: the *sympathetic* system expands energy, mobilizing the body in stressful situations, increasing blood sugar, raising heart rate and blood pressure, while the *parasympathetic* system dominates when we are relaxed and works to conserve the body's energy. Because these systems operate more or less automatically, without our conscious thought, they are considered involuntary. Most people, for example, cannot control the beating of their hearts or the expansion and contraction of their intestinal muscles.

I find it fascinating that the word *sympathetic* is used to describe functions of the autonomic nervous system. For sympathy is, in truth, an automatic, involuntary response to another person's emotional state, while empathy requires a much more complicated integration of thought and feeling. In that sense, then, the interactions between the central nervous system and the autonomic nervous system could be called the empathetic nervous system, for the ongoing communication between these systems is responsible for all the expressions of empathy used to signal our thoughts and feelings to each other. Empathy is, in fact, an integrated mind-body response in which thoughts interact with feelings in an empathetic nervous system response.

I knew that my physical response to Gordon—the immediate, automatic rise in my heart rate and the sudden sensation of feeling intensely focused, all my senses on high alert—signaled physiological empathy. My body was mirroring the changes in Gordon's. Understanding the nature of physiological synchrony, I was able to use my sensations to gain important information about Gordon's emotions. My body's physical reactions gave me insights into his emotional state; they also triggered memories of my own experiences with anger and my understanding, gained through many years of experience, that feelings of resentment and hostility are often related to inner distress stemming from fatigue, emotional strain, or general feelings of insecurity.

Our bodies are tuned in to other people's bodies. We have an automatic built-in system for picking up their physical reactions, and that information provides us with important clues to their thoughts and emotions. Facial mimicry offers a classic example of physiological synchrony. Suppose you are talking to a friend who is sad and begins to cry. Your facial muscles automatically, without your conscious awareness, start to mirror or mimic your friend's expressions. But then something even more astonishing happens—you feel the same emotions your friend is feeling. Just by putting your facial muscles in certain positions, you can come to know what a person is feeling, both physically and emotionally.

Actors and writers understand the power of facial mimicry, using this technique to create specific emotional states. From this passage we can see that Edgar Allan Poe, the classic horror writer, used facial mimicry in an attempt to read other people's minds:

> When I wish to find out how wise or how stupid or how good or how wicked is anyone, or what are his thoughts at the moment, I fashion the expression of my face, as accurately as possible in accordance with the expression of his, and then wait to see what thoughts or sentiments arise in my mind or heart, as if to match or correspond with the expression.

Your moods are altered by your body's physiological responses. Thus, just by smiling you can calm your nervous system and put yourself in a better mood, while putting a frown on your face will make you feel more negative or critical. In one psychological experiment researchers attached two golf tees to subjects' foreheads and asked them to try to move the tees closer together, automatically creating a frown. When the frowning subjects were shown unpleasant photographs, they were much more likely to have a negative reaction to them. In another study subjects who held a pen between their teeth—an action that put the facial muscles in the smiling position—were significantly more likely to laugh at funny cartoons.

Physiological synchrony is a key element in any relationship, including therapeutic interactions. In therapy I know I can drive my patients' emotional states with my facial expressions and body movements. If I get angry or frustrated, for example, patients generally will match my intensity and pick up on my negative emotions. If I am calm, their bodies will respond to my composure. In general, if I smile they will feel happier, and if I frown they will be adversely affected by my negative mood.

This is powerful knowledge, and I approach it with the utmost care and caution, knowing how a stern look or impatient gesture can be devastating to someone who is feeling uncertain or vulnerable. I pay careful attention to my facial expressions, vocal inflections, gestures, and even posture, knowing that my physical reactions can trigger intense emotional responses in others. At the same time I carefully monitor my own physical reactions, using that information to give me clues to other people's emotional states.

In therapy and in life it is critically important to know how our emotions affect our bodies and how, in turn, specific physiological reactions can alter our feelings. A smile, for example, is one of the most powerful expressions of empathy available to us, for when we smile other people experience an automatic, almost irresistible desire to smile, too; and when our facial muscles move into a smiling position, physical changes occur that improve our mood. It's a truism, supported by numerous research studies, that even if you're feeling sad or anxious, putting a smile on your face will make you feel better.

Changing the position of the muscles in your face signals changes in your autonomic nervous system, which in turn initiate emotional transformations. Watch a mother and an infant exchanging smiles, the joyous feeling between them spreading almost in a contagion, and you will understand the power of the body to influence the mind and the simultaneous power of the mind to alter the body's experience.

Step 5: Learn from the Past

Empathy works its miracles of connection and intimacy in the present moment, but it always keeps an eye on the past. We need to know and understand what happened in the past not in an effort to guide our present-day interactions or predict the future but in order to see how old patterns, judgments, theories, and idealizations interfere with what's happening in this moment.

Understanding Gordon's past was critically important in helping him sort out his present feelings of anger and humiliation. Gordon grew up with a father who was, in Gordon's words, the "perfect human being in virtually every respect." According to Gordon, his father looked like a graying Mel Gibson, graduated with highest honors from Yale, earned "megabucks" as the vice president of a major cosmetics firm, and was respected (and often feared) by everyone who knew him. While Gordon was handsome, athletic, smart, happily married, and financially secure, he grew up believing that, no matter how hard he tried, he could never match his father's accomplishments.

As Gordon began to realize how his past was intruding on his present-day behavior, he was able to gain greater mastery over his emotions. I will never forget one incident that Gordon described, when he was giving a speech to the shareholders of his company. He was extremely nervous and kept clearing his throat. In the middle of his speech the company's president stood up and left the room. Gordon was devastated, automatically assuming that his boss was displeased with his performance. His anger began to build, his heart raced, and he was soon perspiring profusely. A few moments later his boss walked to the podium and handed Gordon a glass of water. "It's awfully hot in here," he said, giving Gordon a friendly pat on the back. "Maybe this will help."

As we learn to separate the past from the present, we gain objectivity. We can see that another person's strong emotions are not necessarily linked to what's happening right now but often emanate from previous unresolved conflicts or difficult life circumstances. Suppose, for example, that the receptionist at the dentist's office is curt and unfriendly. Your feelings of animosity toward her undergo a complete transformation when you take a moment to examine your emotional reaction and realize that she reminds you of your cold, critical mother. Not only does the receptionist look like your mother, she even sounds like her and uses similar gestures and facial expressions. Empathy allows you to gather the facts, reach a deeper understanding, then step back a little, gaining the objectivity you need to respond in a balanced, thoughtful way. With empathy's enlarged perspective, you realize that the receptionist's behavior has nothing to do with you personally, and you are able to let go of your anger toward her.

I once had a patient, Kelly, who was the world's worst critic; it seemed that nothing could please her or make her feel better about herself. One day Edie, a social worker at the hospital, found herself alone in the elevator with Kelly. Edie smiled, said a cheery hello, and, in an effort to be friendly, commented on the beautiful suit Kelly was wearing. Kelly swiveled on her high heels to face Edie and let her have it.

"I can't believe you are so shallow," she said, pointing to Edie's name tag. "You're a social worker, you have all that training, and yet you stand there insulting me by commenting on my physical appearance? All my life I have been made to think that a woman is judged by her looks, and here in this hospital, where I come for help, you have the gall to affirm the superficial nature of our culture." With those words the elevator door opened and Kelly stormed off.

Edie immediately took the elevator back up to my office. She told me what had happened and then asked, in tears, if she had been insensitive and even, perhaps, ruined Kelly's therapy. I repeated to her the words my father always said when I came to him with similar concerns: Consider the source. "When someone who is filled with self-hatred lashes out at you," my father would say, "consider the source. Anger usually arises from a long history of humiliation or fear, and that history has nothing to do with you. You just happened to be in the wrong place at the wrong time. Don't buy other people's insecurity, no matter what they're selling it for."

I told Edie that she could have smiled, frowned, coughed, or raised an eyebrow and elicited a similar enraged reaction. In truth it didn't really matter what she said or did because someone, somewhere that day was going to be on the receiving end of Kelly's pent-up emotions. Consider the source. We all have rich and convoluted histories that we bring into our present encounters. If we don't consider the source, we can get confused and leap to the conclusion that we are responsible for the other person's emotional reactions.

Considering the source goes both ways. In addition to honoring the other person's history, we have to pay attention to our own. Whatever past conflicts we have not resolved will be transferred to our present-day inter-actions. Understanding the self and developing awareness of past conflicts are necessary steps to developing empathy for others.

Step 6: Let the Story Unfold

Everyone has a unique story to tell, and every story proceeds at its own pace. When empathy guides the interaction, we can judge with surprising accuracy how fast or how slow the other person needs to go. Timing is everything. Empathy takes us on a journey, and at times the way is difficult and exhausting. At points along the way we need to stop, take breaks, get our bearings, and pay careful attention to the trail markers.

Gordon's intense hostility told me that he was teetering on the edge of an emotional precipice. My timing, I knew, had to be right. I could have pushed him over that edge by responding with aggression, issuing a challenge that would have prodded him to come out fighting. "You're acting like you're entitled to special treatment, Gordon, why don't you stop blaming and start working?" or "You're overreacting, Gordon, and your anger is pointing out your insecurity." Another option would have been to end the discussion abruptly by saying, "You are obviously out of control, Gordon. We will go on to other issues, and when you are calmed down, we can return to this subject." With either of these responses, however, I would have lost a valuable opportunity to help Gordon see, live and in color, how two

men can interact without destroying each other or forcing one to be desig-
nated "winner" and the other "loser."

Like Gordon, I am extremely intense by nature. In fact, many times in
my sessions with Gordon I have recognized in him a younger version of
myself. Unlike Gordon, however, whose father encouraged him to use his
anger to overpower others, I was taught that anger is usually a cover-up for
other emotions—disappointment, hurt, frustration, resentment, feelings of
inadequacy or helplessness—that people might find it threatening to reveal.

Anger is an expression of *perceived* vulnerability or powerlessness. "You
may feel powerless in a certain situation," my father used to tell me, "but I
assure you, there are always resources you can use. Only rarely in this world
are we truly defenseless." If we come to believe that we are powerless, or if
we feel undervalued or unappreciated, our response is to feel frustrated or,
worse, humiliated. Those emotions then lead to anger, aggression and, too
often, violence. In my experience angry or hostile behavior is almost always
fueled by the perception that we are not understood.

For many men, anger is the only emotion they have learned how to master. Psychologists who study the origins of male anger report that parents
frequently use the word "anger" with their sons but rarely with their
daughters. And while parents encourage their daughters to use diplomacy
and tact to mend their relationships, they often accept and even advocate
retaliation when their sons are involved in disputes. "It is very challenging
for most men to express or experience emotions other than anger," writes
the psychologist William Pollack in *Real Boys*, "since, as boys, they were
encouraged to use their rage to express the full range of their emotional
experience."

When boys are treated with empathy and taught how to respond empathically to others, however, intense anger often disappears. William Pollack explains how empathy disarms anger:

> A boy who is cared about will be more likely to care about others. If he
> feels connected to his parents and his family, he will feel more connected to
> other people. If he feels that his parents understand him and empathize
> with him, he will have the ability to do the same with others . . . *When a boy
> feels empathy for another, and diminished personal shame, it is unlikely he
> can so dehumanize that person as to want to commit violence against him.*
> [italics in original]

When I was growing up I struggled, as so many young men do, to understand and control my passionate nature. My parents taught me how to slow
things down, using my thoughts to control my emotions; and over the last
three decades, my training and experience as a psychologist has furthered
my education in learning how to use empathy to balance my natural intensity. When I feel angry or frustrated or when the people around me react
with rage or aggression, I understand that these emotions are driven
by deeper feelings of being misunderstood, discredited, or rejected. That
understanding functions as a kind of "dimmer switch" that lessens the intensity of the emotional interaction. With empathy guiding my way, I can
look beyond the surface behavior to the underlying frustration and fear
and respond in ways that let others know that I am willing to listen and respond to their distress.

In therapy and elsewhere in life, anger and aggression are often misunderstood as the expression of an innate, aggressive drive most common
to males. The theory is that males are inherently violent and sadistic and
need to be taught how to control these spontaneous impulses. With this
orientation, many therapists respond to angry, hostile, or potentially violent patients by suggesting medication. When a patient lashes out in anger
or threatens violence and the therapist feels endangered (often by his or
her own difficulties dealing with aggression), prescribing tranquilizers,
sedatives, or antidepressants is often considered a viable solution. While
some patients undoubtedly benefit from medication, too often this solution says to the patient: "You're too sick for me to handle, let's deal with
this when you're medicated."

And then, of course, there is another choice—the way of empathy. Empathy allows us to stand together at the edge of the precipice—the place
where deep emotions reside—trusting the relationship to guide us to
safety. Empathy teaches us how to let the story unfold, telling us when
to move forward and when to back away, when to run for cover and when to
trust that we are strong enough to deal with the elements. When we are
standing next to another person on that precipice, empathy reminds us
that this is the other person's journey; we are there to serve as companions,
helpers, aides. Our role is not to lead but to follow, not to dominate but to
participate, not to have the final word but to keep the exchange of ideas
flowing. We express empathy by immersing ourselves in the story, doing
what we can to help, and feeling grateful to be part of the experience.

Step 7: Set Limits

When Gordon said, "I tell you all these private truths about myself, and you don't reveal anything meaningful about yourself," he was challenging me to open myself up. He intimated that I wouldn't tell him about myself because I wanted to be perfectly in control. I could easily have accepted his analysis and given him what he said he wanted. I could have said, "What do you want to know about me?"

This is a trap in both therapy and real life. Personal disclosures intended to make another person's insecurities go away rarely work because they divert attention from the individual who needs help. Therapists sometimes make the mistake of sharing their woes with their patients, reasoning that personal revelations create trust and a personal bond. Yet while such interactions may provide instant relief ("I feel better knowing that you have been through similar experiences," a patient might say), they often create long-term resentments. Here's an example.

A thirty-nine-year-old woman suffering from chronic depression comes into therapy and tells her therapist that she is feeling suicidal. "I'm in so much pain," she says. "I feel this overwhelming need to hurt myself."

The therapist responds by moving his chair closer, a look of deep concern on his face. "I need to tell you that I take talk of suicide very seriously," he says. "Three years ago my niece committed suicide."

That revelation may have been intended to create a bond between patient and therapist, or perhaps the therapist hoped to convey his concern for the patient. Whatever the intent, though, the end result is confusion for the patient. *Why is he telling me this?* she asks herself. *Should I ask about his niece? Is that where he wants to go with this conversation?* Flashes of anger may follow. *I want to talk about me, not get involved in my therapist's personal life.* Then the guilt may arrive. *I'm so selfish, that's always been my problem, all I can think about is my own needs.*

People are seldom comforted in an enduring way when we respond to their problems by mentioning our own trials and tribulations. One person's deep insecurities are not healed by the knowledge that other people have serious problems, too. Empathy allows us to listen without bias to the meaning beneath the surface; to listen without bias, we must set limits. Setting limits does not mean that we don't care or that another person's anguish does not affect us deeply; instead it signifies a willingness to maintain our separation in order to offer an objective response.

Setting limits is a way of letting empathy do its work and keeping attention focused on the issue at hand. A middle-aged patient who is experiencing problems with his marriage told me that he believed all men thought about affairs. "Have you ever thought of having an affair?" he asked me. Sympathy might have led me to commiserate with him and share my own thoughts on the subject, but empathy directed me to set limits by focusing my attention on my patient's needs and concerns. "I don't think that speculating on what other men think about affairs is going to tell us much about your discontent in your marriage," I commented, and he immediately agreed.

In therapy—and in everyday life—it is critically important to set appropriate limits. Real trust is developed by moment-to-moment empathic interaction, not by revealing on demand your own thoughts and feelings about a particular subject. We can't alleviate other people's discomfort by becoming as tense as they are; in fact, in most cases doing so only increases their anxiety.

In Gordon's case I tried to convey my deep interest in his anger toward me without allowing the conversation to become focused on me. If my boundaries had been undefined, we might have wandered off on a tangent that in the end would only have increased Gordon's frustration and fury. My role was to absorb the blows without being hurt by them or letting their intensity draw me off course. Guided by empathy, I had no fear of Gordon's anger, for I knew that it was a thin cover-up for long-held resentments and a deep sense of humiliation. By setting limits I was able to keep his emotions focused rather than allowing them to become diffused, the difference between a thunderstorm that lasts for an hour and a light rain that persists for days.

The same truth holds in life outside therapy. While it is important at times to merge with each other, it is also critically important to know that we are separate and have our differences. Empathy allows for differences, and, even more important, empathy helps us tolerate our differences. We are dependent and independent, and the healthiest among us are interdependent. We come together and move apart, always maintaining a balance of involvement and detachment. Guided by empathy, we know when involvement is essential and when detachment is most beneficial for the relationship.

Knowing where I end and you begin is one of the most important challenges facing us in our intimate relationships. If my boundaries get entangled with yours, then I become confused about what belongs to me and what is rightfully yours. In that enmeshment empathy necessarily suffers, for empathy requires objectivity to maintain its balance. In intimate relationships we need to preserve the equilibrium that empathy creates, understanding where we begin and end in relation to the person we love. That state of balance gives us the insights and understanding needed to express ourselves clearly and honestly, always respecting the other person's unique needs, desires, hopes, and dreams.

The most important element in expressing empathy is not the words we speak but the underlying message we communicate. With empathy we hope to send the message that we are interested in the other person's story not necessarily because we are an important part of that story—for strangers can express empathy to each other—but primarily because by immersing ourselves in another person's experience we have the opportunity to reach out, which broadens our perspective and expands our connection to life itself.

A story about Mahatma Gandhi illustrates the interdependence that exists at the heart of empathy. Gandhi was once interviewed by a Western journalist in a small Indian village as he was performing his services for the poor. The journalist said, "How wonderful all the things you're doing for these poor people!" Gandhi replied, "I'm not doing it for these people, I'm doing it for myself." The journalist asked, "What do you mean?" To which Gandhi replied, "How can I have empathy for others without having empathy for myself?"

Chapter 5

Empathic Listening

Empathic listening is always centered on the other person,
and its goal is to make the other feel uniquely understood.

Several months ago I devoted the Boston radio show I cohost to the topic "The Lost Art of Listening Well." After the program a friend asked if she could tell me a story.

"Sure, I love stories," I said.

"It's a true story," she said.

"That's even better," I said.

Her story revolved around a failure in the listening process. "I've been thinking about getting involved again with a married man," she began. "I broke up with him over a year ago, but he's been pressuring and flattering me nonstop. No matter what I say to him—I'm feeling down, I don't have any energy or enthusiasm, I don't like myself very much right now—he always responds with some comment about how wonderful I am, how I need to believe in myself, how nobody appreciates my talents the way he does. Even though I had this nagging suspicion that he was complimenting me in order to get his way, I was getting seduced by his compliments and seriously considering resuming the relationship.

"When I listened to what you said on the radio about empathy and the art of listening, it suddenly dawned on me that he wasn't listening to anything I'd been saying. He was just telling me what he thought I wanted to hear. And then I realized something even more profound—I hadn't been listening to him. I'd just been soaking in all that flattery and praise and letting him manipulate me."

We are given two ears and one mouth, the saying goes, so that we will spend at least twice as much time listening as we do talking. Yet who among us listens more than we talk? When we listen, are we really listening or just rehearsing what we're going to say when it is our turn to talk? Are we picking up certain phrases and ignoring the rest, an ongoing cut-and-paste process in which we pay attention only to the good-parts version? How often do we "hear" the emotions that accompany the words and make a conscious effort to respond to what is left unspoken? How should we listen and, more important, how should we listen with empathy?

Listening seems so easy—you just stop talking and focus on what the other person is saying. Yet of all the skills involved in empathy, listening requires the greatest concentration and focus, for there are so many ways that we can be distracted. Many people listen with "half an ear," waiting for our turn to speak but all the while rehearsing what we are going to say while the other person is speaking. We tend to listen with bias, making up our minds before we hear the full story. We listen with sympathy, connecting everything the other person says to our own experiences and then making comments that do not honor the uniqueness of the other person's thoughts or feelings like, "I understand exactly what you're feeling" or "I know what you're going through." And, finally, we get distracted by the noise of our own internal voices, judging or second-guessing ourselves.

Listening with empathy requires giving up a self-centered view of the world in order to participate fully in another person's experience. Listening with empathy requires focusing in and paying attention, not only to the words being spoken but to gestures, general posture, body position, and facial expressions. When you listen with empathy you make a conscious effort to set aside your biases. You learn how to connect with the other person's emotions without getting carried away by them, to step in and then step back. And you discover how to live with ambiguity and the inability to find answers or solutions to all problems.

Listening with such clarity and depth of feeling that the other person truly feels "heard" is a kind of holy listening, as the Quaker writer Douglas Steere explains:

Holy listening—to "listen" another's soul into life, into a condition of disclosure and discovery, may be almost the greatest service that any human being ever performs for another.

Empathic (holy) listening goes deep into the other person's heart and soul to reveal what is hidden by fear, anger, grief, or despair. This kind of listening can be taught; it can be passed from one person to another. We learn how to listen with empathy by being around people who are empathic and who understand how to listen our souls into life. When we know through our own experience the power of this kind of listening, we begin to grasp how the ability to listen brings us closer, strengthening our relationships with others and with ourselves.

ASSESSMENT

I learned how to listen from my father, who understood both the power of the spoken word and the even greater authority contained in the silent spaces created when we listen with wholehearted attention. I watched my father as he listened to others, observing the way he consciously focused his attention. I saw how he took great care in the phrasing of his questions, in the pauses that signified his reluctance to come up with quick or easy answers, and in the small gestures that told his listeners he was paying wholehearted attention.

My father had what I call a *listening posture* that conveyed his total absorption in the conversation. Like someone in prayer, he had a way of consciously stilling himself, focusing his mind, and making sure that nothing distracted him from the task at hand. Leaning forward, his eyes intent, his hands folded together, he would ask a question, and then he would listen, without interrupting.

When the speaker was finished my father would be quiet. He might light a cigarette or sip his coffee, taking a moment to reflect on what had been said. Then he would ask a question. And another and another. Afterward he would make sure that the other person had a chance to say everything in his or her mind. Then and only then would he offer his carefully considered thoughts.

I loved to watch my father in conversations, for I knew by the way people responded to him that he had a gift. People were changed after a conversation with my father; he had a knack for locating potential and then highlighting the fact that people might have work to do in order to reach that potential. At the end of all of these heart-to-heart conversations, he would say something like, "Of course, this can all come true, Arthur, if you believe in yourself and work hard to make it happen." My father never held back his criticism, but he expressed himself in a way that conveyed his respect for others. His honesty was straight, direct, true to the mark, and always deeply respectful.

One particular conversation stands out in my memory. It was 1965, I was a senior in high school, and football was my life. Nothing in my life compared with the joy I felt when I was running with a football under my arm. I remember one game when I scored the winning touchdown against our archrivals and looked up in the stands to see my father throwing his hat into the air. After that game, in the locker room, a friend invited me to a party and then talked forever about all the great girls who would be there. I remember thinking: Is this guy nuts? Who wants to think about girls just minutes after the most exciting football game of my career? How could there be anything more exciting, more thrilling than the events of the last two hours? What experience could ever touch the glory and wonder of those moments?

If girls came in a distant second to football, academics were not even in the running. My grades reflected my general indifference to studying. I was an "average" student, getting a mix of C's and B's. I had never read a book from cover to cover, although I'd skimmed plenty of them, and I knew how to write a decent paper and get a passing grade with minimal effort. Yet despite my lackluster academic performance, I had been offered several football scholarships to some fairly decent schools. I was trying to figure out whether to play college ball or join a semipro team when I got a call from the guidance counselor, who wanted to see me in his office.

Mr. Martin was pleasant but formal. "I saw your picture in the paper and noted that you've been offered a football scholarship," he said. "Do you want to go to college, Arthur?"

"I'm not sure yet," I said.

He fixed me with a serious stare. "I have to be honest with you," he said. "I'm not convinced that you're college material." Mr. Martin went on to tell me that I probably wouldn't even get into college if I didn't play foot-ball. My grades, he reminded me, were average. He thought there was a good chance I would flunk out of college—and that wouldn't reflect very well on my high school, would it? He ended the conversation by suggesting that I consider other choices, including the armed forces. "In the Army," he said, "you would have the opportunity to grow up, learn about yourself, and discover what you want to do with your life."

That night, when my father returned home from work, I told him about my meeting with the guidance counselor. "So, Arthur," my father said, tak-ing a moment to light up a cigarette, "can you tell me exactly what he said?"

"He doesn't think I should go to college. He doesn't think I can make it."

"Did he say that in so many words?"

"He said my grades were average. He said I'm good at football, but that's probably the only reason I would get into college. He thinks I should consider joining the Army."

My father looked at me for a moment, quietly assessing my mood. "So," he said, taking a drag of his cigarette and gently exhaling the smoke, "why don't you tell me what you think?"

"Maybe I'm not college material, as Mr. Martin put it," I said. I didn't tell my father, but I was feeling pretty confused and disheartened by Mr. Martin's assessment of my skills.

My father waited, watching me.

"I just don't know," I repeated. "He's the guidance counselor—I guess he should know."

Stubbing out his cigarette, my father smiled at me. In that smile I saw all the love in the world. "I know you're not a great scholar, Arthur," he said, "but I'm wondering why this man, who doesn't know you from the butcher down the street, would tell you that you shouldn't go to college. I'd like to hear his reasoning. Let's go in and see what he has to say."

The next day my father and I sat down with Mr. Martin in his office. My father looked at the academic degrees framed and mounted on the wall be-hind the desk and then, very politely, asked Mr. Martin to repeat what he had told me the day before. Mr. Martin went on for quite a while, talking about my average grades, my lack of motivation, the fact that it was his job to determine which students were capable of graduating from college and which students should consider other choices. He noticed my father's rapt attention and the way he nodded his head, as if in agreement with him, and that seemed to encourage him to keep talking. He made some negative comments about sports and extracurricular activities, repeating what he had said to me about the bad reputation so many athletes, particularly football players, were giving our high school.

"Tell me, sir," my father said at one point, leaning forward, his hands folded as if in prayer, "did you play sports in high school? Have you ever coached any sports?"

Mr. Martin's answer was to blow some air out of his nose in amused surprise. "I have no interest in athletics," he said. "My concern is academics." And for the next ten minutes he talked about his philosophy of life and education.

When he was finished my father asked the question he always asked when he was involved in an important discussion. "Have you said everything you wanted to say?"

Mr. Martin said yes, he thought he had pretty well covered the territory.

"Well, sir," my father said, in a very calm voice, "I can see that you are a well-educated man. From the degrees on your wall I see that you graduated from college. You even have a master's degree."

Mr. Martin smiled, proud of his accomplishments.

"So, this is the way I look at it," my father continued. "If someone like you, who clearly has difficulty seeing the potential of a talented kid like Arthur, can go to college and even get a master's degree, then I'm convinced that there's no stopping my boy. Thank you for your time." He stood up, put out his hand to Mr. Martin, shook his hand firmly, and took his leave.

That encounter thirty-five years ago taught me the most important lesson there is about the art of empathic listening—always give other people a chance to explain themselves fully and reveal their thoughts and feelings. Then, after learning everything you can about the person's goals, motives, intentions, fears, dreams, and desires, use that information to make an assessment. Only through this process of listening and assessment can you discover whose advice to take and whose advice you can dismiss. Only by carefully appraising another person's character can you determine whether their advice is sound and respectful of your needs and desires or if they are speaking from a biased position, hoping to influence your thoughts and feelings in order to fulfill their own agenda.

Watching my father as he listened to Mr. Martin and asked his carefully worded questions, I realized that he was sizing up the man. Who is this guy, and where's he coming from? my father wanted to know. Does he have some predetermined agenda? Is he interested in Arthur as an individual or does he think that all football players—or all band members, chess players, cheerleaders, rich kids, poor kids, black kids, white kids—are alike? Those were the questions going through my father's mind as he sat in Mr. Martin's office, trying to determine if the guidance counselor had something to teach him or if he was so full of himself that he had no room left for the thoughts and opinions of others.

"I was listening to his reasoning to see if it made sense, trying to figure out how he came to these conclusions about you," my father told me after that conversation. Now that I've been to college and graduate school I have a fancier word for that process of measuring the breadth and depth of another human being. I call it *assessment*. In terms of developing and expressing empathy, assessment is the most important skill we can cultivate. Assessment is at the very heart of empathic listening.

What is assessment? Simply put, assessment is the ability to discover the truth about a particular person or situation, using empathy as your guide. Assessment is especially important in the early stages of a relationship, when you don't know people very well and you need to determine fairly quickly who they are and what motivates them. You might assess your children's teachers, for example, by sitting in their classrooms for several hours, noticing the way they talk, the way they listen to the students' concerns, how they answer questions or deal with discipline problems, and so on. If you were hiring an employee, you would interview various candidates and ask questions about their background, education, likes, dislikes, work ethic, values, and so on. You would listen for what is said and not said, what is emphasized and what is downplayed.

Assessment is also critically important in our personal relationships, although we tend to overlook its significance. Leigh, a thirty-eight-year-old homemaker who is involved in a nasty divorce process, told me about a conversation she had with her lawyer after the first court hearing. "After my lawyer listened to my husband for fifteen minutes, he told me that in twenty-five years of practicing divorce law, he had never met a man so self-absorbed and with so little compassion. What did I miss? Why couldn't I see what my lawyer noticed after spending fifteen minutes with him? Why did I waste five years of my life doting on this man?"

If Leigh had been taught how to listen empathically and use that process of focused attention to assess her husband's character, she might have saved herself a lot of misery. Empathic listening helps us avoid trivial conversations and keep our distance from people who are interested solely in their own needs and desires. If we don't know how to assess other people, we end up making poor decisions. We pick the wrong people to trust, to love, to work for us, and to take care of our children. We make decisions based on our own vulnerabilities and insecurities. We let other people control us or make decisions for us, when we should be using empathy to create our own pathway in life.

The assessment process in empathic listening consists of two distinct but connected stages. First, listening involves assessing the person who is speaking in order to learn everything you can about his or her perspective, history, character, and motivation. Second, through careful, attentive listening you learn how to assess yourself, being aware of your moment-to-moment emotional state, including your needs, vulnerabilities, biases, and self-interests.

Assessment of Others

To judge another person's character and motivation accurately, you have to be able to adjust your perspective to encompass her or his viewpoint. This ability to expand in response to our interactions with others is how we learn and grow. When we move out of ourselves and into the other person's experience, seeing the world with that person, *as if we were that person*, we are practicing empathy. Empathy requires that we let go of our own theories and judgments and start anew. Listening wholeheartedly, we enter the other person's thoughts and feelings and then move back into ourselves with our perspective altered by what we have experienced. Empathy in all senses of the word involves an ongoing, ever-changing process of self-transformation.

Sometimes when I am trying to explain to a patient or colleague how empathy works, I hold my hands just a few inches apart, palms facing each other. "This is a narrow empathic range," I say, "something like putting blinders on a horse. With limited empathy that is how we go through life, seeing only what is directly in front of us. Empathy gently removes the blinders and expands the range"—I slowly move my hands apart—"allowing us to see into another person's world. With that expanded vision we can see better how we fit into the larger whole."

Listening with an open mind can be a humbling experience, for you can't fall back on tried-and-true (but also weary-and-stale) ways of interacting. You have to be willing to admit not only that you don't have all the answers but that there may not be any satisfactory answers to a particular problem. I was recently talking to Deborah, a forty-one-year-old homemaker, about her desire to have a child. She had been trying to get pregnant for six years and came into counseling after her second miscarriage.

On this particular day Deborah began to plead with me for an answer to her pain and confusion. Her friends were advising her to try new fertility drugs, and her doctor had recently suggested surgery. As I listened it became clear to me that she did not want me to tell her what to do— she wanted me to help her cope with the possibility that she might never be able to have a child. She needed to know that I understood her despair. She wanted me to be with her, to stand by her as she struggled to deal with a painful reality.

"Please, tell me what to do," she said, tears running down her cheeks. "It's too painful, I don't know how I can live with this grief. I don't know if I will ever be able to have a baby—how can I live with this hole in my life?" She was sobbing now, barely able to speak. "Please, Dr. C, help me, give me something I can hold on to, tell me something that will make me feel better."

I knew that all the platitudes that are available to human beings in times like these—I understand how much this means to you and how painful it is for you; it will be OK; try not to worry; everything will work out for the best; you still have time to get pregnant; don't give up hope; you never know, there are constantly new advances in this field—would hurt her more than they would help her. Sympathizing with her would only diminish her experience by taking it over. In truth, of course, I could not know what she was experiencing, because I do not know what it is like to be childless, nor do I know what it is like to be a woman who desperately wants to get pregnant but can't. I can imagine what it would be like for Deborah, but I can't know for sure.

I knew she was in pain—I felt her anguish in my soul—but I had no words that could solve her problem or ease her torment. As she begged me to help her, I remember thinking, I don't know what to do. I don't know what to say, I don't know how to help her. I looked at her, and I felt tears come to my eyes. A moment passed. Deborah took a deep breath.

"Thank you," she said.

"For what, Deborah?"

"For listening. I guess that's really what I needed, someone to listen to me, to feel this with me, to let me put words to my pain."

Later, when I thought back on that conversation, it hit me how difficult and demanding empathy can be. Deborah initially wanted answers, but with empathy providing its quiet resonance, she realized that being understood emotionally was infinitely more soothing than any words could be. Still, during that interaction I wasn't at all sure that I was giving her what she really needed; I only knew that offering sympathy or platitudes would not ease her pain. Empathy guided me to respond with silent respect for her pain; understanding that my feelings were genuine, Deborah responded to empathy with gratitude.

The empathic process sometimes reminds me of critical moments in my football career when something completely unexpected happened—a pass play was called, all receivers were covered, and suddenly I found myself running down the sidelines, heading for the end zone. That's the point where you have to put all the theories and standard plays aside and trust your instincts. Football strategists call it broken field running, and that's a great metaphor for empathy, too. With empathy you can't just rely on the rulebook, because real flesh-and-blood people are always breaking the rules. Real life often doesn't follow our well-laid plans; we have to think on our feet and always be prepared to take off in some unexpected direction.

In a wonderful scene at the end of the first Star Wars movie, Luke Skywalker is flying through a narrow tunnel in a desperate, last-ditch attempt to destroy the Death Star. As he makes the final adjustments on the plane's computer screen, he hears Obi-Wan's voice calmly advising him: "Use the Force, Luke. Let go. Trust me. The Force will be with you, always."

"The Force" is nothing other than empathy, the innate capacity to "see" what lies beyond sight and to "feel" what lies beyond touch. To put the force of empathy into practice, we must rely on our natural instincts, the wisdom of our experience, and the ability to cool down our emotions through careful reflection. Listening to the voice of empathy within us, we learn how to trust our inner powers and at the same time commit ourselves to the hard work involved in expanding the powers within us. This process of self-transformation leads us directly into the second part of the assessment process: assessing the self.

Self-Assessment and Biased Listening

Learning how to listen to the self is as important as learning how to listen to others. Self-interests or biases interfere with the ability to listen carefully and with an open mind, diminishing empathic abilities. When my father talked to the high school guidance counselor, he was well aware of his biases and how they might influence his decisions. He knew that in order to make an accurate assessment of Mr. Martin's thoughts and feelings, he would have to "come clean" with himself, openly acknowledging his preconceptions and then working to set them aside as he listened and tried to learn.

My father had strong feelings about my future. He wanted me to go to college; it was, in fact, one of his greatest dreams. As the first member of his large, extended family to graduate from high school, he believed in the value of education, and he wanted me to have the opportunity that was denied him—to earn a college degree.

Yet my father also knew that pushing me beyond my abilities or circumventing my own dreams would not be wise. He knew me well. I had told him many times that my passion was football, and someday I hoped to play semipro ball. He also knew that I wasn't particularly interested in academics. So maybe, he thought, maybe this guidance counselor has a point here. Maybe he can teach me something, maybe with his help I can offer better advice to my son.

Only through listening with empathy—which requires listening without bias and refusing to control or direct the conversation—could my father get the information he needed to make a decision. He had to enter wholeheartedly into Mr. Martin's point of view; only then could he know if his opinions were based on full understanding, knowledge, and insight.

My father's refusal to prejudge Mr. Martin allowed him to avoid the trap of biased listening. *Biased listening* is listening with your mind already made up. After hearing a few words, you begin to fill in the spaces based on your own experience, and you stop listening to the unfolding story. "He's talking again about his always-critical father, and I know exactly where this conversation is going," you might say to yourself, or "She's going to tell me how wonderful her kids are, I've heard all this before." Your listening is halfhearted—you let the other person talk, responding as if you are listening, nodding your head and saying yes and no in all the right places, but in truth you are convinced that you know all there is to know about this particular topic.

Biased listening can lead us to false conclusions, as this story reveals. Several years ago my cousin Pasquale (we call him Pat) was hospitalized after a serious automobile accident damaged two of his vertebrae. The large window in Pat's hospital room was cracked, and cold air was coming in, so he asked the nurse to pull down the shade.

That evening a psychiatric resident walked into the room, looking very serious. He asked Pat if he would like to talk.

"Sure, yeah, I'll talk," said Pat, always a friendly, sociable kind of a guy. "What would you like to talk about?"

The resident gave him a worried look. "I'm concerned about your state of mind," he said.

"Is that so?" said Pat.

"I think you might be depressed."

"You think I might be depressed," Pat repeated. "Sure, OK. I'm curious, though—how did you come to that conclusion?"

"It was beautiful outside, but the shades have been drawn in your room all day," the resident said.

Pat burst out laughing and then enlightened the resident about why he was sitting in the dark on a beautiful day. When I visited him later that night, he ribbed me. "So, Arthur, what's with you guys with these fancy degrees? You think you know everything that's going on in other people's heads?"

The psychiatric resident wasn't really interested in what Pat had to say because he had already made up his mind. When someone assumes he knows all the answers, you can be fairly certain that his power of empathy has been seriously diminished. Biased listening is unempathic—it is listening with a closed mind. Psychologists sometimes call this distanced listening, which makes me think of people standing on the other side of a busy street politely nodding their heads while I'm talking but, of course, not hearing a word I say.

Here's another example of biased listening. In a recent group therapy session, Elizabeth was talking about her separation from her husband and the problems they were having determining how to split up their property. Two other members of the group, Tom and Teresa, had been through nasty divorces, and they immediately seized on the idea that Elizabeth's husband would try to take advantage of her gentle nature and generous spirit. When Elizabeth insisted that her husband was a decent, good-hearted man who would never take advantage of her financially, both Tom and Teresa jumped on her.

"Elizabeth, you are so naive," Teresa said, rolling her eyes upward. "I can tell you from my own experience that you can't trust anyone, least of all your former spouse."

"Teresa is right," Tom chimed in. "I was overly trusting just like you, and my wife got everything—the house, the car, the kids. She drained my whole life away."

Later we talked in the group about how Tom's and Teresa's experiences had biased them so that they couldn't accurately understand and sensitively respond to Elizabeth's situation. Their biases prevented them from empathizing with Elizabeth and realizing that her situation was unique. It may be a broad, generalized truth that divorces are nasty and both partners are out for themselves, but it is certainly not a universal truth, and there are always variations on the theme.

Biased listening, in contrast to empathic listening, tends to make conclusions based on historical experience. For example, you might enter a relationship with a personal injury lawyer with the idea that all lawyers in this line of work are smooth-talking con artists interested in making money off other people's trials and tribulations. From an empathic perspective you would work hard to hold your preconceived notions in the back of your mind until they are validated by the present communication. This is a conscious process, driven by the empathic desire to be fair and open to new experiences. "I know I have biases, but maybe this particular individual really is interested in the welfare of his clients and cares about truth and justice," you would say to yourself. (Meanwhile, you would also be assessing your motives in the case—do you want "truth and justice," or are you primarily interested in the money you can make off a lawsuit?)

Prejudice

We all have developed general theories based on our experiences in life, but empathy urges us to keep our prejudices in mind so they don't get set in concrete. Fluidity and flow are central to empathy, while rigidity and inflexibility will always diminish empathic abilities. Biases based on titles, ethnic heritage, race, or religion invariably cause confusion and hostility, making it difficult for us to relate to each other.

On my first day of work at Leonard Morse Hospital in Natick, Massachusetts, twenty-five years ago, I had an orientation meeting with the staff. I gave a short speech, introducing myself and describing my general approach to my work, and after some discussion we took a lunch break. A young woman walked up to me during the break, introduced herself as a social worker, and said, "You know, I can't quite believe you're Dr. Ciaramicoli."

"Why is that?" I asked.

"Well, to tell you the truth, I was expecting someone completely different," she said. "I always thought Italians had white T-shirts with cigarettes rolled up in their sleeves. I've never seen an Italian in a three-piece suit!"

The comment surprised me, and for a brief moment offended me, but there was something about her warm smile that didn't go with the intent to hurt. I could tell that she didn't mean to be insulting, so I decided it was my place to expand her understanding of Italians. "I am Italian," I said, "but I don't smoke, I wear T-shirts only when I exercise and they're not always white, and I always—there has never been an exception—show up on my first day of work dressed in a three-piece suit." We had a good laugh, and that empathic moment marked the beginning of a strong and enduring friendship. I learned to value her tendency to say exactly what she was thinking, and I soon realized that by putting her biases on the line, she was trying to get beyond them. What she was really saying that day was, "Hey, this is what I've heard about Italians, but now I'm not so sure—what's the truth?"

Overt prejudices are not the only obstacles to empathic listening. We all have developed ways of organizing our world by putting people in categories and attaching labels to certain behaviors. We live our lives, in truth, by following certain theories of human behavior based on generalizations or abstractions. For example, a prominent cultural stereotype holds that women are more intuitive or perceptive than men. The truth, according to psychological researchers, is much more complex: While women are generally more accurate in interpreting emotions from facial expressions, at least ten studies have shown that men are equally adept at reading other people's thoughts and emotions.

The innate empathic ability is virtually the same in men and women—the difference appears to be in motivation. As the psychologists Tiffany Graham and William Ickes point out:

> By learning to "tune out" or ignore other people's feelings and needs, men could effectively mask or suppress a social sensitivity which—if expressed—could cause them to be perceived as insufficiently strong and masculine. Thus, as Hancock and Ickes have noted, "If men appear at times to be socially insensitive, it may have more to do with the image they wish to convey than with the ability they possess."

Our theories about life in general and relationships in particular are also strongly influenced by certain standardized formulas or models—the belief that healthy marriages and friendships, for example, are based on unconditional love or that strong physical attraction is an essential element of a sexual relationship. These theories are then mixed with our own, often painful life experiences to generate a complex set of stereotyped beliefs and mental biases that can distort our ability to understand the unique experiences of others.

EMPATHY IS NOT SYMPATHY

In a recent group session, Roberta, a fifty-five-year-old widow, was describing Joe, a man she had been dating. She mentioned that he could sometimes be patronizing and overly controlling, guiding her to respond in ways that he believed were most appropriate rather than allowing her to come to her own decisions.

"Sometimes," she admitted, "he treats me like a child. I know he means well, but I'm not used to being treated like this. Fred [Roberta's deceased husband] was always so gentle and accommodating, he never interfered and always let me make the decisions."

As Roberta talked I noticed that Marilyn, forty-two years old and twice divorced, was getting agitated, sighing, shifting in her chair, even at one point putting her head in her hands. After Roberta was finished I asked Marilyn if something was bothering her.

"I think Roberta's boyfriend is being abusive," Marilyn said forcefully. "So many women stay in abusive relationships for years, until their self-esteem is completely destroyed. I hate to see Roberta being abused by this man."

A discussion ensued between Marilyn and another woman in the group about the unequal division of power between men and women. After a few moments I interrupted and focused attention back on Roberta. I asked if she would mind telling the group what she had been thinking and how she'd been feeling when Marilyn labeled her relationship abusive.

Roberta looked at Marilyn, smiled gently, and said, "The word doesn't fit my relationship. Joe isn't abusive. Sure, he can be controlling, but he's also kind and giving."

"You just don't want to look at the whole picture," Marilyn said, her tone defensive, her voice quavering. "You're afraid to admit the truth."

I turned my attention to Marilyn. "I wonder if Roberta's situation might have some meaning for you," I said.

"I don't know," she said.

"Could you tell me what was going on in your mind when you listened to Roberta?" I asked.

"I was thinking about my father." Tears began to roll down Marilyn's cheeks, and several minutes passed before she could continue. "Like Roberta's husband, he was kind at some times and controlling at others. When I was a teenager he was always there waiting for me when I got home at night. Everyone else was asleep, and he would lock the door so I couldn't sneak in. He would wait for me, and then he would make me sit on his lap, and then he would touch me."

That was the first time Marilyn had told anyone in the group, including me, that she had been sexually abused.

In this interaction we can see the distinction between empathetic listening and sympathetic listening. Empathy, as we have learned, is an innate capacity that motivates us to acts of compassion and altruism. Sympathy is an emotion, the passive experience of sharing another person's fear, grief, anger, or joy. Sympathy means "to suffer or experience *with.*" Empathy means to "suffer or experience *in.*" This may not seem like much of a distinction, but it is analogous to mixing oil and water versus mixing water and milk. With sympathy, the oil and water stand next to each other, touching and interacting, but always maintaining their separate identities—two people are together in their separate experiences. With empathy, the water and milk intermix so that each becomes the other and together they create a whole—two people are both in the same shared experience.

Empathic listening is always centered on the other person, and its goal is to make the other feel uniquely understood. This means moving away from generalities to specifics, from dull to sharp, common to rare, old to new, ordinary to extraordinary, familiar to strange. Sympathy goes back to the past, expressing a general feeling of understanding based on common experiences. Empathy always focuses on the present, on what is happening right now, at this very moment.

Sympathetic listening can be destructive to relationships because it is so generalized. When people are in pain or trouble, their deepest longing is to be understood as exceptions rather than rules. Generalizing from their experiences to similar situations can do more harm than good. When a parent says to an adolescent child, "I was a teenager once, honey, I know exactly what you're going through," it doesn't do much for the suffering adolescent, who wants to be seen and heard as a unique individual rather than being lumped into a category with every other teenager who ever lived.

Sympathy allows us to suffer with people without ever getting close to them. "I feel so sorry for the people in Kosovo" is a sympathetic statement based on a general understanding of world events. "I understand what you are going through," or "I know exactly how you feel," we say to our friends when they tell us about their frustrations with the opposite sex, their fears of turning fifty, or their emotional ups and downs as they deal with their aging parents. But empathy knows—its heart is full with the understanding— that you cannot immediately know what I am feeling because you are not me. So empathy seeks to go deeper, to listen with rapt attention, to understand, to mix in, and, even if it is for just a brief moment, share another person's heart and soul.

Ruth, forty-six, has breast cancer. The cancer has spread to her bones and, her doctors fear, to her spinal cord. She has to use a cane, her leg is in a brace, and eventually, she has been told by a neurologist, she will need a wheelchair.

On a recent spring day a specially equipped bus picked up Ruth at her home and took her to the recreation center for a swim in the therapy pool. The female bus driver was cheerful and inquisitive. "Hey, what's up with your leg?" she asked. Hearing that Ruth has bone cancer, the bus driver gasped. "Oh my. Let me tell you, I am so thankful for my life and my little problems. There is always someone else worse off than me." Ruth's gentle smile hid her pain.

At the recreation center a middle-aged woman walked out of the locker room and extended her hand to Ruth, who expected a friendly handshake. Instead the woman sandwiched Ruth's hand between her own, closed her eyes, bowed her head, and prayed, begging the Lord to drive this curse out of his servant. Then the woman walked away, a pious look on her face.

Ruth was speechless. She didn't know what to say, but she knew what she felt. She wished she could kick off her brace, sprint after the woman, tackle her and drag her to the ground. "I don't need your prayer performance or your 'oh poor thing,' " Ruth wanted to scream. "I am not even a person to you. I'm a novelty, a story to tell your girlfriends at the next church supper about how you prayed over that poor, pitiful, handicapped woman at the pool."

But Ruth did not sprint after the woman. Instead she took the bus home and sat down to write a letter to her friends and relatives. Balancing her emotions with thoughtful consideration, Ruth offered suggestions about how to speak and listen to someone who is gravely ill. She spoke with great empathy and asked her loved ones to return the favor by listening with empathy.

> Light a candle for me; if it comforts you, say a prayer, think good thoughts, a couple of novenas or rosaries are all right too; but don't grab my hand and pray over me. Ask me if this is something that will give me comfort. It may the day you visit, who knows? If I say no, let's just be together, you can always pray in my driveway or on your way home.
>
> Be ready to laugh and cry together. Expect our visit to be intense—if I didn't have cancer, our visit would probably be intense anyway. I am not just a cancer patient, you know. Don't tell me I am a poor thing. Your intention may be to empathize with my situation and comfort me, but the effect of "Oh, you poor thing" on me is that I am worse off than you, and you

are glad you aren't having to deal with this stuff. If you need to cherish your good health and fortune, please do this in my driveway or on your way home.

Be willing to take a risk: call me, E-mail me, visit. Work out your own stuff about intruding and feeling uncomfortable if I say this is not a good time. If you can't, get some counseling. Work out what it is to have a friend so ill and then come see me. I am really not in a position to take care of people's stuff. This is not to say I am not interested in what is going on in your life; I mean it when I ask you, "How are you?"

If you feel the need to share cancer horror stories with me, do so only if you are willing to really honor the person you lost or witnessed through this horrible disease. Also, don't tell my cancer story to anyone without honoring who I am. I don't want to be a friend of yours who has taught you so much about dying; I'd rather hope I could be one of your friends who taught you about living.

PERFECTION

Listening is an art, and listening with empathy is the highest expression of that art. With time and a considerable amount of patience, discipline, and effort, we get better at it all the time, but there are always lapses; there are always reminders of the fact that we are human and therefore imperfect, which means that we will make mistakes. I was working recently with Andrea, a friend and colleague whom I supervise. (In clinical psychology licensed clinicians sometimes ask senior colleagues for supervision in an effort to keep improving and to make sure they are maintaining their objectivity, particularly in difficult cases.)

On this occasion I was preoccupied with personal thoughts, and apparently I kept drumming my fingers on my knee. My eyes, Andrea told me later, were looking at her, but I wasn't blinking or responding. I was clearly somewhere else in mind and spirit. Andrea stopped talking and waited a moment.

"What's wrong?" I said.

"You're not here with me today," she answered. From her tone of voice and the expression on her face, I could tell that she was feeling hurt and abandoned. In that moment of failing my friend and colleague, I was reminded once again how difficult and demanding the art of empathic listening can be. We can never say that we "have" it, for we are always having to seek it out. Each interaction is different; every relationship is unique.

Yet those moments when we falter or stumble can be just as instructive, for this is where our empathy for each other and for ourselves deepens and widens. We all make mistakes. I make them on a daily basis. If we think of empathy at its best—when it is mutual and reciprocal, shared by two or more people—then we can appreciate how difficult it can be to maintain, and we are not insulted when a friend says, "Hey, you're not with me today, where are you?" At that moment we may feel a slight twinge of embarrassment, but we quickly recover, knowing that with empathy, as with everything in life, perfection is impossible. No one can be perfectly empathic. We all make mistakes.

But those times when we reach out once again with empathy can also be most instructive. "I'm sorry," I said to Andrea, "I've been worried about my daughter. She's been sick with bronchitis, and her right knee has been bothering her." With that explanation Andrea understood where I had been, and we pulled each other back on track. All social interactions feature give-and-take. On certain days one person may do most of the listening, and on other days that same person may do most of the talking. We give, we take, we listen, we talk, we make mistakes, and we apologize—but we always keep trying to understand and respond with sensitivity. This is how we join together, not in our desire to perfect the art of conversation but in our willingness to acknowledge that we cannot do it alone, for we need each other. Empathy is an interactional process, a commingling of souls. Individual streams join with other streams, and together they create a powerful river that flows on, strong, purposeful, inner-directed.

Several years ago I invited Dr. Paul Ornstein, a Holocaust survivor and famous "self psychologist" to speak to the staff at the hospital where I work. Self psychology focuses on how our sense of self develops through our interactions with others. From the perspective of empathy, self psychology is interested in how empathy enlivens the self and how a lack of empathy leaves us with a depleted sense of self and a deep yearning for connection and intimacy.

After a short talk Dr. Ornstein asked if anyone in the audience would be willing to present a recent case so the group could discuss it in terms of self psychology. For several moments no one moved, intimidated, perhaps, by the thought of discussing their work with a famous psychologist. Finally, a hand went up. Ilaria, the hospital's chief social worker, said she would be willing to discuss "a difficult case." The daughter of a Russian Orthodox priest, Ilaria escaped from Russia with her father during World War II, leaving behind her mother, sister, and brother. After the war the family was reunited, but the anguish of those years continues to haunt Ilaria, one of the most loving, compassionate people I have ever had the privilege to meet.

Ilaria presented her case as good clinicians always do, describing her patient and his presenting problem, offering insights into his family of origin, and detailing various interactions in therapy. Then she turned to Dr. Ornstein and asked directly for his help. "I wanted to discuss this particular case with you because I know that I wasn't doing my best," she said. "I wasn't listening to my patient. I don't know why, but I couldn't get my mind focused."

"What did you do with your confusion?" Dr. Ornstein asked.

"I admitted it," she said. "I turned to my patient and said, 'Do you get the feeling that I'm just not getting it?' And he said, 'Yes, you are totally not getting it.' Then he pointed out very clearly where I had missed the point." Ilaria laughed nervously. "I have to tell you, I'm embarrassed to present this case, because I know that I was just fumbling all over the place. But I really didn't know what else to do."

"I think that was a wonderful intervention," Ornstein said with a broad smile. "You asked the patient if he felt heard, if he got the sense that you understood what he was saying. You gave him the opportunity to speak his mind, and he knew by the way you asked for his help that you sincerely wanted to hear the truth. So he felt free to tell you that you were missing something, and then he pulled you back on track."

That interaction reveals an effective listening strategy that can be used in both therapy and everyday life experiences. Every so often ask your friend, spouse, child, or patient: "Do you get the sense that I'm listening to you, that I'm hearing what you have to say?" Often in my sessions with patients I will preface my statements with words like, "Correct me if I'm misunderstanding you, but I think you might be saying . . ." or "My impression is, and I want to emphasize that it's just an impression . . ." or "Help me fill in the blanks, so far it seems like you might be saying . . ." With these words and phrases I offer an invitation, asking for the other person's help in the invariably complex process of empathic listening. In the attempt to accurately understand their thoughts and feelings, I ask my patients to let me know if I've missed something, to reassure me that I am on the right track, and to guide me back if I've lost my way.

In his classic book *On Becoming a Person*, the psychologist Carl Rogers suggested a similar strategy as a means of testing your listening skills.

> The next time you get in an argument with your wife, or your friend, or with a small group of friends, just stop the discussion for a moment and for an experiment, institute this rule. "Each person can speak up for himself only *after* he has first restated the ideas and feelings of the previous speaker accurately, and to that speaker's satisfaction." You see what this would mean. It would simply mean that before presenting your own point of view, it would be necessary for you to really achieve the other speaker's frame of reference—to understand his thoughts and feelings so well that you could summarize them for him. Sounds simple, doesn't it? But if you try it you will discover it is one of the most difficult things you have ever tried to do. However, once you have been able to see the other's point of view, your own comments will have to be drastically revised. You will also find the emotion going out of the discussion, the differences being reduced, and those differences which remain being of a rational and understandable sort.

Empathic listening leads us to a place of intimate understanding where thoughts and feelings interact in a reasonable, rational way. In this empathic space we reach a deeper understanding of ourselves and our relationship to others. Empathy reveals the intimate subtleties of our mirrored worlds, reflecting back both the uniqueness and the commonalities of our shared experiences.

In the effort to understand others and appreciate their world, we are obliged to give up our self-centered viewpoint. With the other-centered perspective that empathy brings, our problems do not loom so large or seem so insurmountable. Our world expands, becoming a more complicated but definitely more interesting place to be. Free to explore this world, we transform ourselves in the process of immersing ourselves in the lives of others.

This is the power of empathy.

Chapter 6

Sex, Intimacy, and Empathy

We touch bodies when we have sex, but we can only touch
hearts and souls with empathy guiding the way.

In his classic book *Love and Will*, Rollo May described sexual intercourse as "the most powerful enactment of relatedness imaginable." While I am convinced that can be true, I have talked to hundreds of men and women who tell me that sex—even great sex—can't fill up the empty spaces inside them. The mechanics may be good, but with the empathic connection missing, the end result is unsatisfying. May acknowledged the problem later in his book when he discussed his patients' complaints about the lack of feeling and passion in their lives with the comment "So much sex and so little meaning."

How do we put *meaning*—feeling, passion, heart, and soul—back into sex? Empathy is the sole answer, for only with empathy can we reach true intimacy, that state of understanding the thoughts and feelings of another human being while simultaneously knowing that the other understands our inner experience. Touching souls is what we seek in all intimate relationships, sexual or otherwise, but you can't get anywhere near another person's soul without the guidance of empathy.

Sex is not just a hunger, a thirst, or an itch that must be scratched. If it were, masturbation would satisfy all our sexual longings. What we seek in the sexual experience is not simply the release of tension but the momentary merger of two souls that simultaneously confirms and expands the relationship between us. This is ultimate intimacy, the moment when two hearts and two souls join together as one.

How does empathy create intimacy, going beyond physical attraction to encompass the heart and soul? Rather than try to describe the perfect human relationship, I believe we can learn about the power of empathy by witnessing how it can lead us from superficial connections to deep, heart-felt relationships that accept the whole person, imperfections and all. That acceptance is both internal and external, for at the same time empathy embraces others it leads us to accept ourselves with all our limitations and shortcomings. Through empathy we learn how to love each other deeply and truly, and we discover why the search for the *real* person rather than the *right* person is central to our quest for happiness.

CAROLYN'S STORY

My patients are my greatest teachers, and in every session I gain a deeper understanding of the power of empathy to create intimacy. Carolyn is a poignant example. A single mother of two adolescent girls, Carolyn was raised by an alcoholic father and a chronically depressed mother. Her most vivid childhood memories revolve around her efforts to please her father; in therapy she often recalls the hours she spent in a cold, dimly lit base-ment ironing her father's shirts, hoping to win his approval. When she handed him the freshly ironed shirts, he would be pleased, at least for a lit-tle while. Then, inevitably, he would start criticizing her or dismiss her with a scornful comment and an impatient wave of the hand.

As so often happens with children, a lack of empathy in Carolyn's relationship with her parents led to certain distorted perceptions about herself and others. Rather than being able to see her alcoholic father realis-tically as the selfish, insecure man he was, Carolyn grew up idealizing him, confusing his anger with strength, and punishing herself for not being good enough, smart enough, or creative enough to stop his drunken tirades. Her inner voice, like her father's real-life voice, was harshly punitive as she scolded herself for her inability to be the perfect child (and, later, the per-fect adult) who could create and maintain the ideal relationship.

Now in her late thirties and divorced from an alcoholic husband, Caro-lyn is an associate professor at a small liberal arts college. Sex has come to play a central role in her life. One affair quickly succeeds another, but they all follow the same general format. She meets a man, often in a bar, she idealizes him, they end up in bed, and then she repeats her childhood pattern of doing everything in her power to please him. In the end she is overwhelmed with fear that he will see through her and is inevitably disappointed by the shallowness of their emotional connection. After a few weeks or months the affair ends, and a new one begins.

"I understand Monica," Carolyn told me one day during President Clinton's impeachment trial. "She's not interested in the whole man—she just wants thirty percent of him. And that's what he wants, too." She shifted in her chair, a beautiful woman with long, dark hair and dark eyes, seductively dressed in a short-skirted designer suit, makeup perfectly applied, nails painted bright red. She adjusted her skirt and flashed me a winning smile. "That's what I'm interested in, too—I don't care about Mr. Right. I want Mr. Right Now."

Carolyn gave up the search for Mr. Right five years earlier, when she flew to Iowa to be with her dying mother. Her husband, left alone for several weeks, had an affair with his secretary. When Carolyn found out about the relationship, she confronted her husband, who couldn't understand her anger. "You left me for almost a month!" he howled in protest. "What was I supposed to do with myself?"

Carolyn rolled her eyes when she told me this story. "Do you believe it? This man is an engineer, he's not dumb, he understands how things work—why couldn't he use his own two hands to relieve 'the accumulating tension,' as he put it, instead of finding someone to do it for him?"

With her characteristic quick humor, Carolyn attempted to hide her anguish at her husband's betrayal. She told me once that she decided to leave her husband after a couple's session with her previous therapist. Carolyn began to sob, and her husband continued to talk about how selfish she was and how she never paid enough attention to him. "I'm lying here bleeding on the floor," she cried out at one point, "and you just keep stomping on me!" The therapist attempted to calm her down, but her husband interrupted. "Don't even try," he said. "When she gets to this point, there's no turning back."

After the divorce proceedings began, Carolyn started her long series of affairs. Her sexual liaisons always started out with great excitement. "He looks just like Tom Selleck," she said of one conquest. A month later, describing a different man, she said, "This guy is so high-powered, so charming, and he's even better looking than the last one!" A few months later she would tell me about another man who was "sweet and uncomplicated and never puts any demands on me."

And so the pattern continued, as Carolyn initially idealized the new man in her life only to discover several weeks or months later that he was, in her words, selfish, inconsiderate, a liar, scoundrel, drunk, or cheat. After severely criticizing herself for being "stupid" or "naive," she would start over again. She always chose men who were handsome, flirtatious, charismatic ("the kind who can really work a crowd") and who were also aloof, undemanding, and, inevitably, unwilling to get emotionally involved.

"I like having affairs," she told me once, "because you never have to take off your makeup." That statement seemed to sum it up for Carolyn. If you don't take off your makeup, she reasoned, then you still have a shield to hide behind; you can be completely naked but remain emotionally unexposed. She lived in great fear that someone would see through her mask to discover that the perfect outside didn't match the imperfect inside.

One day Carolyn divulged a secret. "I've been having an affair with a younger man," she said, looking down at her hands folded neatly in her lap. "He's half my age. He's married." A pause. "And his wife is expecting their first child."

I waited, knowing she had more to say. "I didn't want to tell you," she continued, "because I thought you might judge me." Another moment passed. "No, no, that's wrong, I'm judging myself. I guess I'm afraid you will make me look at the truth."

"The truth?" I said.

"You know, the whole picture." She pouted, sticking out her lower lip. "I'm afraid if I think too much about this, it will spoil the fun."

"How do you think the truth might ruin the fun?" I asked.

"I don't want to look at this affair," she said. "I'd have to face what I'm doing, sleeping with a man who has a wife and a baby on the way. It all seems so sad, so desperate, so hopeless."

"That doesn't sound like much fun," I said.

"It's not," she admitted. "Even the sex—even that's not fun anymore."

In conversations like these Carolyn began to let down her guard, revealing parts of herself that she was afraid to show to others. My empathy for her—my drive to understand her thoughts and feelings and my ongoing effort to respond sensitively but honestly to her moment-to-moment experiences—gave her the freedom to express herself openly, without fear. She knew that I would be truthful with her, and she desperately wanted to be honest with me. She wanted to "take off her makeup" and reveal the whole of herself, not just the 30 percent she showed to the rest of the world.

When Carolyn accepted that I wouldn't run away from her by judging her or trying somehow to control her behavior, she began to feel more secure about discussing her fears and insecurities. She was able to "borrow" my empathy, using it as a mirror to see inside herself. My understanding, empathic voice—nonjudgmental but always insisting on the truth— gradually began to replace the punitive voice she had been listening to all her life. This is what psychologists refer to as *internalization*, taking in another's voice and ultimately making it your own. We see this process evolve in children all the time, as they take in the tenor of the parent's voice; if it is a reproachful voice, like Carolyn's father's voice, the child's self voice also becomes self-censuring. Adopting my empathic voice, Carolyn was able to speak to herself in a more understanding, soothing way.

One day Carolyn arrived for our weekly session looking very reflective. Her quick, sharp humor had given way to a visible softness, a vulnerability I had not seen before. "I saw my father today," she said. "He was walking down the street ahead of me, and even though I hadn't seen him for years, I knew it was him. He looked so scared and lonely, just a little old man. I realized as I watched him that he had no power over me anymore— he couldn't ever hurt me again."

She leaned forward, excited by a sudden insight. "It was an amazing moment, Dr. C, like that scene in *The Wizard of Oz* when the small round man comes out from behind the curtain. All through the movie you're trembling in anticipation of seeing this guy, you think he's all-powerful, and then you find out that he's just a little old man who has to wake up every morning, look at himself in the mirror, and admit that he's not omnipotent. Standing on the street, it hit me like a bolt from the blue that I wasn't afraid of my father, I wasn't angry, I didn't hate him anymore." She sighed deeply and added, "I just feel sorry for him."

Several months later, just before Christmas, Carolyn arrived at my office laughing, her cheeks bright red with the cold. "You won't believe this," she said. "Last night I went out and bought a fifteen-foot Christmas tree, the biggest tree I ever saw in my life. I had to move all my living room furniture into the garage. My kids think I've gone off the deep end. We laughed about having me committed."

The story behind the tree revealed why Carolyn was in such good spirits. For months she had been involved with the vice president of her college. "I swear, he looks and acts just like Bill Clinton," she said. "A real charmer, the same ingratiating smile, that way of touching your elbow, rubbing your back, looking into your eyes like he really cares about you." She did a little mock shudder and then laughed good-naturedly. "I'm taken in by his little games, you know, just looking at the thirty percent and ignoring the rest of it. But then I start to think—hey, who is this man, what is he really interested in? I force myself to look at another ten percent, and suddenly I see the salesman in him—the wink, the pitch, the fake smile. Then I see another ten percent, the part where he lies to me when he tells me he loves me, and then another ten percent, the part where he lies to himself and his wife and his kids . . . and suddenly I see this man in all his emotional nakedness, and I realize I can't stand the sight of him!

"So then, the night before last, I wake up in the middle of the night, and say to myself: 'Carolyn, you don't want to spend the rest of your life repeating the same old pattern. You deserve better than this.' I thought for some crazy reason about my ex-husband, who never let me buy a Christmas tree—he said he was allergic to them, have you ever heard of someone being allergic to a Christmas tree?—and so the next day I went out and bought myself a fifteen-foot tree to celebrate. I'm telling you, Dr. C, it's the most beautiful tree I've ever seen."

All her life Carolyn had worried about living up to the image established by the men in her life, first following her father's directives and then, because she had so little empathy for herself, acquiescing to the demands of her husbands and lovers. The towering Christmas tree signified her break with her old pattern and her readiness to accept herself as a complicated, imperfect, but wholly human being who could escape from the restricting images she had created for herself.

Through the power of empathy, Carolyn learned that sex by itself cannot create intimacy. She discovered that we touch bodies when we have sex, but we can only touch hearts and souls with empathy guiding the way. Empathy takes us deep into the truth of the other person, giving us the insights and understanding to know where his or her reality ends and ours begins. Empathy tells us who we can trust and who we should avoid, how to protect and defend ourselves, when to move forward and when to hold back.

In every human relationship we go through various stages of intimacy, often bouncing back and forth between the stages on the bumpy but always scenic road called getting to know each other. The first stage is *idealization*, the time when we fall head-over-heels in love and from that upended position see life in distorted ways. *Polarization* is the second stage, when we move from the idea that everything is "wonderful, perfect, all I ever wanted," to the opposite viewpoint, where we become preoccupied with the little blemishes and flaws in the other person. Noticing all the imperfections, we want to run and hide because those weak spots somehow (we're not quite sure how) seem to reflect back on our own vulnerabilities.

From polarization we often make a U-turn and head straight back to the land of idealization, where we begin all over again; or we keep traveling over the potholes and dips in the windy road, hoping that eventually we'll be treated to a smooth ride. With patience, commitment, objectivity, and, above all, empathy, we enter the third stage—*integration*. As our vision expands to encompass the whole picture, we take into account the integrated whole of the other person, which includes both the "good" and the "bad" parts. We learn to see what really matters and let go of what is truly inconsequential. The periodic "bumps" we encounter along the way serve as reminders to slow down and pay attention rather than indications that we have failed and need to start again at the beginning.

Exploring the nature of these three stages teaches us how empathy strengthens our relationships, leading us to develop a deeper appreciation for others and for ourselves.

THE THREE STAGES OF RELATIONSHIPS

Stage 1: Idealization

"Falling in love," pronounced the wonderfully humane psychoanalyst Elvin Semrad two decades ago, "is the only acceptable form of psychosis in our culture." All psychoses, falling in love included, involve an inability to maintain focus and objectivity. We can't, in other words, see straight, think straight, or feel straight. Everything seems to circle around the object of our affection in a dizzying, exhiliarating roller coaster of emotion. Reason is lost in the wild ride, as we get carried away on what seems like the ultimate adventure.

Every time Carolyn fell in love, she believed that this time it would work. *This time* she would choose the right man. *This time* she would be able to change him to suit her needs. *This time* she would do everything possible to please him. *This time* he would realize that he couldn't live without her. But every time, after the idealizations began to fade, she would end up disillusioned and disheartened.

The challenges to empathy in the idealization stage of relationships are obvious, because empathy depends on objectivity for its balance and direction. In fact, in many ways empathy is synonymous with objectivity, which can be defined as the ability to see the world as it is, realistically, without distortion. In his classic work *The Art of Loving*, the psychoanalyst Erich Fromm emphasized the central place of objectivity in the act of loving another person.

> I have to know the other person and myself objectively in order to be able to see his [sic] reality, or rather, to overcome the illusions, the irrationally distorted picture I have of him. Only if I know a human being objectively, can I know him in his ultimate essence, in the act of love.

Why is objectivity so important? Why, in Carolyn's words, do we have to "spoil the fun" with the objective truth? Images are like pictures on the wall, beautiful and inviting but impossible to enter or alter because they are fixed, static. A photograph of the waves breaking against the rocky Maine coast may be a beautiful image, but you can't hear the water pounding against the rocks or feel the salt spray on your face.

Images are things, while human beings are flesh and blood, prone to headaches, toothaches, foul tempers, and bad moods. When we make people into objects, we destroy their spirits. One of my patients told me she can remember the precise moment she began to question her relationship with her husband. He put his arms around her, told her how much he loved her, and then said, "You are the perfect mother, a gracious hostess, and a loving, attentive wife. I want you to stay just like this for the rest of your life."

If we love another person as an object or a thing, we want that person to stay exactly the same in order to match the image we have constructed in our minds, an image that has been carefully crafted to satisfy our needs. This concentrated focus on the self—what psychologists call *narcissism*—keeps us from seeing the other person as a developing, unfolding human being. The other has meaning only in what he or she can give to us. Reality is defined in terms of my needs, my desires, my fears, and my hungers. The world narrows down to the need to be loved. For so many people love is driven wholly by need and not by empathy, which is represented by the yearning to know more, to go deeper, to reveal ourselves, and to know others as they are now and as they will change over time.

Love driven by excessive need is what I call *image love*; it is, in truth, imaginary, for we have fallen in love with the image, not with the real person. This comforts us at first because the image is always unflawed and unblemished, whereas the human being is always, inevitably imperfect. Thus image love protects us from recognizing imperfections in others (or admitting our own) by keeping us from getting too close. Yet if we would love an image, we would also have to be an image. And that is the central point to keep in mind about this stage: If we "take off our makeup," in Carolyn's words, we risk exposing ourselves. That is a risk we cannot take if we remain committed to maintaining the image.

In the idealization stage of relationships, we create images for ourselves and for each other, and these images are always characterizations or stereotypes that deny part of who we are. Stuck in this stage, fearful of moving on, we are inevitably disappointed because, as time goes on, it becomes clear that no one can live up to the ideal image. Some of us have warts, others have acne, fungus on our toes, or spaces between our teeth. We have annoying habits like snorting when we laugh, snoring when we sleep, snapping our gum, or slurping our soup.

We also end up disappointing ourselves. Carolyn said she liked having affairs because she never had to take off her makeup. But putting the makeup on and making sure it always stayed fresh became one of her major preoccupations. What if her mascara rubbed off—what if this new, idealized lover noticed something about her that was flawed, chipped, or cracked? Carolyn's fears of being exposed always flooded her with images from when she was eight, nine, or ten years old, cowering before her father's disapproving eyes. With no makeup (mask) to hide behind, she knew she was not pleasing to him, and she assumed that she was therefore, somehow, substandard, inadequate, never "good enough."

The ideal images we construct for ourselves inevitably take us back to what I call the scene of the crime—the unsolved mysteries of our past that continue to haunt us in the present. Carolyn's ideal images took root in her childhood experiences and the lack of empathy she received from her parents, particularly her father. When she was a young child, Carolyn learned that the way to keep a man happy is to do things for him; the more you do to please a man, the better chance you have of preserving the peace. Her alcoholic father, who had numerous affairs and complained often about the unreasonable demands of women, taught her these lessons. Her husband, who complained that she couldn't satisfy him and had an affair, confirmed the lesson. Rather than realistically assessing her father's and her husband's affairs as reflections of their insecurities, she assumed she was at fault and renewed her efforts to find better ways to satisfy men. Sexual competency became her goal; being a "great lover" became her ideal image.

All children think of themselves in a world where they can do anything they want—the "I can do it myself" phenomenon. Through many empathic interactions with parents, relatives, and teachers, they begin to form a more realistic view of themselves. When treated with empathy and respect, they come to see that they cannot do everything, and they learn to accept their limitations without feeling humiliated by them. When we use empathy to guide our interactions with children, they learn that a flawed performance does not affect our respect for them as individuals nor does it change our love for them.

Empathy helps children cope with their growing understanding of their limitations and their realistic disappointment that, no matter how hard they try, they cannot do everything or be the best at everything they attempt. Children who grow up surrounded by empathy develop a soothing self voice, which assures them that even if they cannot hit a home run to win the game or be voted the most popular person in the class, they are still worthy of love. In contrast, in an environment where empathy is lacking or deficient, the child develops a punitive self voice that continually repeats the message "You have not done enough," which often leads to the self-defeating conclusion "You are not enough" or its corollary, "You are not good enough."

Growing up, we continually underestimate the history we bring to relationships. Even the healthiest people carry their history with them, and only empathy can bring it into awareness, guiding our perceptions and helping us to see where the past continues to guide the present. A recent session with Andrew may help clarify this point. Andrew, thirty-three, came into therapy with a "Big Problem," as he put it. "I'm in love, and really very happy, but I can't make a commitment." With these words he blushed bright red. "This is terrible, I'm so ashamed. You're the only person I could ever tell, and I hope you will understand and not think I'm just a terrible, superficial person. I realized that I can't marry Annie because she has a big rear end. I have this thing about big butts."

Sensing Andrew's deep embarrassment and knowing that he could perceive even a casual gesture or slight change in vocal intonation as disapproving, I was careful to listen very intently and keep my voice neutral. I knew that Andrew's concern with his partner's body went far beyond a superficial interest in the "perfect physique" to something deeper than either of us understood at that moment.

"I wonder what else this might involve," I said, "for your feelings seem to run very deep." With that comment Andrew visibly relaxed, for he understood by my tone of voice and even-tempered approach that I was with him in an important exploration and hoped to understand, not judge, his thoughts and feelings in order to release him from his shame and guilt.

"I don't know," he said with a deep sigh. "I like everything about her. I like her strong body, and I particularly admire her athleticism. But I just can't imagine marrying a woman with a big butt."

At that point I could have offered some insightful but decidedly unhelpful psychological interpretation like, "You are obviously projecting your feelings of inadequacy onto her" or "You are focusing on the superficial aspects of the relationship because you are afraid of commitment." Another direction would have been to ask Andrew directly why he felt "inadequate" in the presence of women. Instead, I used empathy to expand the picture, hoping to set the stage for the truth to be revealed.

"Let me see if I understand," I said. "You like her strong, athletic body, but then you begin to focus on her rear end, and your very positive feelings and perceptions move to a preoccupation with this particular body part."

"That's right," he said. "She's a strong woman, but she's also a large woman, and I've always had trouble with that body type."

"I wonder if you could tell me how it came about that you have trouble with a large body type in women," I said.

"Women like that take charge too much, you know the type, they're controlling, domineering . . ." His voice suddenly trailed off.

"Do you know large women who are controlling and domineering?" I asked.

"Sure, at work, everywhere."

"Do most of the large women you work with fit into the category of the domineering type?"

"No, not all of them," he said after reflecting for a moment. "I know some petite women who are domineering. Well, actually, most of the women I work with are pleasant and considerate of others."

Another long silence ensued as Andrew struggled with his thoughts and feelings.

"Is this a familiar feeling for you, that large women are domineering?" I asked. Asking someone if a thought or feeling is familiar, i.e., customary or habitual, often helps to uncover the historical roots of the behavior.

"Yes," he said without elaborating.

"When do you remember feeling this way?"

"Do you mean when I was young?"

"Not necessarily," I said. "I'm just wondering when this has come up for you before."

"Just talking with you, well, I don't know . . ." Again there was a long pause. "I guess I remember feeling this way a long time ago." Another long pause. "My mother was a large woman."

Later in the session Andrew talked at great length about his mother. "I always felt little in her presence," he told me. "Just thinking about her right now, I feel small. I like petite women, they feel safer to me. I'm not so afraid of being inadequate, and I don't have to live in fear that they will turn out to be like my mother."

And thus we circled back to the scene of the crime, where Andrew as a child was humiliated by his mother, a large woman whose husband left her with four young boys to raise by herself. She took out her frustrations on her children, and ever since Andrew has been wary of large women. From this fear he constructed an image of his ideal woman: trim, petite, with a small rear end—the polar opposite, in looks at least, of his mother.

With empathy leading him to look beyond superficial statements and summary judgments, Andrew was able to gain a new perspective on his fixed perceptions and see clearly how he was confusing the past with the present. He came to understand and accept the fact that a petite woman would not change his past or protect him from feeling inadequate, nor would a large woman automatically repeat the patterns of his past. By returning to the scene of the crime, he could begin the process of putting his old ghosts to rest.

Ideal images are imaginary creations—they are not the real thing. We can only experience true intimacy when we are willing to see other people as the complicated human beings that they are. As we begin to open our eyes and look beyond the image, the challenges to empathy increase, for we often get stuck in "the bad parts" and pay insufficient attention to "the good parts." This is the difficult and demanding stage of relationships that I call polarization.

Stage 2: Polarization

As reality sets in cracks begin to appear in the images we have constructed. Suddenly we see the imperfections we overlooked in the idealization phase, when our eyes were clouded over with image love. As our vision clears we notice our partner's annoying habits, physical defects, and emotional shortcomings. We realize, with a jolt, that the people we've been idealizing laugh too loud, interrupt when we talk, or tell inappropriate jokes. They make negative comments and intolerant remarks. They interject opinions when they're not wanted, or they sit like bumps on a log with no opinions at all. They never want to have sex, or they can't keep their hands off us. They sweat too much, have smelly feet, bad breath, or crooked teeth.

As fissures begin to appear in the ideal images we have invested so much energy in constructing, we find ourselves making snap judgments and speaking in generalizations. He's hyper. She's lazy. He's passive. She's aggressive. He never wants to do anything spontaneous. She's always changing her mind. He's neurotic about cleanliness. She's a slob.

For Carolyn the polarization stage involved a seemingly sudden realization that the man she had been idealizing was not as perfect as she once thought. His jokes, she insisted, were crude. His lovemaking was perfunctory. He paid no attention to her needs or desires. His conversational skills were seriously limited. He was boring, selfish, callous, superficial, and so on.

From the specific Carolyn quickly traveled to the general. "It's not just this man," she would tell me, "it's all men. They're all like that. It always ends up this way." These generalizations would spread in ever-widening circles to encompass all of Carolyn's world, including herself. "I'm such an idiot, I always do this, why don't I learn?" she would say. "What's wrong with me, why don't I know better? My life is so shallow, so cosmetic, everything is on the surface. I guess I should accept the fact that I can't handle relationships with any depth."

Back in the idealization stage, Carolyn could look at herself in the mirror of the other, seeing her reflection as beautiful and unblemished. When her lover's image began to fracture, however, so did hers. Afraid of that image, convinced it represented weakness and disintegration, she would end the relationship and start all over, caught up once again in the fun of the conquest and the flush of idealizing and being idealized.

The polarization stage of relationships can be turbulent and disorienting. With empathy guiding the way, however, we can learn how to take in the new reality and acknowledge that everyone has weaknesses and flaws. With that acknowledgment we are faced with the challenge of sorting through our mutual shortcomings, learning what we can and cannot change, and determining how much time and attention we are willing to devote to the process of change and growth. Recognizing that different people have different orientations to life, we use empathy to find out whether we can adapt to a different perspective and to determine if others arc willing to changc thcir vicwpoints to accommodate our unique approach to life.

When empathy is lacking we try to hold on to the status quo and survive the bumpy ride without fully understanding our power to smooth things out. Or we end the relationship abruptly and start over again, as was Carolyn's pattern. If empathy is not guiding the relationship, we have no hope of progressing through polarization into the integration stage.

The major characteristics of the polarization stage are generalization, the either-or phenomenon, and projection.

Generalization. A fifty-one-year-old man wrote to Ann Landers, desperate for advice. Recently married to a woman "who has been down the aisle three times," he explained that she has an annoying habit of bashing men. She can't stand his male friends, and she constantly makes fun of her

daughters' boyfriends. She seems happiest, he wrote, when she commiser-
ates with other women about how they have been hurt or wronged by men.
Whenever she hears a story about a womanizer, gambler, or heavy drinker,
she comments, "Typical male." When a neighbor visited with a new puppy
and cautioned him to be careful because the dog didn't seem to like men,
his wife commented, "Smart dog."

"How can I make her understand that her constant male bashing is
harming our relationship?" he asked.

Ann Landers responded by asking the man why he didn't notice this
woman's negativity sooner in their relationship, before he decided to marry
her. She counseled him to let his wife know how much her remarks hurt
him. Therapy, she suggested, might help.

The Ann Landers format doesn't allow for long, detailed responses, but
from an empathic perspective I would want to know more about this
woman's background and history with men. Anger is often related to long-
standing feelings of humiliation. How had she been hurt by the men in her
life? When did she learn to lump all men into one category, and how does
that generalization comfort or protect her? When and where in the past
was she failed empathically?

These questions take time to answer, but the process is revealing to all
involved. Treated with empathy, this woman would learn that her concerns
about men would not be dismissed. She would gain new insights into her
thoughts and feelings. She would discover how her broad-brush generalizations hurt her husband by boxing him up with all men and thus denying
him his uniqueness.

Her husband would be helped to understand that her negativity
stemmed from the constricted vision that occurs when people have not
been treated with empathy, meaning that their thoughts and feelings have
not been understood or responded to with sensitivity and care. Empathy
would then help him face the reality of his situation and discover ways to
deal with it. What blinders exist in his history, leading him to miss the obvious? Will his wife change, or is her belief system so entrenched that she
will resist all efforts to revise it? If he accommodates to her, will he end up
subverting his own best interests?

The answers to these questions do not arrive without a great deal of
soul-searching. While empathy usually protects us from investing further
energy in a losing battle, sometimes we choose to stay even when all signs

point to "go." Many, many years ago, when I was still young and somewhat naive, I worked with a couple who were considering a divorce. He openly admitted that he had "lost that romantic feeling" for his wife. Even though she knew his feelings were not going to change, she decided to stay with him. They were both intellectuals and had much in common—discussing current events, reading the classics, attending Boston Pops concerts, going to the theater. Together they decided that even though they might never again be sexual partners, there were other strengths to their relationship that would keep them together.

I must have conveyed my concern that the woman was settling for a relationship that might, in the end, be unfulfilling for her. "I think you are disappointed," she said to me one day. "Maybe when you get to be my age, you will see that although sex is important, other things, including the quality of the time you spend together, are more important."

Empathy does not mean that everything works out for the best, but at the very least the process confirms that you have traveled the road and refused to take shortcuts by reducing the world's complexities to sweeping generalizations. Empathy refuses to label our thoughts and feelings "bad" or "good" and opts instead to weave all aspects of our experience into an integrated whole capable of changing with each new experience and insight. Only with empathy can we discover if we are willing to live with the "whole picture" or if we need to start over again.

The point is to avoid generalizations, for whenever we think in global terms, we are not thinking empathically. Empathy seeks to know the truth about this unique individual or this unusual situation *at this particular moment in time*. When empathy hears a generalization, it immediately wants to pull it apart, knowing that sweeping or vague statements cannot explain individual behavior. Empathy reminds us that there is no such thing as a "typical male" or "typical female." Every human being is an exception, not a rule.

We are drawn to generalizations when we are stressed, tired, confused, or emotionally overwhelmed. Lumping things together makes it easier for us, because we don't have to work so hard to understand. It feels good to take all our ambiguities and uncertainties, wrap them up in neat little packages, and store them away. When we say, "All men are untrustworthy," we can avoid the difficulty of trying to explain why some men can be trusted while others can't. When we say, "Men are from Mars and women are from Venus," we have a neat and tidy way to conceptualize our world and all the people in it. "Men seek to withdraw, women seek to engage" is a sweeping attempt to sum up the differences between men and women in ten words or less. "Women like to talk before they have sex, men just like to have sex" may be a general truth, but it does not fit all individuals. "Men's favorite emotion is anger, women's favorite emotion is sadness" is another generalization that holds some truth but certainly not all.

While it may feel good to simplify our world by generalizing about it, research by the psychologist Vicki Helgeson indicates that adhering too closely to certain stereotypical behaviors could be damaging to our health. In Helgeson's study men who scored high on measures of traditional masculinity, such as competitiveness and hostility, had higher incidences of severe heart attacks than men who were less aggressive and argumentative, while women who fit the classic profile of the self-sacrificing female were more likely to have dangerous heart conditions. Boxing ourselves into certain cultural stereotypes apparently can create imbalances that are not good for our hearts.

Empathy seeks the whole truth, knowing that without it our relationships with others and with ourselves are compromised. Half-truths provide half the picture, because they only go skin deep. Human beings long for a deeper connection (we call it intimacy), where our hearts and minds freely commingle. Only there, at depth, do we feel uniquely understood and truly loved for our whole selves, warts, scars, blemishes, and all.

The either-or phenomenon. Generalizations lead to what I call the either-or phenomenon. Either you love me or you don't. Either you're with me or you're against me. Either you accept me the way I am, or you find someone else, because I'm not about to change.

Either-or behavior shuts out empathy because it reduces the world to black and white. Empathy is always wandering around in the gray areas, the places where ambiguity and ambivalence like to hang out. Empathy and ambiguity are friends—they understand each other. Both empathy and ambiguity know the complicated truth of human beings—that we can be both this and that, both twisted *and* straight, prejudiced *and* tolerant, grateful *and* greedy, honest *and* deceptive, forgiving *and* resentful, hopeful *and* despairing. Empathy sniffs out the inconsistencies and wonders why? Why am I so mixed up? Why am I kind in one moment and cruel in the next? Why should I change? Why shouldn't I change?

There is always room in empathy's world for the complex twists and turns of real life. By embracing ambiguity empathy keeps our minds open and allows us to sort through our conflicted feelings. The end result, ironically, is greater clarity. When we accept the fact that the world and all the people in it—including, of course, ourselves—are not black or white but, as one of my patients put it, "full of gray," we can move away from fixed perceptions into much more fluid, mobile, interactive relationships with others. We realize the error involved in putting people in categories and instead commit ourselves to the more demanding work of seeing them as wholly unique and individual. In this way and in so many others, empathy leads to tolerance of differences—the ability to expand the world to incorporate more than one viewpoint.

The antidote to the polarization of either-or is to adopt an attitude of both-and. We are mixed up—that is the nature of being human. We are unique, we are even exceptional, yet we are also ordinary. In that realization we discover humility, which is the recognition that we cannot be everything, but we can, at least, be something. What do you want to be? That is empathy's soulful question. And how do you plan to get there? That is empathy's heartfelt response.

Empathy won't automatically give you the answers, but it is always happy to keep pushing you further into the question. Since we are not where we want to be, since we obviously have so much work to do, what should we try next? This adventure of getting to know ourselves is at the very heart of creating intimate relationships.

Falling down and getting back up again is the thread that holds together the fabric we call life. Empathy counsels us to dust ourselves off and keep moving, to search for that place of balance where we can accept ourselves for who we are (all mixed up) and for who we want to become (still all mixed up but somehow more comfortable there). If we can look in the cracked mirror and humbly accept that imperfect (but real) image staring back at us, we can also learn how to accept the imperfections of others. Humility leads to tolerance. Acceptance of our own conflicted, complicated nature leads to acceptance of other people's similar but different mixed-upness.

Empathy requires flexibility. Indeed, the very nature of empathy is the ability to bend and flex, which allows us to contemplate the possibility of change and transformation. As the research psychologists Sarah Hodges and Daniel Wegner put it, empathy involves "a thoroughgoing transformation."

To empathize with a person in a situation involves more than simply changing one's spatial viewpoint; it also involves changing one's judgment of the situation, one's memory for events and one's emotional responsiveness to them, one's conception of the person's traits and goals, and even one's conception of oneself.

Projection. "Are you angry with me?" Derek, a fifty-two-year-old certified public accountant who recently separated from his wife, asked me.

"No," I answered honestly. "But can you tell me what you are perceiving that makes you think I'm angry with you?"

"Well, you looked angry with me when you came into the waiting room," Derek said.

"I did?" I asked with real interest, not as a challenge to his perception. "What did you notice about me?"

"I noticed that you didn't make eye contact," he said. Suddenly he frowned. "Now that I think about it, I don't know why I thought you were angry with me. Maybe it had to do with last week's session, which I didn't think went very well."

"How come?" I asked.

"I thought you were blaming me, not my wife, for the fight we had last week."

"So you felt blamed?"

"I was irritated with you for not seeing my position," he said. "I was upset with you. I was angry with you. I guess I'm still angry with you."

In that interaction my patient expressed his belief that I was angry with him when, in truth, he was irritated with me. That's *projection*—seeing in another person certain thoughts, emotions, or behaviors that you deny in yourself. My patient was projecting his anger onto me because his emotions felt overwhelming to him and he wasn't sure how to handle them.

Projection is often unconscious; psychologists sometimes call it *projective identification*, which means that I (the projector) identify with something in you and then I can complain about it without having to look into or evaluate myself. Projection is a defense mechanism, but ultimately it is self-defeating. When we project we attempt to disown or deny certain parts of the self and attach those unwanted parts onto others. Projection is closely related to the phenomenon of image love so often experienced in the idealization stage of relationships. With image love I see you as the perfect mate, the ideal person who can lead me to salvation. When I realize that you are not perfect or when no one comes along to save me, I am tempted to blame everything on you (or someone else). So I project, meaning that I take my problems, paste them on you, and then blame you for making life difficult for me.

Image love and projection represent attempts to feel at ease with ourselves. Both strategies backfire, however, for they distance us from reality, from ourselves, and from the people we care about. We idealize others because we want to be idealized ourselves; we project our feelings onto others because those feelings don't fit with the image we have constructed for ourselves. How painful, then, when we realize that the ideal image is cracked—for that image reflects directly back on us. Only with empathy can we look in that cracked mirror and learn to accept both the imperfect other and the imperfect self. Only with empathy can we decide that the reflection in the mirror is part of us but not all of us. Only with empathy can we make the commitment to devote our energy and effort to alter the image to match reality.

Carolyn was always looking for the ideal man, the handsome, political type who knew what he wanted and was relentless, even ruthless at times, in pursuing his goals. Perfection was her ultimate destination, and Carolyn pushed herself to achieve it, seeking the ideal mate, trying out the latest fad diet, filling her closet with expensive clothes, pushing herself to run thirty miles a week.

Early on in our therapy sessions, she idealized me and tried, in subtle but unmistakable ways, to win me over. With empathy I tried to communicate that I was interested in the real Carolyn, not the image she so carefully constructed of the beautiful, sexy woman who was always in control, always living up to expectations, always keeping her makeup on. I wanted to know and understand the human being who lived, yearned, hoped, and despaired underneath all those beautiful but superficial outer layers.

I hoped, through empathy, to enlarge Carolyn's image of herself and increase her openness to new experiences. I sought to shift her way of evaluating herself from what she had come to believe other people wanted to what she found most valuable in herself. *Who am I? What do I want from life?* These are the questions empathy finds most compelling. Through empathy Carolyn learned to seek the answers inside herself rather than letting other people tell her who she should or shouldn't be.

In this empathic process Carolyn learned to value herself and trust her instincts. This is what the process psychologist Carl Rogers called "becoming a person." He writes:

> The individual increasingly comes to feel that this locus of evaluation lies within himself [sic]. Less and less does he look to others for approval or disapproval; for standards to live by; for decisions and choices. He recognizes that it rests within himself to choose; that the only question which matters is, "Am I living in a way which is deeply satisfying to me, and which truly expresses me?" This I think is perhaps the most important question for the creative individual.

Expressing the self truly and openly means embracing those parts of the self that we would just as soon excise or ignore. In this process of acknowledging our imperfections, empathy shows us a way out of the polarization stage. For if we accept the fact that we can use some improvement, we have to acknowledge the fact that others have work to do, too. In the ongoing process of self-knowledge and other-knowledge that characterizes all healthy relationships, empathy helps us come to grips with who we are and how we are related (imperfectly) to others.

This process of understanding, acceptance, and commitment to change does not come easy. With empathy the accent is always on growth. When patients get stuck and demand acceptance and forgiveness ("I'm not perfect, you know"), my job is to acknowledge their need for understanding but keep attention focused on the places where they can change and grow. "I understand why you are preoccupied," I might say to a patient who has poor listening skills, "but I need you to focus when I talk." "You are trying hard," I might say to a patient who refuses to take responsibility for her actions, "but as long as you continue to blame others for your problems, I am convinced that you will make slow progress."

In the novel Lonesome Dove by Larry McMurtry, two aging cowboys discuss their polar-opposite approaches to owning up to their mistakes. Call says he tries to avoid being wrong because then he doesn't have to worry about acknowledging his flaws. Augustus reminds him that we all make mistakes, whether we admit it or not.

> "You're so sure you're right it doesn't matter to you whether people talk to you at all. I'm glad I've been wrong enough to keep in practice."

"Why would you want to keep in practice being wrong?" Call asked. "I'd think it would be something you'd try to avoid."

"You can't avoid it, you've got to learn to handle it," Augustus said. "If you come face to face with your own mistakes once or twice in your life it's bound to be extra painful. I face mine every day—that way they ain't usually much worse than a dry shave."

Facing up to our mistakes is the first part of the process. Taking action to change what can be changed is the second, equally important step. If we tend to blame others, lie, cheat, listen poorly, or consistently act in self-centered ways, it is not enough to acknowledge those imperfections— we have to do something about them. Our imperfections can be the roots of our strength and the agents of our growth, but only if we use them as springboards to action. Only when we accept the fact that we have more work to do (that the work, in fact, never stops) can we progress into the final stage of mature, ever-changing, self-transforming love— integration.

Stage 3: Integration

Integrated love is the love we yearn for because it is the only kind of love that fills up the "empty spaces" inside us—those parts of the self that we ignore or hold in contempt. In the idealization stage of relationships we hope and pray that the ideal other will fill up those gaping holes. In the polarization stage we realize (often with a howl of pain) that other people are not ideal and, besides, they have their own work to do. In the integration phase we make a commitment to further each other's growth through honest interactions, realistic expectations, and a genuine respect for each other's uniqueness.

Integrated love is the product of *mutual empathy*, a process that involves both the willingness to merge and the ability to detach. You enter the other's experience in a wholehearted way, but you always come back to the self. In their book *The Healing Connection*, the psychiatrist Jean Baker Miller and the psychologist Irene Pierce Stiver emphasize the power of mutual empathy, which they define as "a joining together based on the authentic thoughts and feelings of all participants in a relationship." They write:

Because each person can receive and then respond to the feelings and thoughts of the other, each is able to enlarge both her [sic] own feelings and thoughts *and* the feelings and thoughts of the other person. Simultaneously, each person enlarges the relationship.

Once again we see the expansive nature of empathy. As each person works hard to expand the relationship, the possibilities for growth and transformation are endless. Empathy enlarges our world by opening our eyes and allowing us to see what we could not see before. Integrated love is possible only when mutual empathy inspires the relationship, for empathy needs to flow both ways if the relationship is to remain harmonious. How do you create and maintain mutual empathy in your relationships? The following three suggestions may help.

Constantly reevaluate your theories. We all have theories (psychologists sometimes call them cognitive maps) about what a good relationship should be. We rely on these theoretical models as we try to tease apart the snarls and tangles that occur in every intimate relationship. Like road maps, our theories tell us where we have veered off the way.

Relationship theories are often extraordinarily simple, revolving around a general hypothesis:

- People who love each other shouldn't fight.
- A man should always pursue a woman; men do not respect women who chase them.
- Women say "I love you" with words; men say it with their actions.
- Men are ruled by sex, women are ruled by relationships.
- Men are bad listeners, women are good listeners.
- Good relationships are characterized by unconditional love.
- A healthy sex life is essential for marital happiness.
- If I don't feel like I'm head over heels in love, something must be wrong with the relationship.
- A mother's primary duty is to be at home with her children.
- A father's primary duty is to make a lot of money to support his family.

Such one-dimensional theories offer a straight and narrow pathway to follow—just one misstep and we're headed for major disappointment. While a vigorous sex life is an important consideration for many couples, for example, many happily married people do not place a great deal of emphasis on sex. Another theory is debunked when we accept the fact that sometimes men like women to be the pursuers and sometimes women prefer to do the pursuing. And while unconditional love may be fine in theory, what if your partner treats you rudely and with disrespect? Allowing yourself to be hurt emotionally or physically is a perversion of empathy, which insists on respect as a foundation for every relationship.

Carolyn lived for years with the theory that a woman's role is to please a man. Caught in that theory, she didn't have much space. Because she left herself so little room for error, she experienced intense inner turmoil whenever she did something that angered or irritated the men in her life. Dismantling the theory by understanding its origin in her relationship to her alcoholic father allowed her to construct new theories that honored her complexity. She felt free to be herself, to move around within the more expansive theory, and to search for intimacy with people who appreciated her more expansive (less theory-restricted) self.

Watch out for complacency. As relationships stabilize and continue, we can become complacent; as complacency sets in we feel less motivated to engage in the effortful process of empathy.

"I know what she's thinking," a fifty-year-old man said about his wife. He folded his arms across his chest in a posture that said, "Case closed."

"How do you know what I'm thinking?" his wife responded, her cheeks suddenly flushed with anger.

"It's ingrained," he replied with a self-satisfied grin. "I've lived with you for twenty-seven years; I think by now I should be able to predict what you're thinking."

"You don't know anything about me," she said, her tone biting. "You never have, and you never will."

"All I'm saying is that I know you intimately," he said, suddenly feeling confused and misunderstood. "What's wrong with that?"

The "been there, done that" approach can be devastating to a relationship. I have never met anyone, either in therapy or in real life, who wants to believe that every aspect of his behavior can be predicted or all her thoughts and emotions can be foreseen. No matter how long you have lived with someone, you cannot know all there is to know about him or her, for people are constantly changing. Empathy encourages that process of growth and change, of being and becoming.

I was having lunch on the beach one summer day with my wife and Valerie, an old family friend. We were eating turkey sandwiches from the local deli, and they both wondered if I missed my usual tuna fish sandwich. "I've never known anyone who liked a food so much that he had to have it every day," Valerie commented.

"I don't like tuna fish," I said.

Both my wife and my friend looked at me in astonishment. "Why do you have it for lunch every day?" they asked in unison.

"Because it's good for me."

That real-life story offers a simple illustration of how people can surprise us even after we have known them for many years. In therapy I counsel my patients to search for surprises, to ask their partners questions intended to find out what they are thinking about during both the "big" events of our lives (sending a child off to college, dealing with menopause, coping with an aging parent's infirmity, turning forty, fifty, sixty, or seventy) and the "little" events (listening to a friend's chronic complaints about her husband, handling a child's temper tantrums, managing your anger and frustration when confronted with rude people). Life is full of challenges and changes, and even your most intimate friends will surprise you—as long as you are willing to listen without automatically assuming that you know the answer.

Beware of cognitive confounding. Cognitive confounding, sometimes called enmeshment, is marked by the confusion of boundaries between self and other. If you and I are "one"—and some would say that this is the ultimate goal of intimacy—then where do you end and where do I begin? Empathy helps us to understand that while you and I are one, we are also (and must inevitably remain) two. Even in the most intimate and loving relationships, we always come back to the self. Knowing that truth, empathy seeks to expand the self, hoping to make it a place where we feel comfortable being ourselves.

What is important is interdependence. We are separate and exist comfortably in our own skin because we know we will be in union again. Knowing that we are coming together again allows us to tolerate and enjoy the times when we are separated. Remembering the empathy that exists in our relationships when we are together allows us to feel comfortable and secure when we are alone.

I remember scoring a touchdown when I was in high school and looking up at the stands, imagining my father throwing his hat in the air as he sometimes did. That night when I got home from the game, my mother told me that Dad was still at work—there had been a problem with a furniture delivery and he couldn't break away for the game. As my heart began to sink, I wondered, Would I have scored that touchdown if I'd known he wasn't there?

Today I know the answer to that question. My father has been gone for twelve years, but I still imagine that he is with me. I feel his presence many times during the day. At least once a week, for example, I take a long run. I have osteoarthritis in my back, and as the miles go by I begin to feel the pain. I talk to myself, telling myself that I can make it, but sometimes the pain is intense, and I wonder if I can keep going. Invariably at that point I sense that my father is with me. I can hear his voice cheering me on and telling me he believes in me. I keep running, and the pain eventually fades. Even in death my father keeps me company.

I have always been comforted by the philosophical musings of the Hasidic scholar and master storyteller Martin Buber. When Buber discussed the "I-Thou" relationship, I am convinced he was speaking about empathy, specifically about the ongoing process of merging and separation that occurs when empathy guides a relationship:

> The primary word *I-Thou* can be spoken only with the whole being. Concentration and fusion into the whole being can never take place through my agency, nor can it ever take place without me. I become through my relation to the *Thou*; as I become *I*, I say *Thou*.

"As I become I, I say Thou." That is a powerful statement of empathy. Only *as I become I*—as I learn about myself, discover myself, become aware of my thoughts, feelings, and emotions—can *I say Thou*. Only when I am fully "I" can I be prepared to enter wholly and wholeheartedly—as a whole person—into a relationship. The point of developing the self is to put the self into relationship with other human beings. Life is all about relation-ships. As Buber wrote, "All real living is meeting."

"All real living is meeting." Empathy allows that meeting between I and Thou to be fully realized. Recognizing emotions in others, tuning our-selves in to another person's thoughts and feelings, listening carefully to the words that are spoken while paying attention to the silences that sur-round the words, observing facial expressions and body movements, calm-ing the self, learning how to express one's own feelings . . . these empathic actions are the basic building blocks of friendship, intimacy, and love.

An old story reveals an essential truth about the role empathy plays in creating and maintaining love:

> Rabbi Moshe Leib of Sasov learned to love when he went to an inn and heard one drunken peasant ask another, "Do you love me?" "Certainly I love you," replied the second. "I love you like a brother." But the first shook his head and insisted, "You don't love me. You don't know what I lack. You don't know what I need." The second peasant fell into sullen silence, but Rabbi Moshe Leib understood: "To know the need of men and to bear the burden of their sorrow, that is the true love of men."

Time and time again I have witnessed in therapy sessions similar inter-actions between two people who love each other but do not have the un-derstanding or the skills needed to fully express their feelings and enter wholeheartedly into each other's experience.

"You don't love me," one person will say.

"Of course I love you," says the other.

"But you have no idea what I'm missing," comes the response. "You don't know what I need, you don't even know who I am—how can you say you love me?"

Empathy gives us the insights and the knowledge needed to understand the needs of others, sharing in the depth of their sorrows and the height of their joys. Without the understanding and active involvement that em-pathy bestows, love is an empty intellectual construct, a simple word de-void of meaning. Empathy gives love its height, its weight, and its balance. Empathy is love's flesh and blood, its beating heart and its questing soul.

Empathy is love's reason for being.

Chapter 7

The Dark Side of Empathy

Empathy can help us sense danger. It can let us see into the hearts and minds of people who intend to deceive, manipulate, or harm us.

In the middle of the day in a large city a twenty-seven-year-old woman named Kelly walks home to her apartment, her arms loaded up with heavy bags of groceries. Aggravated that the building's main door is unlocked—Why doesn't anyone else care about safety? she wonders—she makes sure it latches behind her. Walking up the three flights of stairs to her apartment, she struggles with the groceries and one of the bags rips open, sending cans of cat food bouncing down the steps.

"Got it! I'll bring it up," a male voice calls out. I don't like that voice, Kelly thinks, something about it doesn't sound right. A young, friendly-looking man runs up the stairs with the cat food in hand, smiles, and offers to help her carry the heavy bags. She politely declines. "What floor are you going to?" he persists. She doesn't want to tell him for some reason, but she doesn't want to seem unfriendly either.

"The fourth," she says.

"I'm going to the fourth floor, too," he says, reaching for one of the bags. Again, she resists, insisting that she can handle the groceries.

"There's such a thing as being *too* proud, you know," he says.

Despite her misgivings Kelly lets go of the bag. The thought runs through her mind—I don't want to be the suspicious type, the kind of person who distrusts everybody she meets. At the door to her apartment, she thanks the stranger for his help, but he brushes past her, promising that he will leave as soon as he puts the bag down.

He walks into the kitchen and puts the groceries on the table. Then he turns, the smile gone. He pulls out a gun, and he rapes her.

Afterward, he gets dressed, picks up the gun, and warns her to stay where she is. He promises he won't hurt her, adding that he will leave as soon as he gets a drink of water from the kitchen.

Now, for the first time, Kelly senses that her life is in danger and feels truly afraid. All her senses are on high alert as she watches his every move. On the way to the kitchen, he glances at his watch and seems to be in a hurry. Yet he takes the time to close the open window and turn up the sound on the stereo. He turns to look at her and tells her not to look so scared. Once again, he promises not to hurt her. And suddenly she knows— there is no doubt in her mind—that he is going to kill her.

She gets up from the bed, taking the sheet with her. The rapist is in the kitchen opening drawers, looking for something; knives, it turns out. Unnoticed she walks slowly out of her apartment and across the hall, where she opens a neighbor's door (somehow she knows it will be unlocked), steps inside, raises a finger to her lips to signal the need to be quiet, and bolts the door behind her.

This story leads off Gavin de Becker's best-seller *The Gift of Fear*. Fear was Kelly's ally, de Becker explains, telling her exactly what she needed to do in order to save her life. When she finally listened to her fears, she was able to recognize the danger lurking in the shadows and escape from it. Fear is a gift bestowed on us by nature, de Becker concludes, "a brilliant internal guardian that stands ready to warn you of hazards and guide you through risky situations."

I believe there is more to this story. I am convinced that it was not fear that saved Kelly's life but empathy. Empathy was the source of her fear and the power of its motivating energy. Empathy, not fear, gave her the insights that motivated her to actions that would save her life. Even more important—and an essential insight for all who hope to protect themselves and their loved ones against manipulative, deceptive, and potentially destructive people—empathy was also being used against her. In this violent encounter empathy was both a weapon and a defense, used by both attacker and victim. In the end the person with the greatest empathy won.

Let me go back to the beginning of the story and analyze it from the viewpoint of empathy. The rapist, de Becker points out, had probably been observing his potential victim for days, even weeks. He stalked her, watching her every move, carefully assessing her vulnerability and then, through a combination of instinct, hunger, and surging adrenaline, chose precisely the right moment to make a move.

Empathy was the rapist's most powerful tool, more potent than the gun he held in his hand or the knife he searched for in the kitchen. Using empathy, he was able to "read" Kelly's thoughts and emotions from her facial expressions, the way she walked, talked with friends, and interacted with strangers. From observing her he knew that she lived alone; he knew, too, that she was timid and feared for her safety. From his preparatory prowling he felt confident that she would give in to pressure from a friendly, helpful stranger. Perhaps he had seen her smiling at strangers on the street, or inferred from her shy but genuine smile that she would be easy to manipulate.

Relying on empathy—the ability to adopt her perspective in order to understand what she was thinking and feeling—the would-be murderer concluded that Kelly was a good target. He used his insights into her character to predict her reactions and manipulate her into doing exactly what he wanted. Playing the nice guy, using specific words and phrases intended to shake her confidence, he systematically dismantled her defenses.

"There's such a thing as being *too* proud, you know," he said to her on the stairs when she initially refused to let him help with the groceries. Those words got under her skin, disturbing her sense of self with the implication that she might appear standoffish and arrogant. She didn't want to be the kind of woman who sets herself apart from others. Excess pride is a character trait our culture discourages, particularly in women. According to hackneyed but still prevalent stereotypes, women are supposed to be soft and compliant, open and trusting with friends and strangers alike.

Although we have come a long way from the image of the ideal woman as meek and submissive, the would-be rapist's viciously brilliant wordplay pierced Kelly's vulnerable psyche, blocking her empathy from performing its protective function. Without empathy's guiding hand, Kelly could not see through the man's deceptions even though the clues were right in front of her. When she said no and he refused to listen, empathy would have led her to ask: Why isn't he paying attention to me? Why does he keep pushing me? Relying on empathy, she would have come to the conclusion that even though he looked like a nice person, genuinely good-hearted people don't keep pestering you after you have declined their help. But her fear of being "too proud" combined with her longing to be kind and trusting sapped empathy's power. Ignoring her intuition and instincts, she chose to believe the young man had good intentions. That choice almost cost her her life.

In that first encounter on the stairs, the stranger's empathy was more powerful than his victim's. After the rape, however, complacency set in. Believing he was in complete control, the rapist let down his guard. Perhaps he was relying on experience with other victims (there had been others, it turned out), who were so overwhelmed with fear and so willing to trust his promises that he wouldn't hurt them that they offered no resistance. Falling back on a general theory of human behavior learned from previous assaults, he assumed Kelly was "his," for he had wounded her and now, he believed, fear would paralyze her. He simply stopped paying attention.

While his empathy was draining, hers was replenishing. She watched him as he moved around the apartment, reading his thoughts and emotions just as he had read hers moments earlier. Sensing the danger, she focused her attention, using empathy to figure out his next move. She watched him go to the window and close it. She heard his promise not to hurt her, a promise that "came out of nowhere." She noted that he turned up the volume on the stereo. She heard him opening the drawers in the kitchen. Putting all the clues together, relying on empathy to predict his behavior, she knew that he was planning to kill her.

Empathy led Kelly to insight, and insight moved her to action. Calming her down, focusing her fear, sharpening her intelligence, empathy guided her to safety.

Empathy saved her life.

Kelly's story offers a dramatic look at the dark side of empathy, showing how it can be used destructively to manipulate others, breaking down their natural defenses. Empathy can also, however, help us sense danger. It can let us see into the hearts and minds of people who intend to deceive, manipulate, or harm us. With that knowledge we can walk away from potentially destructive situations or relationships without getting so much as a scratch.

The dark side of empathy is extremely powerful, though, and a particularly potent weapon when people are feeling vulnerable or desperate. Adolf Hitler understood the power of the dark side of empathy, using his keen insights into the needs and desires of the German people to manipulate their emotions. Alternating between cold ruthlessness and furious tirades, Hitler exploited his people's fears of poverty and humiliation, portraying himself as the answer to their prayers, the embodiment of hope for their future.

In the finale to a speech given in 1933 and broadcast to an estimated 20 million radio listeners, Hitler spoke of love, hate, honor, and glory with the passion of a religious zealot:

> I can't free myself from belief in my people, can't get away from the con- viction that this nation will once again arise, can't distance myself from the love of this, my people, and hold as firm as a rock to the conviction that some time the hour will come when the millions who today hate us will stand behind us and with us will welcome what has been created together, struggled for under difficulty, attained at cost: the new German Reich of greatness and honor and strength and glory and justice. Amen.

Several years later the news correspondent William Shirer described the tumult that followed an impassioned speech Hitler delivered in the Kroll Opera House in Munich:

> They spring, yelling and crying, to their feet. . . . Their hands are raised in slavish salute, their faces now contorted with hysteria, their mouths wide open, shouting, shouting, their eyes, burning with fanaticism, glued on the new god, the Messiah.

And once again, in a speech given at the Nuremberg "Party Rally of Honor" in September 1936, Hitler demonstrated how the dark side can be used to create a sense of solidarity and purpose, pumping up pride and rais- ing emotions to a fevered pitch.

> Not every one of you can see me and I do not see each one of you. But I feel you, and you feel me! It is faith in our nation that has made us little people great. . . . You come out of the little world of your daily struggle for life, and of your struggle for Germany and for our nation, to experience this feeling for once: Now we are together, we are with him and he is with us, and now we are Germany!

A different strategy was employed in the Nazi death camps, where Hitler's subordinates used the dark side to tear people down rather than build them up. Treating the inmates as subhuman, undeserving of the care or concern we would give even to a helpless animal, the Nazis sought to sever the human connections that inspire hope, faith, and the will to live. The most devastating poison of the death camps was not in the gas chambers where so many millions died but in the atmosphere of complete dehumanization where people's hearts and spirits slowly suffocated from lack of empathy. Eliminating empathy from the environment was as lethal to the camp inmates as removing oxygen.

The only hope for the prisoners was to turn to each other for solace and strength. In his book *All Rivers Run to the Sea: Memoirs* the concentration camp survivor Elie Wiesel offered this eloquent statement about the power of relationships to keep the human spirit alive:

> If anything motivated me, it was my father's presence. . . . We depended on each other: he needed me as I needed him. Because of him, I had to live; because of me, he tried not to die. So long as I still lived, he knew he was useful, perhaps even indispensable. In my eyes, he was the same man, the same father, he had always been. If I was gone, he would lose his role, his authority, his identity. And conversely: Without him my life would have neither meaning nor goal.
>
> In this the Germans' psychological methods often failed. They tried to get the inmates to think only of themselves, to forget relatives and friends, to tend only to their own needs. . . . But what happened was just the reverse. Those who retreated to a universe limited to their own bodies had less chance of getting out alive, while to live for a brother, a friend, an ideal, helped you hold out longer. As for me, I could cope thanks to my father. Without him I could not have resisted. I would see him coming with his heavy gait, seeking a smile, and I would give it to him. He was my support and my oxygen, as I was his.

Only when we understand that empathy is our support and commit ourselves to doing everything in our power to live by that truth can we successfully disarm those who seek to deceive or destroy us. If we think only of ourselves, forgetting the needs of others, retreating into a space restricted to our own desires, we sever empathy's power supply and cut ourselves off from the meaningful world.

I have been talking about extreme examples of the dark side—rapists, wartime speeches intended to inflame passions and dull reason, concentration camp experiences—but the dark side is not always sinister or death-dealing. Weaving its way into everyday life in subtle, often unrecognizable forms, the dark side can be discovered in brightly lighted rooms, practiced by people just like you and me. Every day we encounter the dark side, even though we are often unaware of its presence.

I was leafing through a *Newsweek* recently when I came to a full-page advertisement featuring a photograph of a beautiful Asian woman gazing into her rearview mirror at the headlights of the car behind her. Her facial expression conveys fear and confusion.

"PREDATOR," the ad states in bold block letters. "How to avoid being the prey." Then comes the small print. "You're being followed. Even after you turn, he's close behind. You're frightened. What do you do? Don't go home. You don't want to lead him to your loved ones. Instead, drive to a well-lighted place where there are lots of people."

This advertisement (which looks like a public service announcement and even offers a free booklet titled "Alone Behind the Wheel") is sponsored by Shell gasoline. The closing words are "COUNT ON SHELL." Playing into our fears of being alone and vulnerable, Shell hopes to lure more customers—definitely a creative use of the dark side.

We are surrounded by these kinds of subtle and not-so-subtle manipulations in print and broadcast advertising. Father and son are fishing, the dad takes a sip of beer, the son moves closer, smiles affectionately, and says, "I love you, man." The father sees right through his deceptions and says, "You're not going to get my Bud Light." Funny thing about that advertisement—the dad sees through the son's ruse, but the viewer ends up laughing and thirsting (the advertiser hopes) for a cold brew. Bud Light separates the men from the boys, so why not reach for a Bud?

The radio personality Paul Harvey recently told a story about an elderly woman in the checkout line at the grocery store. Turning to the middle-aged man standing behind her, she tells him that he looks exactly like her son.

"He died recently," the woman continues. The man expresses his condolences. She hesitates for a moment, then she asks him for a favor. Would he mind saying good-bye to her when she leaves the store? Would he just call out in a loud, clear voice, "Bye, Mom!"? "I just want to hear those words one last time," she explains.

Touched by her sweet smile, he agrees, and when she reaches the exit and turns to look at him, he calls out, "Bye, Mom!" She waves, flashes him a bright smile, and then she is gone.

The man chats with the cashier for a few minutes as she tallies up his groceries, a loaf of bread, some cheese, a gallon of milk, cat food. "That will be one hundred and twenty-six dollars," she says pleasantly.

"There must be some mistake," he says, still suffused with good feeling from his interaction with the old woman. "I only have this one bag."

"Didn't she tell you?" says the cashier.

"Who? Tell me what?" asks the perplexed customer.

"Why, your mother. She said you would pay for her groceries."

This unsuspecting man learned an expensive but valuable lesson about the dark side of empathy: it can sneak up on you at the most unlikely moments, dished out by people who look for all the world like kind, compassionate, considerate human beings. When I heard Paul Harvey tell that story, I was immediately reminded of an event that occurred more than a decade ago when I was working as chief psychologist at Leonard Morse Hospital in Natick, Massachusetts. Every day after lunch I led a group psychotherapy session with staff and patients from the open psychiatric unit. Joe from New Jersey was a new patient on the unit. A cocaine addict who had gambled his life savings away and then turned to burglary to support his habit, Joe was charming, talkative, instantly chummy.

Several days after Joe arrived at the hospital, patients started complaining about valuables missing from their rooms—cash, jewelry, watches. After the third or fourth report, I called a special community meeting.

"The thief is among us," I said.

"Hey, Dr. C," Joe called out. "Let me tell you what's happening here."

"This is serious business, Joe, we don't have time for a tangent," I said, feeling a little impatient with him. Like others on the staff, I suspected Joe might be the crook.

"I'm trying to help you out here, okay?" Joe said. I nodded, feeling a little guilty about my suspicions. "Look, everyone here thinks I'm the crook," he continued. "Now don't tell me that thought didn't go through your mind, because I know it did. But I have to tell you something—only a crook can understand another crook. I know who's been stealing from the rooms—it's Marjorie, the cleaning lady."

No one believed him, because Marjorie was a little white-haired lady in her midsixties, sweet-tempered and always eager to please. A few weeks later, however, we found out that Marjorie had a criminal record—she was not only a burglar but a heroin dealer.

After Marjorie was caught I took Joe aside and asked him how he knew she was the culprit. He gave me a crooked grin, pleased that the educated doctor was willing to admit he might have something to learn from the high school dropout turned thief. "I could tell just by talking to her," Joe explained. "Look, Dr. C, everybody here knows my history. The nurses and doctors, they don't like to talk to me, they don't feel comfortable with me. I understand—I'm an addict and a crook. Now I know you don't mind talking to me, but you're not the kind of guy I'd go bowling with either. But from the day I got here, Marjorie joins me outside for a smoke. Now there's no way someone my grandmother's age is going to sit down for a heart-to-heart with somebody like me unless she feels like we're kindred spirits. You know what they say, Doc, birds of a feather flock together. I knew Marjorie was a crook from the moment I met her."

That incident reinforced for me several essential lessons about empathy. Lesson 1: Don't jump to conclusions. Lesson 2: Watch out for biases that might prevent you from seeing the whole picture. Lesson 3: Be ready and willing to learn about the complexities of human nature from anyone and everyone, even those who may seem ill-prepared to be teachers.

The dark side is alive and well in our society, and nowhere is it more prevalent than in the health-care field. Because we don't expect to find it there, we are even more vulnerable to its snake oil charms. We're a nation obsessed with health, and hucksters are everywhere, hawking their herbs, vitamins, antiaging potions, natural antidepressants, and weight loss products. The people selling these products know how to play on our fears of extra pounds, wrinkles, disease, aging, and death; for every physical or emotional complaint we have, they can design a "miracle cure" with a hefty price tag attached.

(This is not to say that herbs and nutritional supplements can't be beneficial. I am a firm believer in holistic health, and I direct an alternative medical center in a major Boston hospital, where I spend a great deal of my time trying to help patients determine which products are beneficial and which are useless or, worse, detrimental to their health.)

One day on the way to work I was listening to a radio show featuring a well-known physician who was fielding calls from listeners concerned about their health. The doctor made a blanket announcement asking for his listeners' help. If they would send him postcards with the names and addresses of their pharmacies, he promised that he would send them, free of charge, identification cards they could use to list their various medications. (He did not explain that he would use the pharmacy addresses to sell his new line of herbal products.)

When an elderly woman called in with a health concern, he listened for fifteen or twenty seconds and then interrupted to ask if she would send him the name and address of her pharmacy. "I would love you for it," he said in a soothing voice. She said she would be happy to do that, and then she repeated her question. Again he interrupted her; apparently he wasn't completely convinced that she understood the importance of his request. "Would you be sure to send me that address, sweetheart? Would you do that for me? Promise?"

"Yes," she said, "I promise."

He never did answer her question.

I would love you for it. Would you do that for me, sweetheart? When people you have never met call you "sweetheart" and tell you that they will "love you" if you do just this little favor for them, red flags should start flying all over the place. I don't mean to imply that strangers can't be authentically kind to each other, but when people ignore your problems and then fall all over themselves to make sure you will respond to their concerns, it's a pretty good bet that there's some darker motive for their affectionate displays. Somebody's profiting from the interchange, and chances are good it is not you.

A few years ago I was invited to speak to a group of senior citizens about the benefits and potential dangers of common nutritional supplements and herbal remedies. After my talk a woman in her midseventies introduced herself and asked for my help. Gently taking my hand (and never letting it go during our twenty-minute talk), Emma told me her story. Recently widowed, with children and grandchildren living thousands of miles away, Emma was struggling with depression and insomnia. When she asked her doctor for help, he prescribed antidepressants and sleeping pills. Wary of taking too many prescription drugs (she was already on medications for high blood pressure and a blood clotting disorder), she asked if herbs or vitamins might work just as well.

"I don't believe in any of that stuff," her doctor responded with a scornful expression and dismissive gesture. "Herbs, vitamins, supplements—it's all quackery."

Feeling abandoned by her doctor and even more confused about her choices, Emma drove to her local health food store. The young saleswoman was kind and listened with obvious sympathy to Emma's story. She told Emma that physicians have little or no training in nutrition, and even if they did they wouldn't recommend alternative products like herbs or vitamins, which cut into their profits. Following the saleswoman's advice, Emma spent forty-five dollars on five herbal remedies: garlic for immune support; ginkgo for memory loss; St. John's wort for depression; melatonin for insomnia; and a weight loss product containing ephedra.

The saleswoman did not tell her (most likely because she didn't know) that garlic and ginkgo should not be taken along with blood thinners, and St. John's wort should not be taken with high blood pressure medication. Ephedra is a strong central nervous system stimulant that can contribute to high blood pressure and heart palpitations and should never be used for weight control. And, according to physicians at MIT's Clinical Research Center, the "standard" 3-milligram melatonin pills Emma was taking were ten times the amount needed to induce sleep; furthermore, older people require even less melatonin because their livers metabolize the hormone at a slower rate.

Every day I hear stories like Emma's, and every day I experience the same fury and frustration. This kind, gentle woman asked for help from the worlds of conventional and alternative medicine, and both let her down. I have no doubt that Emma's depression and insomnia (and even to some extent her immune suppression, memory loss, and recent weight gain) were primarily caused by her grief over her husband's death and her struggle to find ways to deal with her loneliness and fear. Emma's doctor completely ignored her emotional distress, offering prescription drugs for her symptoms and quickly dismissing any "alternative" approaches to her problems. The health store employee took advantage of Emma's helplessness by encouraging her to buy a different herb for each symptom. She also lacked the training and education needed to counsel Emma about potentially harmful interactions between herbs and prescription medications. Neither the doctor nor the saleswoman mentioned that it might be "normal" to feel depressed, anxious, lonely, and afraid when you are elderly, widowed, and separated from the people you love most in the world.

Learning how to deal with the dark side of empathy is as critical to your physical and emotional health as knowing how to treat others with kindness and consideration. How could Emma have protected herself? How can any of us negotiate our way through the hype and hucksterism of our increasingly commercialized world? How can we use empathy to defend ourselves against those who would use their insights and intuition to take advantage of us?

I believe the answers to these questions can be found in the following ten steps. Study these steps, become familiar with them, and make a concerted effort to implement them in your life. Always keep in mind the fact that empathy is a biological drive that evolved to *protect* us from danger. Using empathy to deceive or harm others is a perversion of its life-sustaining energy and reflects a weakness rather than a strength. In the end the positive, protective aspects of empathy will always overshadow its dark side.

TEN STEPS TO PROTECT YOU AGAINST THE DARK SIDE OF EMPATHY

Step 1: Learn the Difference Between Authentic and Functional Empathy

Adrienne walked into my office, threw her leather briefcase on the floor, and said, "I'm sick to death of my scumbag clients. I know, I know, that's not very charitable, but they're dumb, they think only about themselves, and they're all trying to make a fast buck." Her voice trailed off, and she began to pout.

"You don't think I have any empathy," she said.

"I know you have empathy," I said gently. "I've seen it many times before. At this moment, however, I would not say you are displaying a lot of empathy."

We talked for quite a while about the stress of her sixty-hour workweek as a personal injury lawyer, her troubled marriage, and her adolescent son's impulsive behavior. When she left that day she told me she was committed to finding a balance in her life and being more understanding in her relationships with her clients.

A week later Adrienne repeated the briefcase-tossing introduction to the session, only this time she wasn't upset with her clients—she was furious with me. "You ruined my week," she said. "A few days ago this disabled man, a World War II veteran who can barely walk, showed up in my office with a story about his son being killed by a drunk driver. Now you have to understand, I was thinking six figures, easy, this guy is old, he's got a war injury, he lost his only son . . . a real dream case. So he's crying, he's all upset, and I take him to lunch. He orders the most expensive thing on the menu—crab on the half shell, can you believe it? After lunch he tells me he doesn't have any money for a cab. I want to tell him to take the bus, but I give him the cab money, I'm still thinking this case is going to make me rich."

Adrienne sighed heavily. "This damn job," she says, rolling her eyes toward the ceiling. "So, okay, the old guy is supposed to show up the next day with his son's death certificate, but he walks into my office and says he forgot it. He wants to go out to lunch again, and when I tell him I already had lunch, he insists that I give him the cab fare to get home. I finally figure it out—he's scamming me. There's no drunk driver and no dead son. He just wanted as many free lunches as he could get."

Adrienne leaned toward me, her eyes bright with the secret she was about to share. "Listen to me, Dr. C, this is important—empathy did me in. Empathy doesn't work."

"It worked for him," I said.

"How do you figure that?" she asked. "Tell me—how exactly do you define empathy?"

"I define empathy as the capacity to accurately understand another person's thoughts and feelings," I said. "I think he did that pretty well."

"So you're saying he understood me better than I understood him?" she asked, leaning back in her chair and narrowing her eyes.

"From what you've told me, it seems pretty clear that he read you like a book. He knew you were going to be drawn in by thinking about this as a big case, and he used your desire to make a lot of money off his situation to get a free lunch and a cab ride."

"But I was being humane," she protested. "Didn't I tell you that all my clients are scumbags?"

I decided to tease her a little bit. "You never know when a scumbag might have an empathic streak."

Authentic empathy is motivated by a genuine concern for others and a desire to help them. *Functional empathy* is primarily concerned with what other people can give you (or what you can manage to weasel out of them). With authentic empathy we treat other people with care and respect, always seeking the truth in the moment-to-moment interaction. When functional empathy guides the interaction, the other person's thoughts and feelings don't really matter because we are seeking personal gain or satisfaction.

Functional empathy can be relatively benign and predictable, like the salesman who wants to sell you a car with expensive extras you don't really want or need. When my wife and I bought our last car, we agreed on a deal, shook hands with the manager, and arranged to pick up the car a week later on our way to Maine for the weekend. We arrived at the dealership around seven o'clock on a Friday night; it was dark and cold, and a winter storm was threatening. When the salesman drove up with the new car, I took one look at the ski rack on top and said, "We didn't order a ski rack." The salesman said he was sorry about that, but this was the only car they could get in such a short time; if we didn't take it we would have to wait two more weeks. Karen was almost in tears, the girls were freezing in the backseat, and I knew we had been "had." I paid for the car, including the extra two hundred dollars for the ski rack, and told the manager I would never do business with that dealership again, and I never have.

Functional empathy often has a sinister side. The handsome tennis player who befriended wealthy widows, offering them love and companionship only to steal their money and disappear from their lives, is one notorious example. Then there's the lawyer who forgets to mention that he bills twice as much for working on weekends; the insurance agent who convinces a newly married couple to pay thirty dollars extra a month for bogus coverage; the sweepstakes people who prey on the elderly, convincing them they will win a big prize if they keep subscribing to different magazines; the gas stations that try to convince young, female, out-of-state drivers that they are taking a big risk if they don't buy new shock absorbers; or the casinos that identify compulsive gamblers and lure them back with expense-paid trips. (I recently saw a television show about a compulsive gambler who spent every penny he owned, more than $2 million, at a Louisiana casino; the casino owners attended his mother's funeral and offered him the use of their Learjet for an expense-paid gambling vacation.)

Most often, however, functional empathy and authentic empathy coexist, even in healthy relationships. Hoping to entice his wife to have sex with him, John offers to give her a backrub. He sincerely loves his wife and hopes to make her feel good, but he also has an agenda—he wants to have sex. Here's another example. Kate and Josh are old friends who haven't seen or talked to each other for many years. Kate's mother dies, leaving her a large inheritance. Confused about what to do with the stocks and cash, Kate sends an E-mail to Josh, who is a financial planner. For several paragraphs she updates him on her activities, telling him how much she values his friendship; then, in the final paragraph, she mentions her dilemma and asks for his advice. She truly cares for him, but she also wants something from him—authentic and functional empathy are operating simultaneously.

In therapy, too, authentic and functional empathy often coexist. I get paid for my work with patients, so some people might argue that my empathy is wholly functional—I listen attentively and respond with sensitivity because that's what I am paid to do. I don't know many therapists who would continue being therapists, however, if they were working just for the money. Most people in this line of work are inspired by a desire to lessen the suffering of others. We do the work, in large part, because we care about people and want to do what we can to make the world a better place for all of us to live. That may sound like a good line, but I assure you it is the simple truth.

It is easy to get confused about empathy's dual roles, because most of us believe that empathy can't be genuine if someone hopes to gain something from the relationship. But with empathy there is always a gain, because even if we give empathy away with no thought of getting anything back, we always profit. Responding with empathy, we strengthen our relationships with others and with the world at large, expand our horizons, broaden our perspective, and get the added bonus of feeling good about ourselves. Those are definite gains, and they help to explain why it is so easy to "sell" empathy—once people put empathy into practice, they discover that they feel better about themselves, experience less anxiety and stress, and are much more closely connected to the people around them.

So there is always a balance with empathy, and it is that state of equilibrium that we seek. A relationship based on authentic empathy feels steady, solid, and substantial, while relationships primarily driven by functional empathy begin to feel, at some point, unstable and off balance, like sitting on a seesaw with someone twice your size on the other end. Because the power differential is off, the relationship is lopsided, and you never know when you're going to be upended.

The goal is to discover the balance. If functional empathy powers the relationship, you need to protect yourself, knowing that the other person is driven by his or her self-interest. If the relationship begins with functional empathy as its motivating force—as most work associations do, for example—be attentive to the way it evolves. Functional relationships can develop into authentic relationships, just as authentic relationships can become primarily functional relationships. The power of empathy is discovered in its ability, over time, to reveal the truth.

Step 2: Know Your Longings

Longings, yearnings, dreams, desires, hopes, cravings: they all represent the same thing—what you hope for in your life. Do you long for security? Marriage? Children? Long-lasting love? Peace and quiet? Independent wealth? Serenity, spiritual enlightenment, material possessions, a house in the country, a condo in Hawaii? Your longings, which reveal the empty spaces in your life, can make you vulnerable to the dark side.

To understand your longings you will need to ask what has been most important to you throughout your life; you will also need to link your historical longings to your present-day desires. The past always influences the present, and our secret wishes and expressed desires often point to the places where history intrudes on present-day life.

Oscar, thirty-eight, is a gifted and enormously successful artist whose watercolors grace the homes of the rich and famous. Yet no matter how many paintings he sells or how many rave reviews he receives, Oscar still yearns for something more. In therapy he talks about his relationship with his father, a German immigrant who was a gifted but unrecognized sculptor. His father had a mild but debilitating heart attack when he was thirty-five years old, and he looked to Oscar, his oldest son, to fulfill his dreams. "You have the talent," his father used to tell him. "If you work hard enough, you could be a modern-day van Gogh."

Pushing himself to excel, Oscar hoped to make his father's dream come true. Twenty-five years later, more than a decade after his father's death, he continues to drive himself, longing for stardom, always seeking something he can never quite reach. "I want to be the best," he explains. "I want to make my father proud and imagine him smiling at my success, knowing that his life was worthwhile."

Oscar's historical longings reflect his desire to revise the past. In therapy he discovered empathy for himself in the past (the child who grew up believing that he could change the world for his father) and in the present (the man who continued to push himself beyond his capabilities in an ill-fated attempt to alter the pain of the past). With empathy guiding his way, he could break free from the tyranny of the past.

Historical longings are also related to efforts to duplicate the past. Within six months after my father died of a heart attack at age sixty-six, I bought two houses, one in the Boston area, where I work, and one in Maine; the Maine house is on the street where my family vacationed (the only vacation my father ever took) when I was ten years old. I couldn't afford two homes, but that fact had no influence on me. I was driven by my longing to duplicate my past and preserve the sense of family solidarity that characterized my childhood. I wanted to give our children all the love and tender care that my parents had given me.

Motivated by grief and a longing to create the perfect environment for my wife and children, I was vulnerable to the dark side. Contractors, real estate agents, lawyers, bankers, carpenters, plumbers, electricians, and all the other people involved in selling, building, renovating, and financing these houses could easily have taken advantage of me. I wasn't thinking straight because I was driven by a longing to honor my parents' and my brother's memory.

Empathy helps us understand our longings and gauge their influence on our lives. Ask yourself: What do I want? What do I need? What material possessions will make a real difference in the quality of my life? What accomplishments will satisfy me and put my heart at rest?

Many of us want to excel in our chosen fields; most of us want to be admired, respected, loved. "I want to be the kind of person who people walk up to in a restaurant and ask for their autograph," one of my patients told me.

"What would you be famous for?" I asked him.

"I don't know," he said with a shrug and a smile. "It doesn't really matter. I just want people to ask me for my autograph."

Longings for fame, success, admiration, and unconditional love are often generated by the desire to compensate for a disappointing past. To understand your historical longings, you will need to revisit the past, searching for where empathy may have been lacking. Remember, longings are often attempts to fill the empty spaces. Where are those spaces, and what original voids do they represent? When and how were they created? Why were they never filled up?

Empathy should always guide this journey into the past. You are not seeking someone to blame (see Step 7); instead you are working to gain more insight into who you are and why you think and feel the way you do. Once you understand your longings, you can put some of your old ghosts to rest.

Step 3: Learn to Trust Your Natural Instincts

When you are in danger your natural empathic instincts will protect you—as long as you pay attention to them. Kelly, the rape victim whose story begins this chapter, heard the static of empathy but decided to tune it out. Her desire to be friendly and trusting overruled the warning signals raised by empathy, leaving her vulnerable to the rapist's deceptions and manipulations.

When we are in danger our emotional brain immediately triggers alarms, pumping adrenaline through our systems, flooding our bodies with hormones, and speeding up our heart rate. When a cat is frightened it arches its back and its hair stands on end. Humans don't have long hair all over their bodies, so we get goose bumps instead. If you feel a sudden chill, if you get goose bumps, or if your heart starts to race, a primitive part of your brain is telling you to beware. Our brains pick up the seemingly insignificant signals that don't consciously register—a fleeting facial expression, a remark that doesn't quite fit the conversation, a smile on the lips that doesn't show up in the eyes, a nervous tapping of the foot, a rustling in the bushes, a squeal of the brakes.

All these potentially dangerous omens are processed by the emotional brain before they register in our thinking brain. Thus, we often feel fear or sense danger before we can find any rational reason to believe we are at risk. The emotional brain sometimes overreacts, however, sensing a threat where there is none. A creaking of the stairs triggers a major panic attack; a squirrel scampering up a tree sends the heart racing.

In Chapter 4, I talked about the need to slow things down, and the same general rule exists in times of danger. While it is important to heed our natural instincts, we also need to bring the logical, thinking brain into action. The thoughtful responses of empathy can release us from our paralyzing fears into lifesaving action. When Kelly realized she was in grave danger, she relied on her thinking brain, watching the rapist as he moved around the apartment, accurately interpreting his intentions, and determining what she needed to do to save her life—a perfect example of how the thinking and feeling brains depend on each other to guide us and keep us safe.

Step 4: Pay Attention

Fear, anxiety, anger, and frustration inevitably restrict our focus to isolated parts of the landscape. Psychological research shows, for example, that high levels of emotional arousal cause a steep decline in our ability to process information and store it in memory. Thus, if someone threatens us with a gun or knife, our attention is riveted on the weapon, which results in a reduced ability to notice other details. If we are stressed by work, parental responsibilities, athletic competitions, or relationship woes, our vision also narrows, and empathy necessarily suffers.

Our ability to see the wider picture can be further restricted by our longings and motivations. Standing on the stairway with the stranger who offered to carry her heavy grocery bag, Kelly had strong misgivings but chose to ignore them. She didn't want to be the suspicious type, so she overlooked the danger signals relayed by both her emotional and thinking brains. Only after she was raped did Kelly's vision expand. Fearing for her life, she began to pay attention to the whole picture, picking up on disconnected, seemingly insignificant details and piecing them into a whole. She knew the rapist planned to kill her because she was able to ignore her fears and rely instead on empathy's expanded perspective.

While violence is definitely part of our world, the great majority of us will never face a gun-wielding assailant. We will, however, face lesser (but not necessarily less damaging) threats to our health and well-being. In the introduction to Norman Cousins's book *The Healing Heart*, Dr. Bernard

Lown tells a story from his own experience about a middle-aged woman with congestive heart failure who had survived for more than a decade with her disease, raising her children, continuing her work as a librarian, and staying active in her community.

Every week she visited the cardiac outpatient clinic for a checkup, and on this particular occasion her doctor arrived with a group of attending physicians, greeted her warmly, and then announced to the other doctors, "This woman has T.S." Minutes later she was hyperventilating, drenched with sweat, her pulse racing. Dr. Lown, one of the attending physicians, was astonished at the patient's rapid descent from apparent health to serious illness and asked her if she could explain what had caused her so much anxiety. "I know what T.S. means," she said. "It means I'm a terminal situation." Dr. Lown reassured her that T.S. is simply an acronym for tricuspid stenosis, the medical term for her heart condition, but his words came too late to save her. She died later that day of intractable heart failure.

This woman's heart was weak, but it was the intense shock of fear that killed her. Believing that she was a terminal situation, she imagined that hope was lost; with hope gone her will to live faded, and she died. Such moments are not uncommon in our modern medical world. When a physician says to a cancer patient, "Your disease is untreatable, there is nothing more we can do," the patient's world instantly narrows to one seemingly inescapable fate—death. The physician's lack of empathy restricts the patient's world, hope drains, faith withdraws, and darkness descends.

In therapy and in life I am always reminding myself to rely on my peripheral vision. What is it that I haven't noticed? What am I missing? How can I enlarge my perspective so that I can understand more and respond with greater sensitivity? I will never forget a patient who came to me in despair because her husband was having an affair. We worked together for several months, and I remained focused on the issue she presented to me—her husband's betrayal. Not until the end of her therapy, when she brought her husband into the session, did I learn the whole truth. She tearfully confessed to both of us that she had had a brief affair with her boss several years before her husband became unfaithful to her.

I learned that day to keep my eyes wide open and to be more aware of my biases and preconceptions. I was definitely influenced by gender bias, assuming that the husband would cheat on the wife while the wife would remain loyal and devoted. I also learned that I was vulnerable to the damsel-in-distress syndrome, automatically buying into my patient's explanation of being mistreated and figuring that I could teach her what she needed to know to protect herself.

Empathy expands our vision to take in the whole panorama of our experience, offering a wide-angle lens that includes even the peripheral details. Empathy also operates through time, allowing a moving picture to take shape so that we can watch the sequence of events. In the case of the woman who blamed her husband's affair for all their problems, never explaining that she had also been unfaithful to him, I failed to see certain telling, sequential details. I couldn't figure out, for example, why she was willing to stay in such a helpless position. Although I had a feeling I was missing something, I never picked up on my intuition because I was too invested in being her "savior," the one who could teach her how to cope with such a manipulative man.

Empathy always reveals the truth over time. Insights into other people's characters or intentions rarely come in aha! experiences but most often arise slowly, time-release understandings that can be trusted. Pay attention to the subtle shifts in people's moods and behaviors. Watch out for details and facts that don't quite fit. And keep your mind open to all possibilities— as your perspective enlarges, your heart and mind also expand, giving you the patience, flexibility, and wisdom you need to care for yourself and others.

Step 5: Beware of Uninvited Intimacy

When strangers ask you intimate questions or reveal personal information about themselves, beware. Intimacy should always arrive with a formal invitation, an experience you have planned for and feel prepared to handle. Intimacy doesn't occur suddenly, and anyone who tries to make it happen after a few moments of conversation has something other than your best interests in mind.

There are exceptions, of course. A stranger comes up to you at your mother's funeral and without asking gives you a warm hug. "I'm a childhood friend of your mother's," the stranger says with genuine warmth, "and I feel as if I have known you all your life." In this case you can be fairly certain that the stranger is expressing genuine care and concern. By contrast, it's a good bet that salespeople who put their arms around your shoulders after knowing you for ten minutes are getting chummy for self-ish reasons. After you buy the car or the designer dress (or decide not to buy the car or dress), will these people remember you? Will they still want to be your friend?

Think long-term, and be wary of strangers offering affection, effusive gratitude, or "free" gifts. Chances are good they're expecting a return on their investment.

In his most recent book, *Protecting the Gift*, the violence expert Gavin de Becker describes an incident he witnessed during a flight from Chicago to Los Angeles. Seated next to a teenager traveling alone, de Becker observed that the man across the aisle was surreptitiously watching the young woman. Choosing the right moment, the man reached across the aisle, put out his hand, and introduced himself as Billy. Cautiously, the attractive teenager took his hand, told him her full name, and they struck up a conversation. The man learned that she was visiting friends in Los Angeles; they were expecting her on a later flight, and she didn't know how she was getting from the airport to their home. He ordered a Scotch and, when it arrived, offered her a taste; although she initially refused, he eventually coaxed her into taking a sip of his drink. He told her she had beautiful eyes.

When the man got up to go to the bathroom, de Becker politely asked the girl if he could talk to her. She seemed hesitant but nodded her head. "He is going to offer you a ride from the airport," de Becker said, "and he is not a good guy." Sure enough, at the baggage claim area de Becker watched as the man approached the young woman and offered her a ride. When she politely but firmly said no, he made an angry gesture and stomped off in frustration.

The potential for intimacy can often be sensed early in a relationship. We've all known people who make us instantly comfortable, the kinds of people we feel as if we have known all our lives. But true intimacy (intimacy based on authentic empathy) takes time to be developed and trusted. No matter how close you might feel to someone after a brief conversation, a long heartfelt talk, or a successful first date, take your time. If you feel rushed, make sure your boundaries are firmly established and let the person know in clear and unequivocal terms what you expect. If he or she refuses to respect your boundaries and pushes you into some activity that makes you feel uneasy, say no. Trust your natural instincts, and do not hesitate once you have made your decision. Do not allow yourself to be taken in by other people's enticements, no matter how nice they might seem. If they walk away in anger or disgust, don't feel guilty or ashamed for hurting their feelings or ruining a potential friendship—pride yourself on knowing that you used empathy to protect yourself.

Step 6: Beware of Hot and Cold Extremes

Stan, a thirty-nine-year-old restaurant owner, was describing one of his fiancée's "infamous" temper tantrums. She became extremely jealous when he spent half an hour on the phone with his restaurant manager (who happened to be a young, attractive woman). When he tried to explain that they were discussing a business matter, his fiancée slapped him. Later that evening she was contrite and apologetic.

"She can be very sweet at times, but then she loses her temper just like that," he said, snapping his fingers. "Sometimes—maybe even most of the time—I don't know whether I'm coming or going. What do you think I should do?"

"I've been listening to you carefully," I said, "and I'm not sure how it came about that you are so attached to this woman. You told me she has a bad temper and you never know when she is going to be in one of her black moods. Apparently she has alienated many people, including her closest friends and family members. You also told me that, although you care about her, you don't think you're in love with her. Yet you still want to marry her."

This realistic assessment opened the door for a long discussion, as Stan talked honestly about his lack of experience with women, his fears of being alone for the rest of his life, and his belief that this relationship represented his last, best hope for marriage and fatherhood. With empathy putting all the cards on the table, Stan was able to look at the whole picture. At the end of the session he said he wanted to go slow from now on, not making plans for the future until he felt more comfortable that the relationship would last. Months later, when it became clear that his fiancée was not going to change, Stan broke off the relationship.

In general, empathy does not do well in an overheated or chilly environment; it needs a balanced temperature in which cool reflections temper hot emotions. If someone you care about alternates between hot and cold extremes, your emotions will fluctuate with his or her moods, and you will find it extremely difficult to create a balance. Balance is essential for giving and receiving empathy. When the emotional climate is unpredictable, we are constantly on edge, wondering when and if the situation will change. As the tension and anxiety escalate, our thoughts become jumbled, and we find it increasingly difficult to respond in a reasonable, rational manner.

If you often feel off kilter, wondering what to do or say next, thrown by heated expressions of undying love followed by periods of withdrawal and neglect, something is definitely wrong. Extremes are disorienting and disabling. They take more energy than they give and inevitably deplete the power of empathy.

In conflict situations certain characteristic responses are damaging while others help to stabilize the relationship. Researchers who study the way men and women use (or don't use) empathy in intimate relationships have isolated four broad categories of behavior that occur when couples get into an argument. In a scholarly paper titled "Empathic Accuracy and Marital Conflict Resolution," the psychologists Victor Bissonnette, Caryl Rusbult and Shelley Kilpatrick identify four categories of behavior that may occur during conflict. *Exit* and *neglect* are eventually destructive to relationships, while *voice* and *loyalty* help to keep relationships stable and secure.

Exit behaviors include threatening to end the relationship, leaving the room in anger or frustration or reacting abusively (yelling, hitting); this is the "hot" extreme. *Neglect* is a passively destructive reaction (the "cold" extreme), in which you refuse to discuss the situation, avoid further interactions by nodding your head but not really listening, repeatedly withdraw from contentious debates, or criticize your partner for unrelated matters. The researchers conclude that "in terms of long-term couple functioning, it is crucial that they *not* engage in exit or neglect behaviors during conflicted interaction."

The middle, "cool" ground is discovered in the constructive reactions of voice and loyalty. *Voice* involves an active attempt to talk things over and a willingness to search for solutions to the problem, including seeking advice from friends, family members, or therapists. *Loyalty* behaviors are passively constructive and include waiting for the situation to improve, maintaining an optimistic attitude even during conflicts, and defending the partner when others criticize him or her.

Empathy tilts the balance toward constructive behaviors. When we can accurately infer our partners' thought and feelings, we are more likely to accommodate by inhibiting our impulses to react destructively; we work to understand each other rather than retaliate and hurt each other. Empathy helps us leave our self-interests behind. If the relationship is to remain stable and healthy, however, empathy has to flow both ways. If one partner accurately understands the thoughts and feelings of the other but is poorly understood in return, the relationship will become unbalanced and unstable.

The dark side of empathy can exist even in close, loving relationships. With time and patience—but, most of all, with empathy—you can determine whether the relationship has the potential to become more balanced and mutually empathic, or whether your efforts to be accommodating serve only to preserve a tenuous peace. An old saying—"Peace at any price is war"—is applicable in conflict situations. If you put all your energy into preserving a relationship that takes more than it gives, you are surrendering to the dark side and risking your own stability and sense of self.

Step 7: Avoid Blamers

Learning to identify blamers may be the most important step you can take to protect yourself against the dark side. One of the key tools for assessing other people's willingness and ability to take responsibility for themselves (an essential element of empathy) is to look at blaming behavior. Here are a few classic examples:

- There was nothing I could do, it was all so-and-so's fault.
- You won't believe what they did (or said).
- Nobody ever appreciates me.
- They always get their way.
- I did my best, but the rest of the team slacked off.
- Why am I the only one who works hard around here?
- What's the matter with the world anyway?

Understanding the developmental origins of blame is important. In their early developmental stages, children do not experience themselves as separate human beings with a unique sense of self but instead see their parents or guardians as extensions of themselves. When they encounter an obstacle or become involved in a dispute, they tend to hold their caretakers responsible for anything that might go wrong.

When my daughter Alaina was two years old, she bumped into the living room coffee table at the same moment I came down the stairs from my office and opened the door to the living room. "Daddy," she cried out in pain, "why did you do that?"

In Alaina's mind her mother and I were responsible for everything that happened to her, for she had not yet developed a separate sense of self. I soothed and comforted her, helping her to overcome the momentary trauma. I didn't try to teach her that she should accept responsibility for hurting herself, because I knew that this notion was beyond her understanding. With empathy I reacted to her thoughts and feelings at the level she could understand.

As children grow they learn through many empathic interactions with loving adults how to cope with failure and survive. They discover that, even if they make mistakes, they will be accepted and loved. As their ability to accept responsibility for their triumphs and failures grows, their sense of self expands. If their thoughts and feelings are not understood, however, they will continue to blame others as a way of keeping their sense of self intact. Deprived of empathy, they get stuck in the blaming mode.

If you want a really good look at grown-up blamers, tune in to *The Jerry Springer Show*. Men blame women for cheating on them. Women blame their husbands or boyfriends for sleeping with their best friends. Women blame their best friends for having sex with their husbands or boyfriends. Mothers blame daughters for bringing their families to ruin. Next-door neighbors blame each other for their lowered property values.

It's all a blame game. Search for empathy on that program, and you won't find it anywhere—not in the audience members, who take vicarious pleasure in watching people attack each other; not in the host, who inevitably ends up shaking his head at the foolish antics of his guests; and certainly not in the guests sitting onstage, who allow their relationship woes to be exploited for other people's amusement. I wonder if the whole point of this and similar TV talk shows is to let the rest of us off the hook—for no matter how cruel or mean-spirited we might be at certain moments, few of us can claim the miserable experiences of the men and women on these shows. These tell-and-do-all programs give us all a chance to take a break from self-responsibility. We can behave in any way we want—cheat on our best friends, scream at our husbands, physically attack our parents—and there is always someone else to blame.

I love the story (I find it immediately soothing after spending even just these few minutes writing about *The Jerry Springer Show*) of the villager who stood at the gates of his town greeting newcomers. One father arrives with his family, his wagon loaded with his belongings, and asks, "What kind of people live here?"

"What kind of people lived in the village you came from?" asks the villager.

"They were all thieves, every last one of them, greedy, selfish, thought-less, unfeeling . . ."

"You will find the same kind of people here," the villager replies.

The next wagon appears and the father asks, "Tell me, sir, what kind of people live here?"

"What kind of people lived in the village you came from?" the villager responds.

"They were kind, caring, considerate people," the man answers.

"You will find the same kind of people here," says the villager.

You reap what you sow in life, and those who blame everyone else for their problems are sure to find plenty of people willing to blame them, too. Blamers attract blamers, but they need guilty souls in whom to plant their seeds of disapproval and condemnation. Without the fertile soil of guilt, the seeds of blame are scattered to the four winds. So to avoid blamers keep a careful eye on your guilt level. If you always feel guilty when you are with particular people, carefully assess their blaming behavior. Do they blame their problems on others? Are they willing to take responsibility for their own actions? Is everything bad that happens to them someone else's fault?

The persistent blaming of others for one's problems is an entrenched behavior that signifies a lack of flexibility and a definite deficit in empathy. (Psychologists also believe that the more people blame others for their problems, the more disturbed their personalities are likely to be.) Blaming and empathy are opposite behaviors, because blaming is based on false-hoods while empathy is always grounded in the truth. Blaming seeks to hand over responsibility to others, while empathy requires the willingness to take responsibility for one's thoughts, emotions, and actions.

Step 8: Watch Out for Self-Serving Reinterpretations

Emotions are indeed contagious. Those who know how to inflame our emotions to further their own self-centered needs can take simmering thoughts and feelings and create a potentially devastating brushfire. I recently read an article in the *Chicago Tribune* titled "Hate Rock" about the fast-growing white supremacist (skinhead) music industry and its use of vicious lyrics to spread propaganda messages of racial hatred and murder. Young people are slowly "recruited" to the movement, according to the article, when they listen over and over again to raplike lyrics such as these: "There was no Holocaust but there is one coming / Fire up the ovens! / Fire up the ovens!"

This is the dark side of empathy in action as hate-filled messages are broadcast to thousands, even millions, of young people who may or may not have racist leanings. Dancing to that beat inflames the emotions and numbs the mind. Does such propaganda work? I recently read that "hate sites" on the Internet increased from 1,400 to 2,000 in a five-month period. Hatred is like a virus—it is contagious and can spread through the Internet, the printed page, radio, television, and CD players as easily as it captures the imagination of the dispossessed and downtrodden at camp meetings, rallies, and political demonstrations.

Subtler manifestations of the dark side also infiltrate our lives. Suppose, for example, that you are deeply disappointed with your 3 percent salary increase. After work a co-worker, who is also unhappy with her raise, asks you to join her for a drink.

"Don't you think John [the boss] is more partial to men?" your colleague asks after you both have a few drinks.

"I don't know," you say, adding, "but I'm certainly not happy with this raise."

"I've seen the way he treats you," she continues, gathering steam. "He has no respect for you, or for any of the women in the firm for that matter. I know other women who are as unhappy as we are. I think we should join together and file a complaint."

This is a confusing moment, for while you are definitely disappointed with your raise, you have been working at this company for only two years, and you know you have a lot to learn. Still, you wonder if your co-worker might be right—if so many women are unhappy at work, maybe the boss really does have a problem with the opposite sex. Should you go along with her and complain to a supervisor, or should you keep working and hope you get a better raise next year?

Empathy helps to clarify your thoughts and feelings. The next day, with a cooler head, you consider your situation and conclude that your primary emotion is disappointment, not anger. You had hoped for a bigger raise, but, unlike your colleague, you have no reason to believe that your boss is displeased with you. Hoping to clear the air, you schedule a meeting with your boss, in which you ask him if he would mind explaining how the raises were decided. He is open and straightforward—as it turns out, the company gave a straight 3 percent raise to all employees who had been working for less than three years. He tells you he is pleased with your work, enjoys working with you, and plans to give you more responsibility. You leave the office feeling much better about your future, reminding yourself to make sure he follows through on his word.

When people heat up your emotions in order to fulfill their own needs, the dark side is simmering beneath the surface of the relationship. Here's another example: A depressed thirty-three-year-old woman involved in a conflict-ridden marriage consults a psychotherapist. The therapist, who is thirty-five years old, divorced, and living on her own, immediately identifies with her patient and, as the weeks go by, subtly encourages her to consider separating from her husband. More weeks go by, and the therapist becomes more forceful. She believes, based on her own experience and her theories about men in general (rather than her empathic insights into her patient's unique situation), that her patient can find happiness only if she leaves her husband and sets out on her own. The patient resists and several months later terminates therapy.

In this and many similar cases, we need to remember that everyone teaches her or his own struggle. Just because someone is a therapist, a professor, the CEO of a company, or the president of the United States doesn't mean he or she is absolutely trustworthy. Trust is a wonderful quality, but it must be earned—and it can often be abused. If you feel uneasy in a relationship for any reason, trust your own instincts, listen carefully, and use your assessment skills to determine if the person you are involved with is trying to push through an underlying agenda.

Every week I lead a group therapy session in a hospital outpatient treatment program for alcoholics and other drug addicts. One day a newly admitted patient, who had tried to kill herself several days earlier, broke down sobbing. She told the group that before her suicide attempt she had been in recovery for several months and undergoing intensive psychotherapy in an attempt to work out problems in her troubled marriage. She understood that her husband's heavy drinking and periodic rages were undermining her sobriety, but she still loved him and could not imagine living without him.

Confused about what path she should take, she asked her therapist point-blank if she should leave her husband. Believing that the relationship was not only risky for her patient but also doomed to failure, the therapist advised her to pack her bags and leave. "I don't believe you love him," the therapist counseled, "and in the long run I think you will be better off on your own."

Hours after that session, the patient attempted suicide. When I met with her several days later, she was confused and deeply frightened. "Please, can you tell me what I should do?" she asked. I asked her many questions, and in the process of working out the answers, we both realized how confused and at times chaotic her marriage was. Yet as she talked about her husband, it also became clear that she loved him and was not ready to give up on the relationship. She explained that when her therapist, someone she deeply admired and respected, told her that she should leave her husband, she felt that, no matter what route she took, she was doomed to unhappiness. Feeling trapped and hopeless, she believed that suicide was her only way out.

She also told me that she loved her husband, and she believed there was hope for the relationship. For the moment, she realized, she needed to stay. "Maybe someday I will leave him," she said, "but right now I need him to survive."

These stories reveal that the dark side is not always edged with evil. People who truly care about you and are interested in your welfare can manipulate you in subtle but potentially devastating ways, leading you to accept their interpretations of your thoughts and feelings. When you feel like someone you care about might be manipulating you for his or her own ends, remember that no one knows you better than you know yourself. The only good, true answer is the one you find through the hard work, patience, discipline, and commitment of empathy.

Empathy takes time—it cannot be rushed. In therapy if I try to take control, convincing both myself and my patients that I have the ultimate solutions to their problems, I am playing God. I have no right to give other people *my* answers—I can only offer my honest, realistic assessments intended to help them move closer to *their* answers. Even then I am careful to present my interpretations as possibilities, avenues to explore that might yield new insights. My role is to walk alongside my patients rather than lead them where I think they should go or, worse, follow along behind them, nodding my head knowingly at every misstep or misadventure, refusing to offer any explanation or advice for fear of misdirecting them. Once again empathy finds its balance in the middle way, where we work on our problems together, always seeking the unique truth of the situation rather than some canned theoretical version of the truth.

At home, with our two teenage daughters, I try to follow the empathic way; I don't always succeed, but I always try. Although I may feel that I know what is best for my children, I believe my role is to help them sort through their options and arrive at their own conclusions. Their decisions may not conform to mine, but as long as I am assured that their health or safety is not compromised, I must honor their unique pathways.

My daughter Erica was an all-league varsity runner in eighth grade and captain of her high school track team her junior year. She always loved to run, but the spring of her junior year she was plagued with injuries and illnesses and had to drop off the team. Late one night she came up to my home office and told me she was thinking about whether or not she should run her senior year. "I'm so injury prone, particularly in the long-distance races, and I think it's time to give my body a break," she said. "I love running for fun and fitness, but I'm tired of the stress of competition." Erica talked for a long time, and I listened, asked questions, and tried to help her sort through her often conflicted thoughts and emotions. In the end we both agreed that she had made the right decision not to compete her senior year.

That interaction easily could have veered off in another direction. With my love of athletic competitions and my firm belief in her talent, I could have attempted to influence Erica's decision by suggesting that she try intensive physical therapy, offering to counsel her when she felt stressed, or meeting with her coach and asking for special treatment. Instead I listened to her, and she showed me the way that was right for her. I honored the soul-searching she went through, and I had respect for her ultimate decision.

Empathy always seeks out an individual answer to questions or problems, respecting the fact that every human being is unique. Not one of us fits cleanly into a standard theory. We can't be neatly labeled, identified, stamped, or stacked on a shelf. And we can't select the pathway that someone else should take, no matter how much wisdom or experience we may have accumulated. That doesn't mean that we should avoid the responsibility of offering our honest feedback—but any explanation or interpretation we give should leave room for reinterpretation and expansion in the ongoing attempt to understand the truth.

Step 9: Watch for Inconsistent Behavior

Consistency is one important way to assess other people's character (not to mention your own). In a wonderful scene in the movie *The Wedding Singer*, Drew Barrymore asks a grieving Adam Sandler if he had any idea that his relationship with his fiancée was headed for trouble. Without a moment's hesitation Sandler says, "I remember we went to the Grand Canyon one time, and we were flying there, and I'd never been there before and Linda had, so you would think that she would give me the window seat, but she didn't. Not that that's a big deal, you know, but I guess there were a lot of little things like that. I know that sounds stupid."

"Not at all," Barrymore says. "I think it's the little things that count."

"Little things" like inconsistent behaviors can destroy a relationship. When someone is loving in one moment and selfish in the next, kind then suddenly inconsiderate, thoughtful and then, inexplicably, thoughtless—and when this is clearly a repetitive pattern—empathy asks us to beware. People tend to be inconsistent when they are preoccupied (for whatever reason) with their own needs and desires. When it suits them they can be kind and considerate; when it doesn't suit their needs they lapse into selfish and thoughtless behaviors.

We all have occasional lapses of inconsistency, but a continuous pattern of inconsistent behavior indicates a deficit in empathy. Empathy depends on a willingness to invest time and energy in understanding other people's thoughts and feelings. When consistency is lacking, empathy's power is draining. Be on the lookout, then, for consistency in all your relationships. If you are just getting to know someone, pay attention to the way he acts when there is nothing observable to gain. Watch her with waiters, bus or cab drivers, strangers waiting with her in lines at the supermarket. Does he treat the people who work for him with the same care and consideration that he treats his supervisor? Is she pleasant and cordial in face-to-face interactions with her in-laws but then does she spend the next few days tearing them apart? Is he as friendly to the garbage collector as he is to the auditor from the Internal Revenue Service? How does she speak on the phone with strangers? Is he sensitive and understanding with everyone he encounters during the day or only with those he considers useful?

In therapy inconsistent behavior is often revealed when a conflict arises. Christopher, for example, was gracious, pleasant, and considerate for the first eight weeks of therapy. Then one week he didn't show up for his session and never called to explain. The next week he arrived as if nothing had happened. When I asked why he didn't call, he became irritated and defensive. "Something came up," he said, putting his hand in the air, palm out, warning me to back off. He refused to talk about it further.

Three weeks later Christopher skipped another session, and the hospital held him responsible by sending him a bill for the skipped session. Every day for the next week, he called me, shouting at me over the phone, threatening to sue the hospital, demanding that I "make things right." When I explained that he had agreed to the hospital's cancellation policy before he started therapy, he abruptly terminated our sessions.

Patients sometimes ask me for extra sessions, and I oblige them whenever I can. Sometimes, however, especially during the holidays when so many people experience emotional upsets, I simply have no time to fit in extra sessions. A patient's reaction to that disappointment often reveals a great deal about his or her character. Julie, for example, often complains about how she gives more than she gets. Everyone takes advantage of her, she says, and no one takes any time to listen to her. "Life stinks" is one of her favorite sayings.

Three weeks before Christmas Julie told me she was depressed and needed an extra session. I didn't have any time in my schedule, but I assured her I would call if something came up. Every day, without fail, she called me, asking if I had a cancellation. Every day, without fail, I called her back to let her know that nothing had opened up but I had not forgotten about her and would call her when and if I had a cancellation. This went on for a week, and then one night I had an emergency at the hospital, did not return home until midnight, and could not return my calls. The next morning there was a message on my answering machine at work: "Obviously, you don't want to help me," Julie said. "I can tell that other people are more important to you than I am. I'm going to look for another therapist."

A friend recently told me a fascinating story about her father-in-law. She and her husband went out to dinner with her in-laws, and her father-in-law monopolized the conversation, talking about his conversion to Catholicism and his new live-and-let-live philosophy of life. "I try to give everyone space to do their own thing," he said in a calm, serene voice. Fifteen minutes later a young man with a pierced ear walked by their table. Her father-in-law turned red in the face. "I'd like to rip that earring right out of his earlobe," he snarled, loudly enough for everyone nearby to hear.

The inconsistency I am trying to highlight is the discrepancy between the way people describe or define themselves and the way they act in real life. It is much easier to talk the talk than to walk the walk, and inconsistency is a sure sign that someone is having trouble putting one foot in front of the other. We will all, of course, behave in inconsistent ways at times, particularly when we are under a great deal of stress. When inconsistency becomes a predictable pattern that continues through both difficult and serene times, however, we can be fairly certain that empathy is lacking, and the dark side is not far behind.

Step 10: Remember: Empathy Is Not Synonymous with Kindness

George, a recovering alcoholic in his midforties, told me a story about an event that occurred a year earlier, the day after his father died of alcoholism.

"I've got five brothers," he began, "and we decided to meet in a Dorchester bar to hold an old-fashioned Irish wake for our father. This is a hard-drinking crowd, mind you, and when I walked in, somebody called out, 'Get George a whiskey!' Without a second's hesitation my older brother Liam bellowed, 'Over my dead body!' So I spent my father's wake sulking and fuming in a dark corner of the bar. Liam, I figured, had no compassion, and the more I thought about it, the madder I got. When I got home I drank myself into oblivion. I wanted to get even with him and pay him back for his lack of understanding."

At this point in his story, George put a hand to his chin, fingers stretched out over his cheeks, and rubbed his two-day whiskers. He looked at me, eyes sparkling, and offered a self-effacing grin. "So you know the rest, right? I relapse, put my sorry butt back into treatment, faithfully attend AA meetings, ease a little wisdom under my belt, and finally get it into my thick head that I had it all wrong. I thought my older brother was putting me down, humiliating me, but now I know he was trying tō save me. He's rough around the edges, works construction, never graduated from high school. Sure, he could have found a different way to tell me he cared about me, but knowing my brother, putting myself in his shoes, I know he did what he felt he had to do. He did the best he could."

Tears were running down George's cheeks, but he made no effort to wipe them away. "My dad died a drunk, two of my brothers are far gone in the booze, and there I was, finally sober. Now I can see the truth—my brother had just lost his dad to the poison, and he was damned if he was going to lose me, too."

Sometimes what appears to be the dark side of empathy is, in reality, the tough but steady hand of insight and understanding guiding us through troubled waters. Empathy doesn't always give us the answers we want to hear—in fact, empathy often asks us to take a good, hard look at ourselves with the goal of altering our self-defeating behaviors. Many times in therapy I have to call attention to some thought, emotion, or action that is causing a patient endless grief. I always try to use empathy as my guide, listening carefully, asking open-ended questions, expressing my thoughts in ways that allow the patient to disagree with me or take off in a new direction. Nevertheless, my main concern, driven by empathy, is to offer explanations and interpretations that will help the patient grow and become the person he or she wants to be. Those realistic assessments can be bitter pills to swallow. Sometimes patients lash out at me in fury or frustration. Sometimes they retreat into sullen silence, and on occasion a patient will abruptly quit therapy.

I used to feel guilty about patients who quit therapy or withdrew in anger for days, even weeks, wondering what I could have said or done that would have given them the strength and will to continue. But patients know that my primary concern is for their welfare; they know, too, that if I believe they are harming themselves in some way, I will not hold back for fear of offending them or hurting their feelings. They understand that the work involved in changing and transforming the self is not easy or effortless but requires dedication and commitment. Weeks or months later they may return to the work, telling me, "You spoiled an affair I was about to have" or "You ruined my drinking binges" or "You exposed my workaholic attitude and now I can't justify spending so much time away from my wife and children." Empathy is the irresistible variable that draws people back to the work, to life, and to growth.

Empathy's strength comes from its commitment to the truth. I am not saying that there is just one truth, for every experience offers different variations of the truth. Searching for truth and meaning can be a difficult and demanding process, but the rewards are valuable beyond measure. We all seek meaning and purpose in our lives. Seduced by the dark side of empathy in its multidimensional forms, we can be waylaid from that journey, spending months, even years off balance, confused, directionless, in despair. Physical harm is only one threat from the dark side; damage to our hearts and spirits is more common and often more difficult to endure.

Empathy teaches us how to protect ourselves and others by striving to avoid deception in everything we say and do. This can be a hard road, requiring commitment, willpower, discipline, patience, and endurance. Yet only through the power of empathy can we discover who we are, who we are meant to become, and how we can help others in their search to find themselves.

PART TWO

As we move around this world and as we act with kindness, perhaps, or with indifference or with hostility toward the people we meet, we are setting the great spider web atremble. The life I touch for good or ill will touch another life, and that in turn another, until who knows where the trembling stops or in what far place my touch will be felt.

—FREDERICK BUECHNER

EMPATHY IN ACTION

Empathy is both guide and guardian, leading us along the way to intimate, long-lasting relationships and at the same time teaching us how to defend ourselves against those who might harm or deceive us. In Part One we investigated the biological roots of empathy and its essential role in our ability to understand ourselves, each other, and the world we inhabit. Empathy is a true survival skill, an inborn capacity to understand other people's thoughts and feelings and an innately powerful drive that inspires us to create close friendships and caring communities. A fundamental element of social, intellectual, and moral behavior, empathy motivates us to acts of compassion and altruism, taking us deep into the heart of what it means to be human.

I know from many years of experience that empathy works. Putting empathy into practice increases our self-awareness, strengthens our relationships, and helps us understand people who might at first seem strange or unlovable. Expanding our perspective and opening our minds, empathy adds immeasurably to the complexity and wonder of life.

In Part Two I will explore empathy in action, showing how we experience empathy through eight behaviors or ways of being that are sometimes classified as moral or spiritual principles—honesty, humility, acceptance, tolerance, gratitude, faith, hope, and forgiveness. Through these realities, which are the visible if intangible expressions of empathy, we come to a deeper appreciation of our innate capacity for intimacy.

These are not new or uncommon concepts. We have grown up with them, listening to lessons about their intrinsic value from our parents, teachers, clergy, and community leaders. The problem is that the terms have been used so often, and with so little explanation of their practical utility, they've lost their meaning. We know, for example, that honesty is a noble goal, but why is it important to our personal development and how will it benefit us in the long run? The moral imperative to "be honest" too often pales next to more immediate practical concerns. If cheating on tests can help me get into college or refusing to disclose an affair can keep my marriage intact, where is the incentive to be honest?

Self-help books urge us to be optimistic, tolerant, and accepting of others, but they rarely explain how we can remain hopeful when we encounter defeat time and time again, or what possible benefit can be derived from tolerating the intolerant or offering our support to someone who makes a habit of hurting others. Be grateful, we hear. Have faith, we're enjoined. Humility is a virtue. Forgive and you will be healed. The words sound good, but with the thoroughly practical prodding of the modern mind, we wonder why we should invest time in pursuits that don't offer immediate dividends. And while we can understand that being grateful, faithful, humble, and forgiving may be good for our moral or spiritual development, we end up frustrated by the broad generalizations and simplistic, step-by-step instructions that in the end bring us no closer to happiness or self-fulfillment.

What we have been missing is a context in which we can see how these realities affect our sense of self and our ongoing interactions with others. Empathy provides that broader perspective, allowing us to see how honesty, humility, acceptance, tolerance, gratitude, faith, hope, and forgiveness influence our ability to understand other people's thoughts and feelings and respond to them in helpful, constructive ways. Empathy removes these concepts from the dusty shelves of philosophy and religion and puts them in the hands of ordinary people like you and me. Even more important, empathy shows us how to employ these skills to achieve our goal of gaining entry into the inner sanctum of another person's soul.

I use the word *soul* with caution, for like the concept "spirituality" it's an abstraction that has been so eagerly hunted in recent years it's in danger of extinction. What makes up the soul? What, exactly, constitutes a spiritual experience? Once again empathy leads us to an answer that has immediate, practical significance. *Soul*, in empathy's dictionary, is that intangible, invisible part of every human being that yearns for attachment to something deeper and broader than ourselves. The human spirit longs for connection, and empathy provides the power necessary to create intimate bonds with others. Without empathy the yearning for union exists but the soul has no means of fulfilling that longing. Empathy is the force that completes the soul's craving for connection, giving us the courage and the energy to reach out to others for solace and the wisdom to know who we can and cannot trust.

As you read these chapters, keep in mind that each of these experiences has its dark-side reflection, as revealed in the following list. Many of us, for example, struggle with perfectionism, spending countless hours wishing for a perfect body, a beautiful face, brilliant children, the ideal job, or the model marriage. The quest for perfection points directly to a problem with acceptance, which in empathy's dictionary is defined as the ability to see, understand, and embrace the imperfections that lie at the heart of every human being—including ourselves.

EMPATHIC BEHAVIOR	DARK-SIDE REFLECTION
Honesty	Dishonesty, deception, deceit
Humility	Pride, conceit, egotism, arrogance
Acceptance	Perfectionism
Tolerance	Intolerance, bias, prejudice
Gratitude	Ingratitude, greed, thoughtlessness
Faith	Cynicism, suspicion, skepticism
Hope	Despair
Forgiveness	Resentment, bitterness, hatred

Perceiving the dark-side reflection of these experiences helps us to focus on areas where we need to strengthen our empathy. If, for example, you are filled with bitterness or hatred for someone you once cared about deeply, you will know that resentments are blocking your ability to forgive and diminishing your capacity for empathy. When empathy is lacking because we hold on to resentments, give in to despair, or set ourselves apart from others through pride, we find it much more difficult to create or sustain intimate relationships. Dishonesty, pride, perfectionism, intolerance, greed, skepticism, despair, and bitterness isolate and alienate us from others. And when we are isolated and alone, we are in great danger—physically, mentally, and spiritually. As modern research so compellingly confirms, loneliness literally puts our lives at risk.

These chapters are offered, then, as lifesaving experiences that will strengthen the power of empathy for positive, constructive purposes, guiding us to deeper, more meaningful relationships with ourselves, with others, and with life itself.

Chapter 8

Honesty

Lying to ourselves is more deeply ingrained than lying to others.

—FYODOR DOSTOYEVSKY

Honesty is empathy's lifeblood, its oxygen, its living breath. If we take away honesty, empathy loses its reason for being. For how can we relate to others in a meaningful way if we can't be truthful with them? If we don't offer sincerity, how can we demand it in return? (I am talking here, of course, about constructive empathy, which seeks to strengthen relationships, rather than destructive empathy, which uses insights into other people's thoughts and feelings to control or manipulate them.)

If we are to be honest with others, however, we must first be honest with ourselves. All true wisdom—and the ability to get along with each other is certainly an important manifestation of wisdom—is rooted in self-knowledge. "Know thyself," Socrates enjoined, a commandment that is as relevant in the twenty-first century as it was in ancient Greece. To know ourselves we must be wholly honest with ourselves, holding nothing back.

We need to be honest not only with ourselves but also in how we perceive those around us. A wonderful story illustrates this point. A group of students approached a renowned Tibetan spiritual master and asked if he would accept them as his followers. "Yes," he answered, "but only under one condition. You must renounce all of your previous teachers."

The students pleaded with him, for they were all indebted to their former teachers, who had taught them many valuable lessons. The master would not budge from his position, however, and eventually all but one of the students agreed to accept his condition.

The master seemed quite pleased and asked the students, including the outcast, to return the next day for their first lesson. When they were assembled before him, he said, "If you would abandon your former teachers, I know you would also someday renounce me. Seeking the truth, you have lost it. I cannot accept you as my students."

As the room emptied the teacher turned to the one student who remained and said, "You have proven that you will be honest with yourself and with others even when you may lose something that you greatly desire. Because honesty guides your way, we have many valuable lessons to teach each other."

The master then knelt before the student, humbling himself. "I will agree to be your teacher," he said, "if you will agree to be mine."

I learned an important lesson about honesty's relationship to self-awareness many years ago, when I was beginning my master's program in psychology. In my first course, Sensitivity Training, I was given the assignment of confronting my parents and detailing the difficulties I had experienced in life as a result of my upbringing. My professor emphasized the value of honest, face-to-face confrontation, assuring the class of eighteen students that the origins of our psychological problems could be traced directly to the way our parents interacted with us during our childhood.

I was skeptical about the exercise, but I pushed my doubts aside, called up my father (I figured I'd practice on him first), and asked him to meet me for dinner. I explained on the phone that I wanted to talk to him about some issues we were studying in my psychology class. When we met at the restaurant (I chose "neutral ground," as my instructor suggested), he was unusually pensive.

"Okay, Arthur," he said, fixing me with his dark brown eyes, letting me know I had all his attention. "Say whatever you need to say."

I cleared my throat and made a conscious effort to still my anxious mind. My father was not a big man—he stood five feet, seven inches—but when he entered a room he occupied the whole of it. Fiercely independent, proud, intense, even at times explosive, he was always a force to be reckoned with.

Working hard to calm myself, I began to detail my criticisms of his parenting skills and basic temperament, following the guidelines laid out by my professor. I told my father that while I admired his passion, he tended to be overly sensitive and impatient. Basically, I continued, he had a very forceful personality. I concluded by saying I thought he demanded too much of me and his unreasonably high expectations were creating ongoing problems in my life.

With mounting anxiety I watched my father's face, trying to gauge how he was taking the analysis. He was uncharacteristically calm, which only increased my nervousness.

When I finished with my evaluation—I couldn't have talked for more than five minutes—my father asked me a few questions. "Tell me, Arthur," he said, "why is this discussion important to you?"

I fumbled around for some answers, trying to sound like a mature, intelligent graduate student, but to tell the truth, I didn't know why I was sitting in a strange restaurant criticizing my father, a man I loved more than life itself. Recognizing my discomfort, my father asked the questions he always asked when we discussed something important.

"Are you finished?" I nodded my head. "Are you sure that you've said everything you need to say?" I nodded my head again.

"Well, Arthur," my father began, "I have to say that I feel very, very bad for you. You have two big problems, in my opinion. The first is that you want me to be less intense—you want me to change. But I'm fifty years old, and I can guarantee you that my temperament, as you put it, is going to be with me for the rest of my life."

He took a sip of water, folded his hands, and took a deep breath. I could see that he was consciously slowing himself down, making sure that his words accurately conveyed his thoughts and feelings.

"The second problem is more serious," he continued. "In time you will realize how much you take after me. I'm guessing, given what you've said today, that this will be a big problem for you. How will you deal with it? My advice would be to stop blaming other people for the problems in your life and start working on changing what you don't like about yourself."

I'll never forget my father's parting words. "I know you'll work it out, Arthur," he said, his gentle smile conveying his love for me, the older of his two sons. "Your greatest strength is that you always rise to the occasion."

My father understood that the power of empathy resides in its commitment to honesty. He loved me enough to offer me the truth as he perceived it; holding nothing back, he trusted me to be able to accept his thoughts and, over time, respond to them. His empathy went far beyond an automatic emotional response ("I understand what you are going through" or "I sympathize with your pain"), because it involved the thoughtful ability to look at the world through my eyes, accurately assessing what I needed to change and grow as a human being.

Here's the honest truth—my father saw right through me that day. He understood that my halfhearted attempts to change him were only a detour and that the most important work confronting me involved a willingness to look inside myself without flinching. He knew that if I continued to blame other people for my problems—and, worse, if they accepted that blame—I would go nowhere. (I'm reminded, as I write these words, of a line in Sam Keen's book *To Love and Be Loved*: "If we did not have a deeply ingrained habit of blaming others for our deficiencies and failures, therapists would starve to death.")

If my father had responded emotionally, with sympathy, he might have patted my hand, told me he understood, accepted my assessment, wondered what he had done wrong, even attempted to make amends . . . and in all likelihood I would have walked out of that restaurant believing that my fears and insecurities were at least in part his fault. With empathy guiding him to search for the truth, my father taught me to look inside my own heart and soul for the answers to my questions. I may be part of the problem, he was willing to admit, but do you really want to change me? Will that be the goal of your life as a psychologist and a human being, changing others to make life more comfortable for yourself?

EMPATHY'S DEFINITION OF HONESTY

Empathy defines honesty as the ability to see oneself clearly, to understand others accurately, and, above all, to communicate those perceptions in sensitive, tactful ways. Heartless truth-telling is not the way of empathy. Many people confuse honesty with a subtle (or, often enough, not so subtle) form of humiliation, believing that only by tearing people down can we build them back up again. Suppose, for example, that it is 5:00 P.M. on a beautiful summer day when a father returns home from work to discover that his thirteen-year-old son has neglected his chores.

"You didn't mow the lawn, did you?" the father asks.

"No," the son replies, hanging his head.

"We've talked about this before, haven't we?" the father says, his voice rising in frustration and anger. "You are lazy and a procrastinator—how do you ever hope to achieve anything in life?"

While the father justifies his harsh assessment by telling himself that he is speaking for his son's "own good," such brutal honesty shames and confuses his son and may well lead to self-defeating behaviors. "I'm lazy and a procrastinator," the child reasons, "so why should I mow the lawn today, when I can put it off until tomorrow?"

Empathy's honesty is not so sure of itself. Empathy never assumes that "my" truth is the best or the only truth but instead asks, "What is the truth at this particular moment, for this particular person?" Empathy seeks to find a fit between "your" truth and "my" truth, knowing that sometimes there is no easy compromise. Empathy does not try to prove itself right but only seeks to broaden, widen, and deepen its perspective. "Explain your truth to me," empathy asks, "and I will try my hardest to understand."

In searching for the truth empathy looks for the words or phrases that will allow the other person to "hear" our concerns. Rather than accusing, insulting, or humiliating, the father could actively adopt an empathic approach, allowing his emotions to settle down before he talks to his son. "I noticed when I came home tonight that you didn't mow the lawn," the father says in a neutral voice.

"I was busy," the boy says, somewhat defiantly.

"Oh? What were you doing?" the father responds, again keeping his tone impartial and refraining from making accusations.

"Well, I read a book, I watched TV, played with some kids . . ."

"That does sound like a busy day. Do you think you might find some time tomorrow to mow the lawn?"

"Sure," the boy says. "But there's still an hour before dinner—maybe I could mow the lawn now."

"It's probably cooler now, anyway, don't you think?" the father says.

Through his questions, comments, and vocal intonations, the father tries to communicate that he respects his son and wants his son to respect him. The honesty that springs from empathy is always respectful, honoring the individual's unique experiences but placing the greatest value on the relationship. Empathy, like respect, appreciates differences but always seeks a common ground.

In her eloquent book *Respect: An Exploration*, the Harvard University professor Sara Lawrence-Lightfoot focuses on the ways respect strengthens and deepens our connections to each other, "creating relationships among equals." In the opening chapter she tells a story about her mother, Margaret, and her father, Charles. The story takes place shortly after Margaret graduated from medical school.

> At her first summer job after marriage, a research position at the Mississippi Department of Public Health, Margaret went to meet the director. "He immediately called me 'Margaret.' . . . This was 1938 in Mississippi, and people did not immediately call each other by their first names." The director was making clear that despite her credentials from Columbia Medical School, she was a Negro talking to a white boss. "Charles was infuriated. . . . He was so angry, he felt destroyed." Her new husband's rage and pain brought home to Margaret their already deep bonds. "For the first time, I knew what it was to be a wife and feel a kind of empathy with someone close to you. . . . You feel something he does."

Empathy and respect are mutually dependent. We can't have empathy without feeling respect for others, and we can't have respect without experiencing empathy as a foundation for the relationship. With empathy we feel what other people feel, and that ability to move into another person's experience is the foundation for respect. Both respect and empathy demand honesty—honest (authentic) dialogue, honest (undiluted) attention, honest (attentive) listening, and a commitment to honest (heartfelt) change. When we honestly (accurately) understand another person's thoughts and feelings—an understanding that extends beyond sympathy ("I feel your pain") and even beyond identification ("I have experienced what you have experienced") to the realization that even though I have not been through the fire of your experience I can see the flames in your eyes and feel the heat in your skin—we gain a deep and abiding respect for each other's unique experiences.

HOW EMPATHY LEADS TO HONESTY

Empathy is, first and foremost, the ability to *accurately* understand another person's thoughts and feelings. The word *accurate* is crucial, for if our understanding is faulty our responses will be misdirected. The accuracy of our perceptions directly influences the sensitivity of our responses. How do we know if our perceptions are accurate? Psychological researchers offer the following insights into the mechanics underlying empathic accuracy:

• To understand other people's thoughts and feelings, we need to be fully involved in the present moment. Empathic accuracy is based on our moment-to-moment interactions—what is happening right now—as well as on our knowledge of another person's personality, character, judgments, and opinions.

• Honest interactions require that we acknowledge any preexisting stereotypes or biases that might impair our understanding of others. In the same way we need to examine theory-driven judgments about others that contribute to mutual misunderstanding. Psychoanalytical theory, for example, tells us that sadism and violence are expressions of an innate aggressive drive—we turn to violence because it is part of our nature as human beings. Yet recent research shows that children whose parents divorce or are alcoholic, physically abusive, or generally unempathic have significantly higher rates of overt aggressive behavior than children who are raised by loving, empathic caretakers. In a twenty-year study the psychologist Cathy Spatz Widom followed 908 children and found that those who had been abused had 50 percent more arrests for violent crimes than did a control group.

Abuse breeds abuse. Violence produces violence. Empathy fosters empathy. Knowing that our behaviors are directly influenced by the way others treat us allows us to move closer to an accurate understanding of our thoughts and feelings and enables more honest, truthful interactions.

• People involved in unhappy relationships are more likely to misinterpret intended positive behavior of their partners, underestimating the incidence of such behavior by as much as 50 percent. In other words, if you're having difficulty in a relationship, the chances are good that you will see the bad even in the good, and honest expressions of caring and concern can easily be misinterpreted.

• A belief in the importance of passion and romance increases our ability to understand each other's thoughts and feelings. Researchers theorize that when we emphasize the importance of passion and romance, we are more likely to work hard to make our relationships passionate and romantic. In this case believing makes it so or, as the psychologist William James put it, "Faith creates its own verification."

• While empathic accuracy tends to increase over time, long-term relationships can lead to complacency and familiarity, which inevitably diminish empathy. Feeling like we know each other's every move, we are less motivated to engage in the hard work of trying to understand changing emotions and complicated thoughts. Complacency is not good for relationships, for if we think we know everything about the other person, we leave no room for growth and surprise. As we stop investing our time and energy in empathizing with each other, we respond to each other with theories and judgments based on the past. Empathic accuracy depends on a lively back-and-forth between individuals who see each other as changing, growing, adapting individuals with plenty of surprises left.

Empathy always insists on the truth, for if we are not honest—if we hide certain truths from each other or if we reach false conclusions about each other because of theory-driven judgments—it is difficult if not impossible to trust each other. Illuminating moments in therapy and life often occur when someone asks a direct question—Am I beautiful? Am I as smart as people think I am? Am I obese? Am I a bad person?—and we offer an honest, empathic answer. Empathy leads us to honesty because it takes us beneath the surface to perceive what another person is really feeling, thinking, and experiencing. The challenge, then, is to learn how to communicate our thoughts and feelings in helpful rather than hurtful ways, expanding rather than contracting each other's perspective.

"Am I really brilliant?" a patient once asked me. "Or am I a fool who comforts himself by imagining that he's intellectually superior?"

With that question my patient asked for a balanced, realistic assessment of his intelligence. In my experience the honest answer to such a question is discovered not at the extremes but somewhere in the middle.

"From what I have come to know about you," I said, "you are not as smart as you want to be nor are you as unintelligent as you fear you might be."

A forty-two-year-old woman who had been trying hard to lose weight recently asked for my opinion. She had lost thirty pounds and was exercising every day, but she still felt uncomfortable with her body. "I can't stand this sagging, flabby flesh under my arms and on my stomach," she said, wrinkling her nose in disgust. "I bought a bathing suit the other day, tried it on for my husband, and his only comment was 'Nice colors.' I was hoping he would compliment me for daring to get into a bathing suit, but he didn't even seem to notice. What do you think? Do I need to lose more weight? Am I obsessing here? I need a mirror of reality."

"I can imagine that it would be difficult for you to lose so much weight and then, when you put on a bathing suit, have your husband not even seem to notice," I said.

"I think he wants me to be drop dead gorgeous," she said. "You know, he wants me to look like the models in the Victoria's Secret catalog."

"That's not very realistic, is it?"

"You mean I'm not drop dead gorgeous?" She laughed.

"No," I said, laughing with her, "you are not drop dead gorgeous, but you are also not the plain, unattractive woman you sometimes imagine yourself to be. You are an intelligent, kind, attractive woman who has worked very hard to lose weight. Could you lose more? I'm sure you could, but I also know it is hard work. Could you be more fit? If you keep exercising, you will continue to see the benefits."

"Thanks," she said with a big smile. "I feel better hearing the truth from you, even if it does mean I'm not drop dead gorgeous."

I will never forget the time when Carolyn, whom I described in Chapter 6, told me that she had had a brief affair with a married man half her age whose wife was expecting their first child. "I find that despicable," she said. "Do you?"

"Why do you want my judgment?" I asked.

"I don't know," she said. A moment later she added, "I guess I don't need an answer—I know what I'm doing, and if I thought it was the right thing to do, I wouldn't be here talking to you about it."

In therapy and in life there is no room for deception. Honesty is what we seek in our relationships, but we need to hear the truth in a way that won't humiliate us and offer the truth in a way that won't estrange us from each other. Even when we reveal thoughts, feelings, or behaviors that make us feel ashamed of ourselves, we want to know the honest facts. The empathic interaction contains the shame and guilt to the situation rather than allowing them to be unleashed in the mind, where they can turn into humiliation and self-censure.

If honesty is cruel it is not guided by constructive empathy, for empathy always seeks to frame its truths in ways that help rather than hurt.

PRACTICING HONESTY

Learn the Difference Between Constructive and Destructive Truth-telling

Empathic honesty seeks to build up rather than tear down. If your comments humiliate or degrade another person, they are not in the service of empathy. Before you speak, learn to ask yourself: Do I have an ax to grind? If the honest answer is yes, assess your impulse to hurt the other person (and therefore, in empathy's equation, yourself) before you engage in conversation. Focus on communicating the truth honestly but tactfully. Make sure that you are offering your honest thoughts in an attempt to help the other person rather than with the hope of furthering your own interests or proving a point. Always seek to communicate your concerns in helpful rather than hurtful ways.

Be Respectful

Empathic honesty is fundamentally respectful. Empathy always conveys respect for other people—respect for who they are, what they have experienced, where they came from, and where they are now. Respect insists that we see other people as they truly are, hearing their concerns, paying attention to their longings, listening to their dreams, quieting their fears. If honesty does not *give* something to another person—if it only *takes away* by criticizing, putting down, making judgments—it is not motivated by empathy.

In your interactions with others, always ask: Am I being respectful? Do my comments convey my respect for the other person's unique experiences and the complexities of his or her thoughts and feelings? Am I offering my strength and support?

Use Honesty to Set Limits

So many of us are preoccupied with being nice that in the name of kindness, unselfishness, or unconditional love we put up with behaviors that are hurtful, even harmful. Years ago I worked with a cocaine addict who lied to me many times and stole medications. One day he called the hospital and told the switchboard operator it was an emergency; she put the call through to my office even though I was in session. On the phone he explained his "emergency"—he had violated parole and needed me to write a letter to the court to bail him out. I was forceful with him, and when he kept pushing, I hung up on him.

My patient was flabbergasted. "You hung up on that person!" she said.

"He lied to me too many times," I said.

"So if someone lies to you, you can cut him off?" she asked. This question led to several conversations in which she asked me, always with intense curiosity, how you can know when it is time to set limits and how exactly you go about doing so. That phone call was a turning point in her therapy, for she had been living with an alcoholic husband who physically and emotionally abused her. Seeing the handwriting on the wall, as she put it, she worked hard over the next few months to develop the ability to set limits with her husband. Several months later she made the decision to leave him and initiated divorce proceedings.

Use Your Thoughts to Cool Down Your Emotions

With empathy we use our thinking brains to cool down our emotional brains. If we give voice to our feelings as they arise, without cooling them down with thoughtful reflection, we circumvent the empathic process.

Be Honest with Yourself, Above All

Sometimes what we imagine to be honesty is merely a thin disguise for disapproval and censure. If you find that you are constantly criticizing others, it is time to take a good, honest look at yourself. Ask yourself: What is it about this person or this group of people that bothers me? What insecurities do they bring up for me? How can I work on my self-doubt rather than focusing all my attention on another person's faults and flaws?

I don't have many fixed beliefs, but let me repeat one theory that I believe applies in most cases: Critical people are insecure people. If you spend a lot of time criticizing or censuring other people's behavior, the chances are good that you also spend a good deal of time criticizing yourself.

Every Day, Without Fail, Ask: What Am I Hiding?

Honesty seeks to reveal what is concealed. Look for the hidden places, first in yourself, only then in others. Ask: What am I holding back? What will happen if I bring my thoughts and emotions out into the open? What do I fear? Can I live with the consequences of being honest?

Establish Safety First

Empathy, safety, and honesty are intimately connected. When you are treated with empathy, you feel safe with others; when you feel safe, you can be honest and expect honesty in return. Empathy creates an atmosphere of safety, for you know that your concerns will be heard and you will be treated with respect and consideration for your welfare. If you feel threatened, exposed, or vulnerable, you will not be able to hear the other person's honest assessment.

To feel safe with another person you have to establish a relationship based on empathy. Listen carefully. Let the other person know that you are trying to understand her perspective. Be patient. Learn how to live with imperfection. Avoid offering ready-made answers. Ask for the other person's help. Take your time. Proceed step by step. Be willing to backtrack. And always, if you make a mistake, be willing to say, "I'm sorry" and make amends.

This is the empathic way.

> *Honesty is stronger medicine than sympathy, which may console but often conceals.*
>
> —GRETEL EHRLICH

Chapter 9

Humility

Imagine that every person in the world is enlightened but you. They are all your teachers, each doing the right things to help you learn patience, perfect wisdom, perfect compassion.

—Buddha

Humility is that place of balance where we know who we are and who we are not. Empathy guides us to a humble position by keeping us focused on the truth of our behavior, gently opening our eyes and allowing us to see who we are so that we can avoid being sidetracked by the struggle to be something we are not. Whenever we put ourselves in a privileged place, assuming our situation is unique or the rules don't apply to us or we're somehow "above it all," we diminish the power of empathy. Presenting ourselves as different or better or smarter than others, we create a distance that can only lead to misunderstandings. Empathy always seeks to bring us closer together, reminding us that we need each other and, in fact, cannot get by without each other.

In many ways the book *Tuesdays with Morrie* is a short but loving treatise on the relationship between humility and empathy. A professor (Morrie Schwartz) is dying, and his former student (Mitch Albom) visits him every Tuesday, humbling himself before his teacher in the hopes of learning how to live a fuller, richer life. The professor, however, is learning his own lesson in humility. Deeply humbled by imminent death, he knows that any wisdom he has to share arises from the knowledge that he will soon be reduced to ashes and dust.

In one memorable conversation Morrie recalls an "interesting question" someone asked him—was he afraid of being forgotten when he died? His answer takes us deep into the heart of empathic humility. "I don't think I will be," he muses. "I've got so many people who have been involved with me in close, intimate ways. And love is how you stay alive, even after you are gone."

Morrie turns, then, to his student and asks him a question. "Do you ever hear my voice sometimes when you're back home? When you're all alone?"

· "Yes," his student answers. Morrie is satisfied, knowing that with this question and answer his own doubts are stilled and the point has been driven home. For if we hear the voices of those we love, even when we are separated by many hundreds of miles—even when we are disconnected by death—then they are still with us, talking, listening, carrying on.

Empathy's humility is discovered in the fact that the most important work we can do in life is to comfort and care for each other. Our primary reason for being is not to be the best or the brightest, the richest or the most beautiful, but to be as concerned about others as we are about ourselves. Through our relationships—through the act of finding each other and affirming that without each other our lives have no lasting meaning or purpose—we make our most significant and lasting impact on the world.

A few weeks before he died, just before "the fourteenth Tuesday," when the professor and his student say their final good-byes, Morrie tells Mitch a simple story about a wave in the ocean. The wave is having a wonderful time in the vast sea, gently rolling along, lifted by the wind, then settled by the still air, lolling and cresting, falling and climbing, rocking and reeling. Then one day the wave takes a look around and realizes that something has changed—the ocean does not go on forever. Up ahead there is a rocky coast, and the waves are crashing against the shore.

"I'm going to die!" the little wave realizes. "For no matter what I do, no matter how hard I struggle, I'm being carried along by the other waves, and I, too, will crash against the shore."

Another wave comes along and asks, "What's the matter?"

"Don't you understand?" the little wave asks. "Look up there, we're headed for disaster, we're all going to crash and break apart on the shore."

"Oh, but I'm afraid you don't understand," the second wave says. "You see, you are not just a wave—you are part of the ocean."

Empathy's humility is discovered in the truth that we are all part of something larger than ourselves. Empathy leads us to that humble acceptance of our indivisibility, for while we are separate and unique, we are also part of a deeper, wider, broader truth: we are all part of the ocean. With empathy guiding the way, as the professor guided his student, we discover that reality long before the distant shore comes into view.

In his classic book *The World's Religions*, Huston Smith tells a story about Oren Lyons, the first member of the Onondagan tribe to enter college. When Lyons returned home on his first vacation, his uncle took him out fishing. Rowing to the middle of the lake, his uncle got to the real business at hand—making sure his nephew understood his place in the world.

> "Well, Oren," he said, "you've been to college, you must be pretty smart now from all they've been teaching you. Let me ask you a question. Who are you?" Taken aback by the question, Oren fumbled for an answer. "What do you mean, who am I? Why I'm your nephew of course." His uncle rejected his answer and repeated his question. Successively, the nephew ventured that he was Oren Lyons, an Onondagan, a human being, a man, a young man, all to no avail. When his uncle had reduced him to silence and he asked to be informed as to who he was, his uncle said, "Do you see that bluff over there? Oren, you *are* that bluff. And that giant pine on the other shore? Oren, you are that pine. And this water that supports our boat? You are this water."

The uncle hoped to teach his nephew that *who* we are is less important than *where* we belong and *how* we relate to each other. Empathy always emphasizes our underlying and overpowering connection to each other and to the world itself. We are no more and no less than the pine tree on the opposite shore, the water beneath us, or the uneducated man sitting on the other side of the boat. We can only give back to the world what we have taken in; realizing how much we have taken in gives us the humility needed to give back in full measure. When Mother Teresa was asked how she could work with lepers, she answered, "Because they give me so much back," she said.

The summer before my senior year in college, I worked with my father in his furniture store, loading up furniture and driving the delivery truck. After ten hours of hard, physical labor, I would come home exhausted, sit down to supper with my parents, and talk. After dinner my father would drift off to read the paper, visit with the neighbors, or smoke a cigarette on the front porch, and my mother and I would keep talking. One night, after a long, heartfelt conversation, my mother told me how much she enjoyed talking to me. Proud of myself and pleased that she had noticed my conversational skills, I offered her what I thought were sympathetic words.

"It must be hard for you," I said, "because you could sit and talk for hours, but Dad doesn't have the time or patience for long talks." I then offered my mother a quick analysis of my father's shortcomings. "He's very intense," I said, "and very impatient, which makes it difficult to engage him in long, meaningful conversations."

My mother was quiet for a moment, gathering her thoughts. When she spoke her voice was gentle. "So now you don't like your father's intensity, Arthur?" she said. "When you need him, and he drives three hours to see you at your college after he just worked twelve hours straight, is that when you appreciate his intensity? Or perhaps when he looks at you with those big brown eyes, seeing right through to your heart, and says, 'I will help you through anything, no matter what, I'll be there for you,' is that when you appreciate his intensity?"

My mother let her words sink in for a moment. The look on her face said, *I don't want to hurt you, but you're just not getting it*. "Close your books, Arthur," she said, "and open your eyes."

Empathy's humility is wrapped up in those three words: *Open your eyes*. My mother, like Oren Lyons's uncle, was not impressed with book learning, but she was even less impressed with people who had "swelled heads." She used to say that the butcher in our town was as good a human being as the local doctor. "The doctor is a kind and generous man who takes care of many people," my mother said, "but he never remembers anyone's name, and outside of the office he doesn't seem particularly interested in people.

"Now the butcher"—and here my mother's eyes would sparkle—"this man makes his living selling meat, but at the end of the day, he gives food to the poor. So both the doctor and the butcher are good men, but true goodness does not stop when you have closed your doors for the day."

A similar story features a conversation between a rabbi and a student. "In the Talmud," says the student, "the stork is known as *hasida*, which means the devout or loving one. Yet in the Scriptures, the stork is classed with the unclean birds. Can you tell me why?"

"The stork gives love only to its own," answers the rabbi.

When we offer our care and concern only to those in our family, our gang, our tribe, our neighborhood, or our country, the love we offer is tainted with arrogance and pride. Empathy demands a humble love, one that cares for all people. Empathy's love issues forth from humility, the understanding that, when we strip away our titles and possessions, we are all more alike than we are different. We are all little waves in the vast ocean of life.

EMPATHY'S DEFINITION OF HUMILITY

Empathy defines humility as that place of balance where we acknowledge both our strengths and our weaknesses, without getting too wrapped up in either extreme. With humility we avoid the trap of getting swelled up with pride in our accomplishments and the equally self-defeating snare of being deflated by exaggerating our faults. The psychiatrist Fritz Perls used to explain the difference between the balanced person, the neurotic, and the psychotic this way: The psychotic insists, "I am Abraham Lincoln"; the neurotic complains, "I wish I were Abraham Lincoln"; and the balanced person says, simply, "I am who I am."

Humility is synonymous with what I call healthy narcissism, which means that we understand how to devote a balanced amount of energy inward toward ourselves and outward toward others. We can say "I am who I am" without pumping ourselves up with pride ("I am who I am, and I'm the greatest") or deflating ourselves with false humility ("I am who I am, and I am nothing"). Humility helps us find the balance between all and nothing.

In his book *Markings* Dag Hammarskjöld offered an empathic exploration of humility's middle position:

> Humility is just as much the opposite of self-abasement as it is of self-exaltation. To be humble is *not to make comparisons*. Secure in its reality, the self is neither better nor worse, bigger nor smaller, than anything else in the universe. It *is*—is nothing, yet at the same time one with everything.

With empathy we find security in our own reality, knowing that we are located somewhere between the extremes of everything and nothing. In a later passage Hammarskjöld wrote:

To have humility is to experience reality, not *in relation to ourselves*, but in its sacred independence. It is to see, judge, and act from the point of rest in ourselves. Then, how much disappears, and all that remains falls into place.

In the point of rest at the center of our being, we encounter a world where all things are at rest in the same way. Then a tree becomes a mystery, a cloud, a revelation, each man a cosmos of whose riches we can only catch glimpses. The life of simplicity is simple, but it opens to us a book in which we never get beyond the first syllable.

Humility is that place at the core of our being where we can settle into ourselves and find a point of rest. From this vantage point we can see that we are not the center of the universe but only one small, insignificant part, and that realization is ultimate freeing. Seeing ourselves within the vast sphere of living things, we understand our relative insignificance. And that realization releases us from the desire to be the best, the brightest, the richest, or the most beautiful, and lets us settle into the humble truth of who we are. Paradoxically, that middle position also releases us from the fear that we may be the worst, the dumbest, the poorest, or the plainest person on earth. Humility puts us right smack dab in the middle, where we're forced to admit that we're not so great and pleased to add that we're not so bad, either.

HOW EMPATHY LEADS TO HUMILITY

Empathy—the act and process of taking another person's perspective on a particular situation or life in general—requires humility. In order to adopt the other's view, we must suppress our own perspective. In a very real sense we have to say to ourselves, "My perspective is not broad enough," a position that conveys not self-criticism ("I'm not good enough") but a desire for self-expansion ("I have so much more to learn and experience"). Humility generated by empathy signifies a commitment to set aside our theories and biases so that we can enter every new situation with an open mind—the beginner's mind that Zen practitioners talk about, a mind cleared of preconceptions, wiped clean of biases, swept, polished, scrubbed to the bone.

Psychological researchers who study "perspective taking" offer the following insights into how a lack of humility can interfere with empathy.

• Egocentrism, which is defined as the inability to prevent your own emotions and thoughts from interfering with your ability to understand others, obstructs empathy. When you and your desires, dreams, hopes, and fears are the primary focus of your world, you will find it difficult to adopt other people's perspectives or differentiate between your needs and other people's desires. It's like the old joke about the man who talks for hours about his problems, then turns to his friend and says, "So enough about me—what do *you* think about me?"

• The ability to take other people's perspectives, accurately inferring their thoughts and feelings, is acquired gradually as you learn about your own emotions, desires, beliefs, and thoughts. Understanding yourself—and, even more important, feeling secure within that understanding—you will be motivated to reach out to others. Anything that prevents you from developing a broader base of self-understanding (grief, trauma, abuse, lack of empathy in relationships) will necessarily interfere with your ability to empathize with others.

• Taking another person's perspective requires suppressing your own—a demanding process that depends as much on motivation as on innate ability. That motivation can stem from both the desire to help others (constructive empathy) and the attempt to manipulate others (destructive empathy).

• Constructive empathy arises directly from humility, for humility leads to the impulse to become a better (more understanding, caring, forgiving, tolerant) human being. Destructive empathy stems from arrogance and pride—the belief that you are the center of the universe and people are valuable only so long as they are useful to you.

• Constructive empathy and the impulse to altruism can be communicated. The first and most essential step is self-knowledge, for the more we know about our own thoughts and feelings, the more skilled we become at reading other people's emotions. Before five years of age children tend to be grandiose in their thinking ("I can do everything"); with experience and continued brain development, they become more self-aware, realizing that they have limitations. Self-awareness breeds humility—when you understand that you have both strengths and weaknesses, a whole new world of emotions opens up to you: jealousy, envy, insecurity, pride, confidence, and, of course, humility.

If you are treated with care and respect for your uniqueness, you learn how to handle these difficult emotions and become socially competent or, as Daniel Goleman puts it, "emotionally intelligent." If, however, you are neglected, ignored, criticized, or mistreated, you can get stuck in the grandiosity stage and, to defend your shaky sense of self, learn to blame others, become obsessed with perfection, project your thoughts and feelings onto others, and practice intolerance, all of which can lead to a host of negative emotions, like anger, hostility, resentment, fear, shame, and guilt.

• Constructive, beneficial empathy can be taught. In a scholarly paper the psychologists William Ickes, Carol Marangoni, and Stella Garcia write: "It appears that empathic understanding is a trainable skill, and that through the provision of immediate, target-generated feedback a 'generalized' or global improvement of this skill can be obtained."

In other words, we can learn—and we can teach others—how to take another person's perspective, listen empathically, control our impulses, regulate our moods, find a balance between emotion and reason, resolve conflicts, and create intimate, long-lasting, loving relationships.

Empathy, as the research shows, is an effortful process requiring a willingness to temporarily give up our own thoughts and feelings in order to more accurately understand the thoughts and feelings of other people. When we remove ourselves from the center, we make room for the perspectives and opinions of others. Empathy expands with humility and contracts with arrogance and pride.

Humility is the very foundation of empathy.

PRACTICING HUMILITY

Ask for Help

When you ask for help, you automatically humble yourself, admitting that you need guidance. Every day practice humility by asking someone for help. Ask a friend to help you with a problem you're facing. Ask your spouse for help with a problem in your marriage. Ask a stranger for directions.

Phrase your questions with humility:

- *I'm having trouble understanding this—could you help me?*
- *I don't know what to do. Do you have any ideas?*
- *I feel lost—can you help me find my way?*

Put Other People's Needs Above Your Own

A married couple decides to share a cheeseburger for lunch. The waitress asks if they want onions on their burger. "Yes," says the wife at the same time as her husband says, "No."

Here's the humble twist to the story: The wife doesn't like onions but said yes knowing her husband's fondness for them; her husband said no recalling how onions play havoc with his wife's digestive tract. As the waitress waits, pen poised, they discuss their options. "I don't need the onions," the husband says. "I can pick them off," his wife counters.

In simple moments like this, when we put the needs and desires of others above our own, we discover humility. Ask yourself: What can I do today for someone I love? What can I do for a stranger? Where can I give up control and let someone else take over? What do I want that I don't really need?

Listen

Listening is at the heart of humility and empathy, for when we truly, deeply listen, allowing the other person to *feel heard*, we leave the self behind. A group of early Christians called the Desert Mothers and Fathers placed great emphasis on the art of listening. According to one story, a newcomer to the desert approached one of the elders. "Can you offer me some words of wisdom to help save my soul?" the newcomer asked.

"If you want to save your soul," the elder replied, "do not speak until you are asked a question."

And then there is Morrie Schwartz's question to his former student. "You'll come to my grave?" Morrie asks. "Yes," his student replies, adding that "it won't be the same not being able to hear you talk."

"Tell you what," Morrie says. "After I'm dead, you talk. I'll listen."

Say Your Prayers

Prayers are a gentle way of humbling yourself and asking for help. As the theologian Simon Tugwell explains in *Ways of Imperfection*, the original meaning of prayer was a petition or cry for help, and the true nature of prayer arises "from incompetence, otherwise there is no need for it." The simple act of asking for help is good for the spirit, but it also benefits the mind and the body; perhaps even more important from empathy's perspective, prayers are good for others. In a series of experiments conducted at Harvard University Medical School, Herbert Benson demonstrated that saying prayers stimulates certain physiological changes leading to "the relaxation response."

In his book *Healing Words*, Larry Dossey, M.D., cites hundreds of studies showing that loving, empathic thoughts and prayers can have a powerful, positive influence on health and healing—not just in humans but also in bacteria, rats, and mice. In one experiment sixty subjects with no known healing abilities were able to slow down *and* speed up the growth of bacteria cultures. In a series of twenty-one experiments with mice recovering from anesthesia, nineteen studies showed "highly significant" results, with the "prayed for" mice enjoying a faster recovery.

You can pray at any time of the day, and you can direct your prayers to just about anyone—God, the Great Spirit, a friend or relative, even yourself. Pray for those who are struggling to find their way. Pray for those who have died, asking that their souls be at peace. Pray for yourself, seeking strength, understanding, faith, forgiveness. Pray for others. Pray for humility.

Consider Your Mortality

Nothing is more humbling than the understanding that we are mortal, and our time on earth is limited. Because our questions about death cannot be answered with any certainty, just asking the questions is humbling. Where do we go? Is there life after death? Does our spirit live on? What is our purpose on this earth?

These are not just religious questions but the basic philosophical questions of life, and they have practical meaning, too. Humbled by our mortality, we can also be inspired by it. The world will go on without us, no doubt about that, but while we are here we do what we can to make the world a better place. That's all.

"There is a crack in everything God has made."

—RALPH WALDO EMERSON

Chapter 10

Acceptance

The fir tree has no choice about starting its life in the crack of a rock. . . . What [nourishment] it finds is often meager, and above the ground appears a twisted trunk, grown in irregular spurts, marred by dead and broken branches, and bent far to one side by the battering winds. Yet at the top . . . some twigs hold their green needles year after year, giving proof that—misshapen, imperfect, scarred—the tree lives.

—HARRIET ARROW

In the aftermath of John F. Kennedy, Jr.'s death in a plane crash off Martha's Vineyard, many stories were told about him. This one is my favorite.

> Many years ago on a ski slope, John Jr. was crying. His uncle Bobby came up to the boy, put an arm around his shoulder, and said, "Kennedys don't cry."
> John looked up at his uncle and said, simply, "This Kennedy cries."

With insight and wisdom far beyond his years, a young boy speaks to the truth of who he is. I am not like everyone else, he announces to the world. I am unique, my own person, my own individual self. Even in my weakness—no, especially in my weakness—I accept myself for who I am.

There is a poignant epilogue to this story. Hearing her son's words, Jackie Kennedy smiled proudly and offered him a hug, an affirming gesture that goes a long way to explaining why John F. Kennedy, Jr., was so accepting of himself. Encouraged by his mother to be himself, he was able to find the courage to stand up for himself and defy other people's expectations of his behavior. In the safe surround of his mother's empathy, he was given the opportunity to become himself.

To thine own self be true. This old adage is the empathic heart of acceptance, which demands that we ask first, *Who am I?* Of all the questions we ask in life, this is the most challenging, for to answer it truthfully we need to give up our self-deceptions and accept not only the strong and admirable aspects of our nature but also the fragile, fallible parts. Only when we have accepted ourselves with all our "good" and "bad" parts can we learn how to accept others with all their strengths and weaknesses.

EMPATHY'S DEFINITION OF ACCEPTANCE

In his classic book *On Becoming a Person*, Carl Rogers offered an empathic definition of acceptance:

> By acceptance I mean a warm regard for him [*sic*] as a person of unconditional self-worth—of value no matter what his condition, his behavior, or his feelings. It means a respect and liking for him as a separate person, a willingness for him to possess his own feelings in his own way. It means an acceptance of and regard for his attitudes of the moment, no matter how negative or positive, no matter how much they may contradict other attitudes he has held in the past. This acceptance of each fluctuating aspect of this other person make it for him a relationship of warmth and safety, and the safety of being liked and prized as a person seems a highly important element in a helping relationship.

While I agree with Rogers that acceptance conveys warm regard, respect, and liking for another person, I believe it is most important to emphasize the process involved in coming to acceptance. Empathy defines acceptance as a three-stage, continually evolving process. In the first stage we learn to accept ourselves with all our contradictions and complications. Self-acceptance leads to the second stage, in which we learn to accept others with all their contradictions and complications. And in the third stage we accept the inevitable contradictions and complications that arise in every human relationship when two complicated, contradictory people meet.

As always with empathy, self-acceptance comes first, for self-knowledge and self-awareness lay the necessary groundwork for understanding others. Looking inside ourselves (eyes wide open), we see both the good and the bad and invariably exclaim, "What a mess!" Strangely enough, that insight is comforting, for giving in to the truth of ourselves is infinitely less painful than constantly fighting our reality. After years of doing battle with ourselves, it suddenly dawns on us that we're not getting much of anywhere. What is empathy's answer to that impasse? Give up, let go, and surrender to the truth of the self.

Empathy makes surrender possible, reminding us that it is okay to not be okay. Being happy is a fine goal, but happiness tends to be fleeting and difficult to duplicate. Happiness is a moment-to-moment kind of thing, and between those pleasureable moments we have plenty of sorrow, confusion, grief, and despair to muddle through. Besides, who said we had a right to happiness? Can any one of us really claim that privilege? Isn't happiness something we treasure for the moment, knowing it is sure to pass?

I'm *not* okay, and you're *not* okay—but that's okay. That's a philosophy that empathy can embrace. Glenn, a thirty-three-year-old concert pianist, once told me that he could not accept making even one mistake when he went on tour. With empathy guiding the way, we talked about his father, an electrician who was always putting down other people (most notably his son) in the ill-fated attempt to elevate himself. When Glenn accepted his father as "not okay" (imperfect, critical, insecure), he could admit that he was also "not okay" (imperfect, self-critical, and insecure). Viewing his insecurities as somehow normal and an everyday part of growing up with an excessively critical, insecure father, he could accept himself as perfectly human, which really meant he was "not okay," but that was okay.

The Jesuit priest and master storyteller Anthony de Mello offered some priceless thoughts on being "O.K." This quotation is taken from *Mastering Sadhana*, Carlos Valles's book about de Mello's teachings.

> The theory of *I'm O.K., You're O.K.* is deadly teaching. It imposes on you the obligation to feel O.K. and unless you feel O.K. there is something wrong with you. That is simply intolerable. I am whatever I am, and I feel whatever I feel, and it's fine. I need not be O.K. in order to be O.K. if you follow me; I may not be O.K., and that is perfectly O.K. with me. You must break free of the O.K. trap. In fact I plan to write someday a book with the title *I'm an Ass, You're an Ass*, which will be the antidote to the O.K. doctrine. Someone has already suggested to me a subtitle for the book: *A book you'll get a kick out of!*

Acceptance, which is available to us only through the wide-angle lens of empathy, is the way that we "break free of the O.K. trap." Acceptance says, "I'm not okay." Oddly enough, when we accept the fact that we're not okay, we start to feel better. We release ourselves into the truth of ourselves, and then something astonishing happens—we begin to change. Slowly, almost imperceptibly, the self begins to cave into the self. The nineteenth-century philosopher and psychologist William James called this process surrender, explaining that "something must give way, a native hardness must break down and liquefy."

The ice inside melts, and without willing it or commanding it, we begin to change. Carl Rogers referred to "the curious paradox" that links acceptance to change:

> When I accept myself as I am, then I change. I believe that I have learned this from my clients as well as within my own experience—that we cannot change, we cannot move away from what we are, until we thoroughly *accept* what we are. Then change seems to come about almost unnoticed.

"A man [sic] cannot be comfortable without his own approval," Mark Twain once said, and truer words were never spoken. Acceptance of the self must come from the self. But only through the power of empathy—only through other people's concern for our thoughts and feelings and their confirmation that we are worthy of their interest—are we able to open ourselves up to the mixed-up truth of who we are.

HOW EMPATHY LEADS TO ACCEPTANCE

Empathy leads us to acceptance by enlarging our perspective. We see ourselves, with empathy's wide eyes, in the big picture. Placing ourselves in the context of our relationships with others, we see how we *fit*, where we belong. Finding our place in the larger community, we learn that we can only accept ourselves if we accept our need for each other.

Acceptance of self is an essential first step in the process of accepting others. Being yourself is a process of learning who you are and where you fit or belong. This process never ends, for the self is always changing, growing and transforming in relationship to others, who are going through a similar evolution. While other people may be moving faster or slower, they are working on the same basic task you are—discovering who they are and where they belong.

Not long ago in a nearby town a ten-year-old girl was killed in a freak accident during a snowstorm. Her father was driving the car when it hit a patch of ice and skidded off into a snowbank. Shaken up but physically unharmed, both father and daughter got out of the car and stood by the side of the road, waiting for help. A pickup truck hit the same ice patch, veered out of control, and struck them, killing the girl and critically injuring her father.

The tragedy threw many people in our area into grief and shock. The day after the accident I got a call from my friend Betty, a minister at a local church; she was scheduled to give the eulogy at the child's funeral service. Devastated by the loss, Betty had no idea how she was going to deal with her own emotions, and she wondered what she could possibly say that would help others cope with their anguish. "I feel this overwhelming need to give the perfect sermon," she told me, "but I just don't think I have the strength."

Betty talked for a while about her old attachment to perfection and the lessons she had learned from her stern, emotionally aloof father about the need to be in control and to hide your deepest feelings from others. Then she began to talk about her parishioners, who were literally begging her for help, sobbing in her arms, desperately searching for a way to make sense of a child's senseless death.

"I'm not God," she said, breaking down in tears. "I'm just a human being."

"I wonder if that's your answer," I said.

"That I'm not God?"

"Yes," I said. "I wonder if you could tell your parishioners what you have just told me—that you are devastated by this loss and you need their help just as they need yours. Perhaps you could tell them that you don't have all the answers, but you believe in the power of the congregation to support and care for each other."

"But if I open myself up like that, won't I be sidestepping my responsibility?" Betty asked. "Aren't I supposed to be the strong one, the one they depend on for answers to their pain?"

"But isn't the most fundamental answer to our pain the fact that we need each other?" I said. "Many, many times you have used those words in the past—our strength is discovered in our need for each other."

"Yes," she said, with a look of hope and growing excitement. "That's what I believe."

Betty gave her sermon without notes, speaking eloquently from the depth of her own pain, admitting her fears of appearing vulnerable and emphasizing her belief that only by joining together would the congregation discover some measure of healing. With the understanding that her strength emerged directly from her weakness, Betty discovered the power of empathy to heal and transform. As she cried openly with the parishioners, broken hearts began to heal into wholeness.

"No one is as whole as he who has a broken heart," said Rabbi Moshe Leib of Sasov. We can only be whole when we accept the fact that we are broken. Every human being on this earth has broken places—hurts, aches, griefs, wounds, unsatisfied yearnings, painful disappointments. These are not flaws we should fear or blemishes we should try to cover up—they are merely the scars that come from living fully, actively, and openly.

Because we live, we hurt. Because we move around in this world, thinking, feeling, acting, and reacting, we get bumps and bruises. How could it not be so? "All real living," to repeat the Jewish scholar Martin Buber's words, "is meeting." And when we meet, we sometimes collide. Perhaps the deepest level of acceptance we discover in life is the wholehearted embracing of both the joy and the suffering that inevitably arise in close relationships.

PRACTICING ACCEPTANCE

Let Go

As the psychologist William James put it more than a hundred years ago, if you "let go your hold," you will gain "inward relief." He illustrated his point with a story. A man is walking alone at night and suddenly finds himself sliding down the side of a precipice. Flailing around, hoping against hope to save his life, he grabs onto a tiny branch. For hours he clings to life, but finally his fingers can no longer retain their grasp. With a final, despairing cry, he lets go—and drops a mere six inches to the ground.

"If he had given up the struggle earlier," James commented in a wry epilogue to this story, "his agony would have been spared."

Ask yourself: What do you hold on to in life that you fear losing? (The answers, of course, are as rich and varied as life itself—wealth, health, marriage, friendships, children, happiness, security, love, peace of mind, houses, boats, jobs, youth . . .) What does the struggle cost you? Can you relax your grip? What awaits you on the ground below? How far is the drop? Will you survive if you let go?

Learn How to Accept Criticism

If you are truly, honestly, wholly yourself, I promise you this—you will encounter people who don't like you, who disapprove of you, and who want to change you. As Antonio Porchia put it in *Voices*, "They will say that you are on the wrong road, if it is your own." Criticisms can be well deserved, and when they hit the mark, they have much to teach us. But critical comments can also be undeserved, unnecessary, and manipulative. Sifting the wheat from the chaff is an important, challenging task.

If you find that you are often critical of others, use your empathy to discover the source of your insecurities. In my experience people who do a lot of criticizing are often insecure; feeling unsteady and unprotected, they tend to lash out at others. Ask yourself: In what situations do I have difficulty accepting myself? With what specific people do I feel apprehensive or off balance? How could I change the situation to feel more secure, more safe?

A tendency to be critical of self and/or others generally points to some unresolved pain, something in your past that continues to disturb your peace of mind. Finding out where your insecurities come from will help you deal with them openly and honestly, in the present.

Remember: Growth Through Suffering

When you open up to others and accept the fact that you need help, you leave yourself vulnerable. Why do that? some people wonder. Why let people into your heart and soul who then might tear you apart?

Understanding the power of empathy, you will know who to trust and who to question. Use your assessment skills. Listen carefully. Watch to make sure that people's actions match their words and stated intentions. Be aware of the ways you can be manipulated. When you are convinced that a person is trustworthy and authentically cares about you, enter the relationship wholeheartedly.

We cannot engage in real, human relationships without getting hurt, but pain, as so many wise men and women have reminded us, is one of our greatest teachers. We grow through suffering. Our deepest wounds are often the source of our greatest strength. Ask yourself: What are my deepest wounds? Where do I feel the most consistent hurt? How can I use this pain to grow, change, become a stronger, more accepting, more tolerant and loving human being?

Pay attention to the healing that has come through your relationships rather than focusing on the harm inflicted. Teach yourself to ask with every painful or disappointing encounter: What can I learn from this experience? How could I have handled the situation differently? What has pain taught me about the resources and resilience of the human spirit?

Find the Places Where You Fit

We accept ourselves when we find others who will accept us. This is what happens so often in therapy—distressed souls who feel alone and misunderstood find a place where they fit and belong. They stop running away from themselves and start accepting themselves for who they are, with all their varied strengths and weaknesses.

Think about home. What does the word *home* mean to you? How do you feel when you go there? Is "home" the kind of place where you fit in because your imperfections are accepted—where you are appreciated and loved in spite of your shortcomings, where you are loved, in part, because of your weaknesses? Where do you feel like you can be yourself? Where is your true home? Where do you feel safe?

Think, too, about those places where you don't feel at home. Are they "bad fits" because you are trying to be what you are not or because others do not accept you for who you are? Are you trying to conform to someone else's expectations of who you should be? How does the effort to fit in affect you? Is it worth it to keep trying? What will you gain? What will you lose?

Spend Time Alone

The ability to be alone is a necessary (if at times painful) condition for acceptance of ourselves and others. Not until we learn how to be comfortable alone with ourselves can we be comfortable with others. In *The Art of Loving* the psychoanalyst Erich Fromm explained this basic truism. "If I am attached to another person because I cannot stand on my own feet," Fromm wrote, "he or she may be a lifesaver, but the relationship is not one of love. Paradoxically, the ability to be alone is the condition for the ability to love."

Here are a few ways to be alone: Take a walk by yourself. Read a book. Write to yourself in a journal or diary. Take a drive by yourself. Take a nap.

You can also talk to yourself. I have little internal self-talks all the time, particularly when I'm tired, stressed, or feeling challenged by a situation or individual. I walk into the bathroom, look in the mirror, see my father staring back at me, and talk to myself internally using his confident voice. "You can do it, Arthur," I can hear him say as clearly as if he were in the room with me. "I believe in you. You always rise to the occasion."

Whose voice do you hear when you are alone? Is it a positive, optimistic, supportive voice, or a censuring, scolding, humiliating voice? When we spend time alone, we learn how to listen to ourselves. Listening to ourselves, we begin to know ourselves. Knowing ourselves, we understand how to put up with ourselves. Putting up with ourselves, we learn to accept ourselves for who we are, and we learn to set realistic goals about who we can become. We give up certain dreams and find new dreams to believe in. We face old ghosts. We find out how the past can intrude on the present.

We find, in the Jesuit priest Wilkie Au's words, "self-love," explaining:

> Self-love establishes the necessary condition that makes going beyond one's self (self-transcendence) possible. The grace that enables us to accept ourselves simultaneously stirs up within us an urge to break down the walls that separate us from others.

Take Your Time

Acceptance does not come easy, and it progresses in stages. Accepting yourself is only the first step. Accepting others is the second, equally complicated step. Not only do you have to accept others with all their flaws and complications, you also have to accept their opinions of the world and (even more difficult) their opinions of you.

Can you live with other people's criticisms? What if their religious or political beliefs are different from yours—can you accept their position as valid from their point of view? What if your dreams for your children's future are not their dreams—can you accept the fact that your children need to go their own way? Can you accept intolerance and prejudice in your friends?

What can you accept, and what do you find unacceptable? What can you change? What do you refuse to change? Why?

> *One can only understand the power of the fear to be different, the fear to be only a few steps away from the herd, if one understands the depths of the need not to be separated.*
>
> —ERICH FROMM

Chapter 11

Tolerance

In a real sense all life is interrelated. All [people] are caught in an inescapable network of mutuality, tied in a single garment of destiny.

—MARTIN LUTHER KING, JR.

Learning how to "put up" with each other is one of the most challenging tasks we face in everyday life. We *need* each other, that much is clear—dozens of psychological studies offer dramatic proof that our physical and emotional health depends on loving, supportive relationships. Psychologists, neurologists, immunologists, and philosophers seem to agree that there is a biological foundation for our need to create close, loving relationships. I am convinced that this basic drive to connect with each other is powered by empathy.

Empathy allows us to communicate with each other, understand each other, and, most important of all for our mental and physical health, learn how to live with each other. We tolerate each other because we can empathize with each other—empathy is the biological basis for tolerance. If we were all alike, feeling the same emotions, thinking precisely the same thoughts, we wouldn't need empathy—we would automatically know exactly what everyone else was thinking and feeling because their thoughts and emotions would be perfect replicas of our own. But we don't think and feel the same; in fact, most of us respond in such wildly diverse ways that it is a wonder we get along at all.

The reason we get along is empathy, which the University of Connecticut psychologists Ross Buck and Benson Ginsburg define as "a primordial capacity for communication that inheres in the genes." Empathy is our common language. Take the words away, and we would still be able to communicate with each other through the expression in our eyes, the shifting muscles in our faces, the touch of our hands, and the capacity for insight that allows us to look into each other's heart and soul and see the truth. With empathy the differences between us fall away, and we see what we have in common—hearts that yearn for connection, souls that long for understanding. Empathy leads to tolerance, which can be defined as the willingness to put up with differences; as empathy expands our consciousness throughout our lives, it works to create an active appreciation and abiding respect for the great diversity of life on this planet.

In my first real job as a psychologist I had an unforgettable encounter with a prison inmate convicted of murder. During the day I taught psychology at the University of Southern Connecticut in New Haven, and two evenings each week my roommate and I counseled inmates at a local prison. On our first night at the prison, the warden gave us a brief rundown on the prisoner he believed was most in need of help.

"This man is a psychopath according to the psychiatrist's evaluation," the warden said, handing me the prisoner's file. "Killed his brother-in-law in cold blood. He's a big man, stands about six feet, four inches, weighs two hundred and fifty pounds or so, works out every day in the weight room." If the warden was trying to scare us, he was doing a heck of a job.

I turned to my roommate, who was seven inches taller than I and fifty pounds heavier. "Hey, Joe," I said, handing him the file, "this one's got your name written all over it."

"Not a chance." He laughed, holding his hands up and backing away from me. "Remember, Arthur, this was your idea. I'm sitting on the sidelines for this one."

The warden led me to a huge, concrete-walled room, wished me good luck, and left me alone with the prisoner, who was sitting at a table, his hands folded on top of an old, well-used Bible. Handsome and powerfully built, he watched me pull out a chair and sit down.

"Did they tell you I was a psychopath?" he said. His voice was deep but surprisingly gentle.

"Yes," I said, knowing he wanted the truth.

"Well, then," he said, his eyes locked on mine, "I guess you might as well leave if your mind is made up."

"My mind is not made up," I said. "I'm here to listen to you."

And so, after several long silences and more pointed questions, he decided to tell me his story. He was married ("to the only woman I will ever love," he told me), and they had a two-year-old son. Six days a week, ten hours a day, he worked at the local shoe factory; every night he got home after dark. One winter night, around 9:00, he returned to his apartment to find his brother-in-law, drunk and in a rage, slapping his wife around while his son cowered in a corner. His wife was bleeding from a cut on her cheek.

"I tried to reason with him," the prisoner told me, "but he picked up his whiskey bottle, broke it over a table, and came charging at me. He was not a big man, but I had to watch out for that broken bottle. I pushed him, and he came back at me. I hit him, and he came back again. Then I landed a punch on his jaw, he fell back, cracked his head against the table, and died right there in my living room, in front of my wife and my son.

"The jury took less than an hour to convict me of manslaughter." He leaned across the table. "Have you ever heard of Claudine Longet?"

I nodded my head. An actress and the wife of the popular singer Andy Williams, Longet murdered her lover, an Olympic skier, by shooting him in the back.

"I'm just asking you to think about that—here's a rich, white woman who follows a man into his apartment, has a lovers' spat, pulls out a gun, shoots him in the back, and never spends a day in prison. For defending my wife and my child, I get six years, and they label me a psychopath.

"Take a look around this prison," he said. "There are no white people here. Everyone here is black except for one drug dealer, who is Mexican." He put his head in his hands and was quiet for a few moments; then he picked up the worn leather Bible and hugged it to his massive chest. "I read this every day," he said. "I try to make peace with myself, but I have a conscience that will never rest. I killed a man. I will suffer forever."

When I left the prison that night, I was a changed man. I had always prided myself on being tolerant. As a second-generation Italian with an unpronounceable last name, I had experienced enough intolerance in my life to know the value of open-mindedness and respect for differences. But that night, sitting face to face with a man convicted of killing and labeled by my own profession as a psychopath, I understood the power of prejudice to close off the mind and the heart. I felt his loneliness and his fear, and I heard the pain in his voice when he told me to leave if my mind was made up. I understood how intolerance holds the spirit captive, destroying hope and diminishing faith. And I saw how one man's belief in himself and his God brought him a measure of peace, even though, as he said, his conscience would never let him rest.

I went back to my apartment that night and searched through my boxes of books for the Bible my parents had given me for my confirmation. I knew the passage I was looking for was in the New Testament, but it took me a while to find it. Reading the words that I felt sure the prisoner had read many times over the years gave me a sense of peace and hope.

> Judge not, that you be not judged. For with the judgment you pronounce you will be judged, and the measure you give will be the measure you get. Why do you see the speck that is in your brother's eye, but do not notice the log that is in your own eye? Or how can you say to your brother, "Let me take the speck out of your eye," when there is the log in your own eye? You hypocrite, first take the log out of your own eye, and then you will see clearly to take the speck out of your brother's eye. (Matthew 7:1–5)

I talked to this prisoner many times before he was released several years later, after spending nearly twelve years in prison. Later I heard that he had been reunited with his wife and son, and became an active, respected member of his community and his church.

EMPATHY'S DEFINITION OF TOLERANCE

Empathy defines tolerance as the ever-expanding capacity to understand human nature in depth. Tolerance goes deep. Looking beyond the superficial outer layers—the color of people's skin, the neighborhood they live in, the degrees they hold, the careers they pursue, the church they attend—to the inner heart and soul, we discover our common ground. We are all human beings. Serb or Albanian, Palestinian or Jew, black, white, yellow, brown, or red, we are all cut from the same cloth.

Empathy, which is the act and the process of enlarging our perspective by looking at the world through other people's eyes, leads to tolerance as surely as a narrow mind leads to hatred and violence. As our vision expands we begin to see people in a new light. Understanding the pain of those who are the victims of prejudice and intolerance, we feel moved to speak out against it. Empathy is the antidote to the poison of prejudice.

During World War II my father was a sergeant in the OSS (Office of

Strategic Services), the precursor to the CIA; he made thirteen parachute jumps behind enemy lines. Although he rarely talked about his war experiences, he repeated one story several times. It was 1944, and my father's unit was in Italy, assisting the partisan forces in their efforts to blow up bridges used by the Germans to transport their supplies. Every night my father would sit and talk with the company cook, a German defector, who would tearfully describe his homesickness and his longing for his young wife and newborn child, who were still in Germany. The German cook and the Italian American sergeant became fast friends.

One moonless night fourteen men from my father's unit set off with explosives to blow up a strategically located bridge. When they got to the bridge the Germans were waiting for them. All fourteen Americans were captured, and the next day they were paraded barefoot through a nearby town while the Germans shouted to the Italian villagers: "The Americans are losing the war! Look at the soldiers' feet—they have no shoes!" The Germans marched the prisoners outside the village, where they dug up a tree and buried the Americans alive.

The next day a group of Italian partisans arrived at the camp and questioned the cook, who eventually broke down and admitted that he was a spy. Looking at my father, the cook begged for mercy. He brought out the pictures of his wife and child, asking for mercy on their behalf. My father turned his back on his friend and walked away; moments later he heard the gunshot.

That sound and the memory of a young man begging for his life haunted my father for the rest of his life. Whenever he told this story he would lean closer to David and me, making sure we were listening, and in a steady, firm voice ask us never to forget that while evil exists in this world (and the Nazis in his mind were the personification of evil) not all Germans were Hitler-loving Nazis, just as not all Italians were Mussolini-loving Fascists. The capacity for good and evil, my father taught us, exists in all people. "Knowing that you are capable of evil," my father would say, "you must try at all times to throw your weight onto the side of good."

HOW EMPATHY LEADS TO TOLERANCE

Empathy leads us to tolerance, for only with empathy can we build bridges to others who seem so unlike us. Only with empathy can we reach out to people we initially want to push away because we imagine that in their brutality or their simplicity or their stupidity they are not like us. Empathy reminds us that the evil in others is a potential that we also carry within our own hearts. The capacity to hate, to exact revenge, to refuse forgiveness, even to take a life is in you as it is in me as it is in all human beings. That humbling realization and acceptance of our own shadow inevitably and unfailingly leads us to tolerance.

Empathy allows us to see the connections between us, making strangers less strange, foreigners less foreign. When we adopt other people's perspectives, we do more than step into their shoes—we use their eyes, we borrow their skin, we feel their hearts beating within us, we lose ourselves and enter into their world, *as if we were them.* I emphasize those words once again because they are so critically important and so often misunderstood. With empathy, we do not step into others' experience to see it with *our* eyes—empathy demands that we see it with *their* eyes. Through that experience we are fundamentally changed, for we see with a sudden, startling clarity that we *are* the other. All the good and the bad that we see in them we can also recognize in ourselves. The hurt, the shame, the fear of humiliation, the desire for revenge—these are as much parts of our own souls as the quest for honesty, the humble spirit, the forgiving heart.

Tolerance begins with the willingness to listen. Listening with empathy means that you put yourself aside and enter the other person's experience. You are, literally, all ears. Tolerance also involves the *ability* to listen, which is not the same as the *willingness* to listen. Many people are willing listeners, but they interrupt, take off on tangents, offer advice, and pronounce judgments—in other words, they cut off empathy through their untutored listening skills. Listening is an art that takes time, discipline, and practice.

A third step in the process of developing tolerance is to look for extenuating circumstances, which means, simply, that we seek a broader understanding of other people's behaviors. When we can see the whole picture, rather than focusing in on one piece of it, we develop a more expansive range of emotional responses. Tolerance can be viewed as a way of understanding the "extenuating circumstances" of other people's lives.

In an experiment conducted by Dolf Zillmann, a psychologist at the University of Alabama, volunteers who ride an exercise bike are treated rudely by an assistant (in reality a member of the experimental team). Later, when the volunteers are given a chance to get back at the surly assistant by writing an evaluation of his performance, they willingly take their revenge.

In another version of the experiment, a young woman enters the room and informs the rude assistant that he has a phone call. When he leaves he is discourteous to her, too, but she takes it in stride; she then explains to the volunteers that the assistant is under tremendous pressure because of his upcoming oral examinations for his graduate degree. In this version of the experiment, the volunteers decide not to censure him in their evaluations and instead express empathy for his situation. Understanding the whole picture, the students were able to tolerate the assistant's inconsiderate behavior.

A fourth essential step for developing tolerance is to remain objective. To be tolerant, we must learn how to see the difference between our image of a person, which is all mixed up with our desires and fears, and that individual's true reality. Anything that makes us focus on another person as an object will undermine our capacity for empathy. In an article titled "Automatic and Controlled Empathy," the psychologists Sara Hodges and Daniel Wegner explain how empathy is weakened by our biases:

> The tendency to adopt another person's perspective is obstructed by anything that makes us focus on that person as an object. When we think about a person's characteristics or group memberships, we are less likely to be able to appreciate the contribution of the person's situation and goals to the person's behavior. This means that when we are automatically drawn to think about a person's personality traits or other characteristics, be it spontaneously or as the result of information that leads to rapid inferences about such traits or category memberships, our ability to empathize will be hindered. The automatic inferences we reach about others' personalities may often be incorrect without adjustment to take their situations into account, and this will automatically damage our empathic accuracy as a result.

The psychoanalyst Erich Fromm, author of *The Art of Loving*, described the need for objectivity in less complicated terms:

> If I want to learn the art of loving, I must strive for objectivity in every situation, and become sensitive to the situations where I am not objective. I must try to see the difference between *my* picture of a person and his [*sic*] behavior, as it is narcissistically distorted, and the person's reality as it exists regardless of my interests, needs, and fears. To have acquired the capacity

for objectivity and reason is half the road to achieving the art of loving, but it must be acquired with regard to everybody with whom one comes in contact. If someone would want to reserve his objectivity for the loved person, and think he can dispense with it in his relationship to the rest of the world, he will soon discover that he fails both here and there.

I once heard a beautiful story that brought all these ideas of love, tolerance, and hope together. It concerns an old rabbi and his students.

"How do we know when night has ended?" an old rabbi asked his students.
"Is it when you look at a faraway tree and see that it is an apple tree and not a pear tree?" asked one student.
"No," answered the rabbi.
"Is it when the stars fade away as the sky grows lighter?" asked another.
"No," said the rabbi.
"Perhaps it is when the light grows greater than the darkness?" asked a third.
"No," the rabbi responded.
"When does the night end, then?" the students asked in unison.
"When you look at the face of any man or woman and see that they are each and all your brothers and sisters—that is when the night ends," said the rabbi. "If you cannot see this, darkness reigns throughout the world."

PRACTICING TOLERANCE

Be Patient

When people ask me what being a psychologist has taught me, I always answer, "Patience"—and patience, I believe, is synonymous with tolerance. As we listen with empathy, letting the story unfold without rushing through or skipping past its more complicated passages, we discover tolerance through patience. As a general rule, patient people are tolerant people, while impatient people seem to have a more difficult time with tolerance.

I recently ran into a Stop & Shop store with twenty minutes to spare before my next appointment and a list of seven or eight items to purchase. In five minutes I had collected everything on my list, but when I got to the checkout stand there were six people in line ahead of me. Thinking about everything I had to do that day and the people I would disappoint if I were late, I began to feel impatient, and my tolerance level dropped like a rock. Why was the checkout person so slow? Why didn't I choose the other line?

At that point I saw an old friend, a retired teacher who has debilitating rheumatoid arthritis, standing in the line ahead of me. I called her name, and she moved back to stand next to me. I asked how she was feeling. "My new medications are causing some side effects," she said, "but I'm not letting it keep me from my garden!" We talked about her dahlias and my plans for the summer in Maine, and before I knew it we were through the line and I was headed back to work. Entering another person's world, I was able to find patience, which led to increased tolerance.

Give yourself extra time. If you are meeting a friend for lunch and it's a fifteen-minute drive, give yourself an extra five or ten minutes to get there. (Take a book or magazine along in case you arrive early.) If you have a long commute to work and traffic jams are common, keep your car stocked with tapes and CDs. (Try listening to a book on tape.) If you get stuck in the slowest line at the grocery store, pick up a magazine and leaf through it or strike up a conversation with the person in front of you.

Take off your watch. Try this on Saturdays and Sundays or when you go on vacation.

Banish the words "hurry up" from your vocabulary. Americans are becoming known as the "hurry up" people. I recently watched a young boy and his mother at a concession stand. He was trying to decide whether to order a blue or green Gatorade. No one was in line behind them, but his mother kept pushing gently at his shoulder and telling him to hurry up. He got flustered; near tears, he finally ordered a Pepsi instead.

Take the other person's perspective. You're in a long line and feel impatient. Look around and ask yourself how it would feel to be the woman in the next line trying to calm her screaming child or the elderly woman leaning on her cane. What would it be like to be the checkout person who has to face a long line of impatient, intolerant customers?

Exhale. Our hearts speed up when we inhale and slow down when we exhale. Practice exhaling when you're feeling stressed and give your heart (literally) a breather.

Smile. Researchers have discovered that putting your facial muscles into a smiling position automatically initiates physiological changes that make you feel better; other people see you smiling and they feel better, too. Smiles can do wonders for impatience and intolerance.

Speak Up

Intolerance spreads through silence as quickly and easily as it does through hateful words or actions. If you witness an act of prejudice or intolerance, speak up. In this story told by Anthony de Mello, you will discover a gentle way to point out a friend's intolerance.

> A woman complained to a visiting friend that her neighbor was a poor housekeeper. "You should see how dirty her children are—and her house. It is almost a disgrace to be living in the same neighborhood as her. Take a look at those clothes she has hung out on the line. See the black streaks on the sheets and towels!"
>
> The friend walked up to the window and said, "I think the clothes are quite clean, my dear. The streaks are on your window."

Whenever I hear gossip—one colleague unfairly criticizing another, a neighbor spreading rumors about a new family that moved in down the street, a teenager whispering behind a friend's back—I think about how we go adrift in the attempt to elevate ourselves. Intolerant actions always backfire, for they reinforce our own fears that we are not good enough and can only raise ourselves up by putting others down. Speaking up against intolerance helps those who are feeling uncharitable to reconsider the reasons for their prejudice as well as easing the burden on those who are being denigrated.

Avoid Criticism and Its Gentler (but Not Less Harmful) Cousin, Teasing

We've all heard the old adage that sticks and stones will break your bones, but words will never hurt you—but that has certainly not been my experience. Words, labels, derogatory names, gossip, and rumors go very deep and sting for a long, long time. I've heard many stories from patients, friends, and family members about childhood taunts that created lasting scars.

Be careful with your words, and teach your children why it is important to speak gently and kindly to others. What should you do when you are teased or taunted? Remembering this truism (which we have repeated throughout this book) may help: Critical people are insecure people. When my daughter Erica was in fifth grade, she came home with a story. "Johnny pulled my ponytail today and told me I was skinny and a weakling," she said.

"What did you say to him?" I asked.

"I turned to him and said, 'Johnny, why are you so insecure?' "

"And what did he do?"

"He stopped bothering me."

Beware of Anger and Hostility

Intolerance and anger are intimately connected. "When we are intolerant, we perceive others as misbehaving," writes Redford Williams, a psychiatrist at Duke University who has conducted groundbreaking research into the psychological and physiological effects of anger. "And most of the time when this happens, we become angry."

Angry, hostile people tend to be unhappy. According to Williams and other researchers, angry people have difficulty maintaining intimate relationships, their sex lives are relatively unsatisfying, they experience greater stress at work (and less job satisfaction), and they are more likely to be isolated and lonely.

Anger is devastating to the body as well as the mind and spirit. Anger slows down the blood flow to the heart, increases blood pressure, contributes to higher cholesterol levels, impairs the immune system, and increases risk of death from a variety of causes. In a long-term study conducted by the psychologists Redford Williams, John Barefoot, and Grant Dahlstrom, medical students took a test to gauge their levels of anger and hostility. Decades later in a follow-up study, the researchers found that the physicians who had scored highest were *seven times* as likely to have died by the age of fifty as were physicians with the lowest hostility scores.

Williams and his colleagues also followed a group of thirteen hundred people who had at least one severely blocked coronary artery. After five years those men and women who were unmarried and had no close confidant were three times more likely to have died than people who were married and/or had a close confidant. In his book *Anger Kills*, Williams offers the following "key points":

1. Hostile people—those with high levels of cynicism, anger, and aggression—are at higher risk of developing life-threatening illness than are their less hostile counterparts.

2. By driving others away, or by not perceiving the support they could be deriving from their social contacts, hostile people may be depriving themselves of the health-enhancing, stress-buffering benefits of social support.

Beware of Too Much Tolerance

Tolerance, like everything inspired by empathy, has its limits. Sometimes in the name of tolerance we put up with actions and behaviors that are hurtful, even harmful to ourselves and others. Women put up with abusive husbands, friends let friends get away with racist remarks, parents patiently endure the behavior of their aggressive, hostile children, spouses tolerate each other's affairs: there are countless instances where in the name of love, loyalty, or courtesy we suffer through various indignities and indiscretions.

Empathy keeps a careful eye on excessive tolerance, knowing that manipulative people can easily take advantage of those who find it difficult to set limits. Always ask yourself: Am I being truly tolerant (in the sense of being open-minded), or am I just trying to keep the peace? Am I so dependent on my partner that I ignore his or her contemptuous behavior, hoping to salvage a difficult relationship?

Tolerance requires discipline and respects boundaries. When we put up with cruelty in the name of tolerance, we threaten to destroy the experience we are trying to protect. Unbounded tolerance can diminish the power of empathy.

> *It is a terrible, an inexorable law that one cannot deny the humanity of another without diminishing one's own: in the face of one's victim, one sees oneself.*
>
> —JAMES BALDWIN

Chapter 12

Gratitude

There is only one real deprivation . . . and that is not to be able to give one's gifts to those one loves most.

—MAY SARTON

A friend recently told me this story about gratitude:

A blind man was begging in a city park. Someone approached and asked him whether people were giving generously. The blind man shook a nearly empty tin.

His visitor said to him, "Let me write something on your card." The blind man agreed. That evening, the visitor returned. "Well, how were things today?"

The blind man showed him a tin full of money. "What on earth did you write on that card?"

"Oh," said the other, "I merely wrote, 'Today is a spring day, and I am blind.'"

What would it be like to be blind on a glorious spring day? That is an empathy-inspired question, as are these questions:

What would it be like to be old and frail, with no one to care for you?

What would it be like to lose a parent, a spouse, a child?

What would it be like to be overweight in a society that worships skin and bones?

What would it be like to be homosexual in a predominantly heterosexual world?

Empathy slows us down so that we can ask such questions and consider their answers. Putting the brakes on our headlong rush through life, guiding us to take a moment and consider how we are related to others, empathy asks us to respond in ways that strengthen those connections. Gratitude is the response that empathy seeks.

When we experience gratitude—and gratitude is primarily an experience, not a feeling—we *see* our innate giftedness. We recognize the gifts that we have been given, gifts bestowed on us without our having to ask for them. What are these gifts? The fragrance of a rose, the touch of a child's hand, the taste of a ripe peach, the V-shaped flight of geese in autumn, the sound of thunder, the crack of lightning, the crash of waves against a rocky shore.

What value can we put on these realities? My father used to tell me that he was a multimillionaire. I would smile (I'd heard these words many times before) and ask him to explain. "Because," my father would say, "if anyone offered me ten million dollars or ten times or a hundred times that much for you or David, I would not consider it. You are beyond value, beyond price, and I am the richest man alive."

Empathy is the spring from which gratitude flows. Without empathy I do not believe we would be able to feel gratitude, at least not in its most meaningful sense of being thankful for all the gifts we have and most especially for those that were given to us without our having to ask for them. Empathy broadens our perspective so that we can see ourselves in the big picture, and from that vantage point we see what we have that is valuable beyond measure. We are part of a universe, a planet, a nation, a community, a neighborhood, a family . . . what price can we place on these "goods"?

Empathy rains its gifts of understanding on all of us; the reservoir fills and spills over, irrigating both near and distant fields. We give because we have no choice—it is part of our nature, as human beings. Grateful to give, grateful to receive—the gratitude that flows from empathy never runs dry.

When I was nine years old, I asked for a Lionel train for Christmas. I wanted that train so much that I couldn't think of anything else. I dreamed about it day and night, imagining what it would look like speeding along its miniature track. Nobody else in my neighborhood had a Lionel train; for all I knew, nobody else in the world had a Lionel. I would be the first to own one, and that, I believed, would make me special.

On Christmas morning I woke up when it was still dark and tiptoed past my sleeping brother. The stairs creaked, so I stayed on the edges, hoping to keep the magic moment to myself. A light was on in the kitchen, and I peeked in to see my father sitting at the table, drinking coffee and smoking a cigarette. He looked up at me, something shifted in my heart, and I knew there would be no train under the tree.

Without a word I ran into the living room and stood before the Christmas tree, blinking back tears, believing in miracles still, hoping the train would just suddenly appear before me. Maybe I missed it, I thought, picking up boxes and shaking them. Maybe it's in a closet or maybe it's outside on the porch.

"Arthur." My father's voice was gentle as he kneeled down next to me. "We could not afford the train. I'm sorry, because I know how much it meant to you."

He put his hand around my wrist and squeezed, a gesture he used only when he was discussing issues of the utmost importance. "You may not understand what I am about to say now, but someday you will," he said. "On this Christmas morning, with just you and me in this room, I would like to give you a gift far greater than anything money could buy. I want you to know that I will always love you. No matter what happens in your life, I will always be with you, believing in you, supporting you, cheering for you. No father could ever love a son more than I love you, and that love will never rust or need repairs—it will always be yours, now and for the rest of your life."

I must have given him a look of doubt and, perhaps, confusion—How can love make up for a Lionel?—for he squeezed my wrist tighter and leaned toward me. I breathed in the familiar, bittersweet odor of Chesterfields and Maxwell House coffee mixed with plenty of sugar and cream. "Believe me, Arthur," my father said, "this will come to mean more than any other gift I could give you. I promise you that."

EMPATHY'S DEFINITION OF GRATITUDE

Gratitude, in empathy's dictionary, is not just a feeling but a way of experiencing and interacting with the world. *Feeling* grateful is fine, but empathy asks that we do something about that sensation. Keeping gratitude to ourselves misses the whole point of the experience, for gratitude, in empathy's book, is a response that links one person to another.

I will never forget an encounter I had very early in my career with Ralph, a patient diagnosed with paranoid schizophrenia. He sat on the edge of the chair, hands tightly gripping the armrests, and said, teeth bared, "I could kill you if I wanted to."

"I know you could kill me, and I thank you for restraining yourself." He looked at me, momentarily confused, his forehead creased in a frown. "And my mother thanks you, too," I added.

The frown lines smoothed out, and he gave me a huge smile. "You're welcome," he said, folding his hands in his lap and leaning back in his chair. Twenty years later I sometimes run into Ralph in the hospital where I work. Not very long ago I saw him in the hospital van in the parking lot. He was pounding on the window trying to get my attention; I was afraid he was going to break the window. "Hi, Ralph," I called out, waving at him. "Hi, Dr. C," he shouted back with a big smile. Whenever he grins at me, I imagine that he is remembering the gift he gave my mother.

I discover gratitude every day in my work with men and women who are suffering yet put one foot in front of the other in a courageous attempt to work out their problems. I'm an eternal optimist—I believe that for those who are willing to stay with the process and do the hard work, life will improve. When I see how people respond when they feel understood, how they relax, ease into themselves, and let go of their struggle to hide their loneliness and fear, I am filled with gratitude for the power of empathy.

When my patients realize that I am grateful for the opportunity to work with them—because what happens in those interactions changes my life as surely as it does theirs—a space is created for empathy and intimacy to work their everyday miracles. What do I mean by "everyday miracles"? A twenty-three-year-old woman who asked for my help with "relationship problems" burst into tears in our second session. "I'm sorry," she apologized, "I don't know what's wrong with me, I just feel so confused. It seems like for every step forward, I take two steps backward. I think I am failing at this."

"Failing at what, Susan?" I asked.

"Life. Relationships. Love. You know, the whole thing," she said. "I'm just so afraid I will never get anywhere, I'll never have a better career, I'll never make better choices in men, I'll never feel better about myself." She cried for a moment and then looked up at me. "Would you mind telling me what you think of me?"

This is always a crucial moment in therapy, for while people want to be comforted with kind words, they are also asking for a realistic assessment. "I can only tell you what I have come to know about you so far," I said. "I won't tell you anything that isn't true just to make you feel better, because I know that would only disappoint you in the end."

She nodded her head, encouraging me to continue.

"I see an intelligent woman who is clearly very capable and talented in understanding others," I said. "I think you have come to see your role in relationships as a caretaker—specifically a caretaker of hard-to-reach men. I think you believe that this is your only salvation. But I don't believe that."

"You don't?"

"I think you have many sources of salvation," I said.

At the end of the session, she took my hand between both of hers and thanked me. I asked her why, genuinely wanting to know what she was feeling grateful for at that moment.

"You got me with that intelligent woman remark," she said. "I think I can coast on that for a while."

In therapy I often use the term *borrowed empathy*. When patients tell me they can't feel any empathy for themselves or others, I try as best I can to lend them my understanding, care, and concern, hoping they will understand my authentic desire to help. In the process of lending and borrowing empathy, we realize that we are not alone; acknowledging that others care about what happens to us, we automatically experience gratitude.

HOW EMPATHY LEADS TO GRATITUDE

Empathy weaves a web of connections that support and sustain us, and gratitude is our response to the realization that we are dependent on each other—that we need each other if we are going to survive. Gratitude always, inevitably, strengthens empathy. And in the true spirit of giving, empathy returns the gift, leading us to see the giftedness of our lives and offer thanks.

Of all the psychological theorists I have studied and admired, the one I hold in highest esteem is Heinz Kohut, the founder of self psychology and the first psychoanalyst to honor empathy with focused attention. In his last public address, in October 1981, Kohut spoke on empathy; he died just a few days later. At the very end of his talk, he told a story about a woman he was treating who was deeply depressed and suicidal.

This is a fascinating case because Kohut was at the end of his rope. Trained as a classical psychoanalyst whose role is to be objective and emotionally removed, Kohut sensed that his patient was dying before his eyes. All his training, all his skills, all his careful observations couldn't help her. Here's how he told the story:

> About fifteen years ago I was engaged in a long, long analysis with a woman who was extremely vulnerable. . . . She said she felt like lying in a coffin, and that now the top of the coffin would be closed with a sharp click. . . . She was deeply depressed, and at times I thought I would lose her—that she would finally find a way out of the suffering and kill herself. But I didn't. At one time at the very worst moment of her analysis, during the first year or perhaps year and a half, she was so badly off I suddenly had the feeling [and said]: "How would you feel if I let you hold my fingers, for a little while now while you are talking? Maybe that would help you." Doubtful maneuver. I am not recommending it, but I was desperate. I was deeply worried. So . . . I gave her my two fingers. She took ahold of them, and I immediately made a genetic interpretation to myself. It was the toothless gums of a very young child clamping down on an empty nipple. That was the way it felt. I didn't say anything. I don't know whether it was right. . . . But [after this one occasion] that was never necessary anymore. I wouldn't say that it turned the tide, but it overcame a very, very difficult impasse at a given dangerous moment, and gaining time that way we went on for many, many more years with a reasonably substantial success.

Breaking the rules of his training, hoping to find a way to bring a lost soul back to the world of the living, the doctor offered his patient two fingers—that's all, but it was enough. Perhaps she understood the risk he was taking. Perhaps she felt in his touch his very deep, authentic concern for her. Or perhaps she simply needed a lifeline, and he gave it to her at precisely the right moment.

How did the patient express her gratitude? In perhaps the most meaningful way possible—she held on, for life.

PRACTICING GRATITUDE

Slow Down

We need to slow down long enough to think about what we have to be grateful for. Rushing through life, we always seem to want more—more time, more money, more respect, more love. I believe that one of the most important functions of therapy is to give people time to slow down and focus on what they have achieved so far in life. When patients tell me that they feel stuck, as if they haven't made any progress at all, I ask them to remember where they were at this time last year. Has anything changed in that year? Do they have new friends? Are their relationships improved? Have they accumulated any wisdom?

When we fail to see our lives as a process—a sequence of events, a work in progress—we tend to feel ungrateful. Gratitude arises not when we measure our lives against a standard of perfection (a predictable way, it turns out, to discover ingratitude) but when we take the time to appreciate our slow but steady gains.

Ask: What Do I Need?

"You can never get enough of what you don't really want," Eric Hoffer once said. Keep an ongoing list of your wants and your needs. What do you want the most? Do you want it because you need it? If you don't need it, why do you want it?

How do your wants and needs change over time?

What do you want that you can never get enough of? Why don't you get filled up? What hole is draining?

Is it possible that what you need is emptiness rather than fullness?

Say Thank You as Often as You Can

Saying thank you will help you to develop an attitude of gratitude, a way of looking at the world with thanks for what you have rather than wishing for what you don't have. See how many times you can say thank you in one day.

Let People Know You Appreciate Them

Instead of saying "I love you" to your spouse, friends, parents, or children, say "I appreciate you." The inevitable answer will be a quizzical "Why?" which gives you the perfect opportunity to think and talk about why you are grateful for their company, help, insight, or support.

Saying "I appreciate you" is sometimes more meaningful than saying "I love you." Speak of your love through your gratitude.

Use Gratitude to Organize Your Life

Joseph Campbell, author of *The Power of Myth*, told a wonderful story about a conversation he overheard at a restaurant.

> At the next table there was a father, a mother, and a scrawny boy about twelve years old. The father said to the boy, "Drink your tomato juice."
> And the boy said, "I don't want to."
> Then the father, with a louder voice, said, "Drink your tomato juice."
> And the mother said, "Don't make him do what he doesn't want to do."
> The father looked at her and said, "He can't go through life doing what he wants to do. If he does only what he wants to do, he'll be dead. Look at me. I've never done a thing I wanted to in all my life."

This is a cautionary tale for all of us. Rather than viewing life as drudgery, a series of thankless chores, how can you organize your days around activities that you feel grateful to perform? What kind of work do you most enjoy? Which tasks do you find the most boring or mind-boggling? What talents do you have that come naturally to you?

Organize your life around activities you are grateful to perform, and your gratitude will grow exponentially.

Learn to Delay Gratification

As important as it is to spend our time engaged in activities we enjoy, it is equally important to learn how to control our impulses and delay gratification. In a fascinating study conducted in the 1960s at Stanford University, researchers offered four-year-olds a "marshmallow challenge." A child was left in the room with a marshmallow while the researcher went on an errand; before leaving the researcher explained that if the child could wait until he returned from an errand, the reward would be an extra marshmallow. Approximately two-thirds of the children were able to wait for fifteen or twenty minutes in order to earn the two-marshmallow reward; the remaining third couldn't resist the impulse and immediately grabbed for the marshmallow.

Twelve to fourteen years later the researchers checked up on the children and discovered some amazing facts. The children who were able to resist temptation grew up into young adults who were more assertive, organized, confident, dependable, and better able to handle stress and frustration than the grabbers, who tended to be more prone to jealousy, envy, argumentative behavior, stubbornness, and resentment about not "getting enough." Even more astonishing, the students who were able to delay gratification were far superior academically and had significantly higher SAT scores.

Learning how to delay gratification (sometimes called impulse control) undoubtedly helps us embrace challenges and cope with the inevitable frustrations of life. When patients tell me they are developing a crush on someone and thinking about having an affair, I always say, "Tell me how you feel six months from now, after we have a chance to talk about your longings, find out what they really mean, and discover how an affair would satisfy them." Those patients who are willing to wait without acting on their impulses often discover that the attraction fades as they work on their problems and learn to appreciate what they have.

Experiencing a sense of gratitude for what we have helps us avoid feeling resentful about the things we lack. Gratitude, as they say, is its own reward.

Nobody can conceive or imagine all the wonders there are unseen and unseeable in the world.

—Francis P. Church

Chapter 13

Faith

As you go the way of life, you will see a great chasm.
Jump.
It is not as wide as you think.

—JOSEPH CAMPBELL,
quoting a Native American initiation rite

Several years ago I was sitting on my uncle Phil's front steps while he smoked a cigarette and drank several cups of strong black coffee. For some reason I can't remember, I was reminiscing about my senior prom.

"Oh yeah, I remember," my uncle said. "Your father specifically asked you not to drink that night because the year before the Melucci boy got drunk and died in a motorcycle accident, and the year before that a football player smashed his car into a tree."

Uncle Phil took a sip of coffee and then patted me on the knee. "You were a good boy that night at the prom," he said, "but others were not so good. Joannie Santori was drinking right out of the bottle. And Chris Adamo—he had so much of that spiked punch his friends had to carry him out to the car. I think everybody was drinking that night except for you."

I looked at him in amazement. "How do you know about Joannie and Chris?"

"We were there!" He laughed, taking a sip of coffee and looking at me over the rim of the cup, his eyes full of mischief. "Your father and I dressed up in our best suits and spent the entire night looking in the window, making sure you were true to your word."

I couldn't believe it. "You were looking in the window at my senior prom? Uncle Phil, are you telling me the truth?"

He nodded his head, clearly proud of his role as my self-appointed guardian angel. My uncle was the kind of man who made you feel that as long as he was nearby the world was a safe place to be. He used to say, "If you need me at two in the morning, Arthur, I'll be there in five minutes," and here he would look deep into my eyes, making sure I got the point. "Do you understand what I'm saying, Arthur? *Five minutes.*"

"What would you have done if you'd seen me drinking?" I asked him.

"Why do you think we wore the suits?" he said, breaking into a huge smile.

The thought of my father and his brother walking into my senior prom and hauling me away because I'd taken a sip of spiked punch was too much for me, even thirty years later. My uncle laughed at the expression on my face. "Arthur, Arthur," he said, "we loved you—what else could we do?"

On the surface this story seems to have more to say about doubt than faith. Didn't they trust me? was my immediate thought. I gave my father my word—why did he doubt me? Approaching the story from empathy's wider perspective, however, I could see the important role played by faith. My father and my uncle Phil had ultimate faith in relationships. They considered themselves my protectors, and they believed that as long as they were there to watch over me, I would be safe. They had faith in me, I don't doubt that fact, but they also had that little edge of doubt that gives faith its authenticity. They knew that faith sometimes needs a friendly push. Their faith was real, but it wasn't blind. As Uncle Phil would put it, "We weren't born yesterday."

EMPATHY'S DEFINITION OF FAITH

Faith inspired by empathy believes in the basic goodness at the heart of human beings. Faith gives confidence that if you work hard, you will see the results. Yet empathy's faith is also rooted in doubt. Let me explain the apparent paradox.

I have faith in the following observations:

- Human relationships are healing.
- Empathy is an innate capacity that can be nurtured through caring relationships.

- Empathy reduces stress, diminishes anxiety, increases self-awareness, reinforces optimism, resolves conflicts, and creates intimacy.

My faith in these observations (which I would call truths) comes from my experience—I have "earned" my faith through my interactions with many people over many, many years. I cannot, however, ask you to accept on faith that these observations are true. I can only encourage you, through my faith, to cultivate empathy in your own life and then observe how it affects your relationships. If you see that empathy works, you will also have earned your faith.

The faith that springs from empathy is realistic, and doubt is its firm foundation. From doubt—which involves wondering, imagining, asking questions, disputing the answers—you set your feet on the pathway of faith. To doubt is to raise a question—and how can you receive an answer if you haven't asked the question?

Doubt is the sign of a questing mind. Explain that to me, says the doubter. Help me understand. And don't just tell me—show me. Show, don't tell—that's a cardinal rule of all teaching. In therapy I encourage doubt. I hope to instill in my patients a questioning attitude that says, Show me. I'm not saying no, but I'm not going to take everything you say for gospel, either. Doubt grows from self-confidence, and self-confidence is an essential ingredient of faith. If you don't have faith in yourself, how will you develop faith in intangible realities like empathy, hope, gratitude, and forgiveness?

Doubt is inherently creative. It puzzles over things, muses on them, turns them over, shakes them up. Doubt is a sign that, in searching for your own way, you are unwilling to accept others' points of view just because they tell you something is so. Only when you doubt can you discover real faith—not the faith of dogma and doctrine ("Do this or else," "Take this pill and you'll feel better," "Listen to me and do exactly as I say") but the faith that comes from having your eyes and your ears wide open. You are willing to travel the way of doubt in order someday to reach the land of belief, knowing that only through the journey can you have faith that what you have found is real.

Faith is often discovered in darkness, when we feel lost and afraid, unsure of ourselves and our place in the world. We are most in need of faith when we seem to have lost any reason to believe. In *My Confessions* the nineteenth-century Russian writer Leo Tolstoy wrote about his struggle with depression, which threatened to extinguish meaning and purpose from his life.

> I felt that something had broken within me on which my life had always rested, that I had nothing left to hold on to. . . . I did not know what I wanted. I was afraid of life; I was driven to leave it; and in spite of that I still hoped something from it.

Two years of torment and unanswered questions followed Tolstoy's crisis of faith. Then, one day in early spring, taking a walk alone in the forest, he experienced a sudden resurgence of the will to live. He called it faith.

> Faith is the sense of life, that sense by virtue of which man [sic] does not destroy himself, but continues to live on. It is the force whereby we live. If Man did not believe that he must live for something, he would not live at all.

Where did Tolstoy's faith come from? On what was it founded? He claimed that his faith was not a new discovery. "And what was strange," he wrote, "was that this energy that came back was nothing new. It was my ancient juvenile force of faith, the belief that the sole purpose of my life was to be *better*." On that simple truth resurrected from his past, Tolstoy discovered his life's work—"to be *better*."

We need faith in times of crisis, but faith also serves us well in the normal activities of everyday life. When we make a mistake, we have faith that in the future we will try to avoid a similar error. When our children fight with each other, we have faith that they will still love each other the next day. When we argue with a friend, we have faith that the relationship will endure. When a loved one dies, we have faith that her love will stay with us for all the days of our lives. Looking ahead, we have faith that the empathy we offer our children will be passed on to their children and their children and their children, forever.

HOW EMPATHY LEADS TO FAITH

Empathy leads us through our doubts (not around them) to discover faith. Tolstoy's search for faith is instructive. First, he accepted that there might be certain truths or experiences that he had ignored or misunderstood. Then he asked questions and searched for answers. Feeling a craving for connection, a yearning for a relationship to something larger and more powerful than himself, he kept searching. He listened. He waited. He watched. And then one evening, while he was taking a walk in the woods, faith came to him unbidden.

Empathy—the yearning to understand combined with the need for connection—is a powerful catalyst for change. Empathy *can* change the world; at the very least it can change our immediate experience of the world and, by altering our experience, directly affect the way we understand and interact with each other. A few years ago I worked with Rebecca, a nineteen-year-old woman who was recovering from leukemia. She was referred to me by an exercise physiologist who invoked the "secondary gain theory" to explain Rebecca's ongoing refusal to go anywhere without her walker; according to this theory, people hold on to their illnesses and exaggerate their symptoms in order to gain attention. Admitting that he was frustrated with Rebecca's continued dependence on the walker, he told me that she could walk if she put her mind to it.

In our first session Rebecca said she was sick and tired of being pushed around by "those behaviorist types" who didn't understand the nature of her physical limitations and didn't believe her when she told them she wasn't ready to walk. "This has been a long and painful illness," she explained with tears in her eyes, "and my body is just not strong enough to walk without support."

She regarded me thoughtfully, obviously trying to figure me out. After a moment she asked if I was going to be like all the others and try to talk her into giving up the walker. I assured her that I would not force her to do anything that would make her uncomfortable and that it would always be her choice when and if she decided to walk on her own.

For the next few weeks we talked about her experiences as a leukemia patient, her fears of dying, the emotional trauma she endured when her high school friends stopped asking her to join them for various activities, and her continued dependence on her parents for emotional and financial support. I listened, and she talked. When she asked for my help, I encouraged her to reexamine certain fixed perceptions about her world and to try to be more understanding and forgiving of herself.

As we spent more time together she began to understand the nature of her fears and the reasons for her slow progress. Whenever she talked about being on her own again and walking without the walker, she was flooded with memories of her disease: the initial diagnosis, the painful treatments, the unpleasant interactions with doctors and nurses, and all the anxieties and fears associated with those memories. Using the walker, Rebecca felt strong and independent, for she didn't have to worry about falling or asking other people for help. Giving up the walker terrified her because it represented a return to a more vulnerable period of her life and brought back all the insecurities she experienced at that time.

At least once every session she would ask me when I was going to push her to walk. I always gave her the same answer: "It's your choice, Rebecca. You will know when the time is right. I have faith that you will walk when you feel ready, and when you do, I will be there to help."

One day, after we had been working together for six or seven weeks, Rebecca arrived with a bad cold and sore throat. "I know I should be at home in bed," she said, "but I just had to be here today. I realized this morning that the fear has become a bad habit—a really bad habit, because it's keeping me stuck and preventing me from moving forward. If I could only get over this anxiety, I think I would be okay. Do you understand? Do you think I'm crazy to be so paralyzed with fear?"

"I don't think you're crazy." I smiled. "I think you're scared, and I think that's normal."

She smiled and looked down at her hands, folded neatly in her lap. "So when do you think I might be ready to walk?"

I could tell by her smile and her question that she had already made up her mind. "I think you're ready right now," I said.

"Right now? Here?" Her tone was more excited than anxious.

"You can walk along the wall," I said, "and I'll be on your other side, right next to you. I promise you—I won't let you fall."

She took a deep breath and stood up, holding on to the wall for support. Taking a few quick steps, she almost stumbled. She leaned against the wall, a panicked look on her face. I helped steady her with words, calmly encouraging her to go slow and take one step at a time.

She nodded her head, and I could see that she was focusing hard on the task before her. She took a step, then another and another. After a few minutes she was walking back and forth in the office, her cheeks flushed with pride and excitement.

Breathless, she sat down in the chair. "We did it!" she said.

"*You* did it, Rebecca," I reminded her. "You found the physical and emotional strength you needed, but even more important, you had the wisdom to know when the time was right."

That day I was reminded of a favorite saying, which expresses for me the real meaning of the therapeutic relationship: "Don't walk in front of me, I may not follow; don't walk behind me, I may not lead; walk beside me, and just be my friend." Empathy is an equalizer, for it always creates a relationship in which two people recognize that they depend on each other and at the same time support each other. In therapy I seek to convey my respect for the inherent capabilities of my patients, honoring at all times their desire for self-transformation. I have great faith in the relationship itself, knowing that people will grow and change if they are treated with respect and offered words of faith in their capabilities.

Faith works—but do not be afraid to doubt it. Scientists, who are trained to be skeptical, are often the last to believe in the healing powers of intangible concepts like faith, hope, forgiveness, and empathy. Before they believe they demand proof. That's what David Spiegel, a psychiatrist at Stanford University, was looking for when he decided to study the effect of psychosocial interventions on women with metastatic breast cancer. Often confused with Bernie Siegel, M.D., who argues in best-sellers like *Love, Medicine and Miracles* that psychological and social factors can prolong life, Spiegel started his experiment with the intention of *disproving* such ideas.

The study involved eighty-six women with advanced breast cancer. The women were randomly assigned to two groups: both groups received routine cancer care (radiation and chemotherapy), but one group also met together for ninety minutes once a week for a year. In these group sessions the women discussed their feelings about their disease and its effects on their lives, helped each other cope with the threat of death, grieved together, supported each other, and shared their gratitude for the gift of each moment in their lives. Their strong relationships in the group helped alleviate the social isolation they experienced as cancer victims.

Five years after the study began, Dr. Spiegel received the computer printouts analyzing the "survival curves," which showed the number of women still alive at a given time. He was literally knocked off his feet.

I had to sit down when I got the first (of what would prove to be hundreds) of printouts. The two survival curves overlapped initially, but diverged markedly at twenty months. By four years after the point at which the women were enrolled in the initial study, it turned out that all of the patients in the control group had died, but fully one third of the patients who had received group therapy was still alive. . . . In other words, on average, patients who had been in the experimental treatment program had lived *twice as long* from the time they entered the study as did the control patients. This was a difference so significant that statistical analysis was almost unnecessary—all you had to do was look at the curves. And I had been expecting no difference at all!

At the end of his experiment, Dr. Spiegel had the proof he needed to state with full confidence that close, loving relationships can prolong and enhance life. His faith in this truth did not come automatically; in fact, he had to see the data with his own eyes. But having doubted and having seen, his faith could not be shaken.

PRACTICING FAITH

Find a Stepping-stone

Faith sometimes needs a launching pad. When I was thirteen years old and finishing eighth grade, I had to decide whether to go on to Catholic school or public school. The public school offered football, and I desperately wanted to play. Hearing about my dilemma, the priest called me into his office one day and asked me if I really thought I should give up God for football. Tormented by doubt, I went to church late one afternoon after school, put my hands together, and with all my energy and faith prayed for a sign. At one point I looked up at the altar, and I swear I saw a statue of Jesus move. That was all I needed. I left the church convinced that Jesus wanted me to play football.

That day was a definite stepping-stone for me, a place at which I look back and think, Ah, a leap of faith. My faith in my decision, I realize now, stemmed from a fierce desire to play football, but it was the intensity of my need that inspired my faith and my will to believe. We can all find many stepping-stones in our lives, places where we made the decision to head off in one direction rather than another. Find the stepping-stones in your own life, the times when you looked for reassurance or advice and found what you were seeking. Where did the response come from? Was it the reply you wanted? How did the answer change your life?

Have Your Doubts

Don't let doubts scare you away from faith. Allow yourself to have misgivings. Harbor suspicions. Be wary. Challenge faith. Ask *why?* again and again and again, but always ask with the goal of moving closer to what you are trying to understand rather than pushing it farther into the distance.

The way to discover faith (and then to practice it) is to have your doubts. Face the crisis, don't run from it. Stand nose to nose with what you hope to understand, and always doubt with your mind opened to the possibility that you might be in for a surprise.

Beware of Cynicism

Cynicism and doubt are not the same experience. Cynicism is a state of disbelief, an active act of *not* believing. Doubt raises questions, but it is not closed-minded. Cynicism shuts off possibilities; doubt leaves room for hope. Cynicism leads to pessimism; doubt leaves room for optimism. Cynicism contracts; doubt expands.

Doubt confronts the world full throttle and dares faith: Go ahead, show me! Cynicism turns its back and slowly wanders away.

Don't Be Afraid to Talk Back to God

Empathy's faith is not afraid to ask questions and express doubts—empathy only asks that we listen carefully for the answers, because it is in the back-and-forth conversations between two caring, concerned people that we learn and grow.

Coming to faith could be described as a way of challenging authority. Express your doubts. Wait. Listen. And then, sometimes, you will hear a voice talking back.

In her book *Everyday Epiphanies*, Mela Svoboda describes a charming conversation she had with God, whom she chastised for being *too* tenderhearted.

> "You love too indiscriminately. You trust people way too much. You're far too forgiving. And you're entirely too patient!"
>
> Having said that, I invite God to tell me what's wrong with me. But all I hear God say is, "You know, Honey, I really get a kick out of you!"
>
> Which only proves my point.

> *Believe in the infinite as common people do, and life grows possible again.*
>
> —WILLIAM JAMES

Chapter 14

Hope

Death is not the ultimate tragedy of life. The ultimate tragedy is depersonalization—dying in an alien and sterile area, separated from the spiritual nourishment that comes from being able to reach out to a loving hand, separated from a desire to experience the things that make life worth living, separated from hope.

—NORMAN COUSINS

At heart we are all optimists. We all want to believe, for believing we can endure almost anything. But life sometimes knocks the wind and the belief out of us, and it is then, in the drifting stillness, that empathy can lead us back to hope.

When my mother was dying of cancer, I visited her every night in the hospital, and there, in the descending darkness, I discovered hope. Late one night she asked me a question.

"Arthur?" she whispered.

"Yes?" I whispered back.

"Do you remember the day we went to the cemetery?"

I knew which day she was talking about. "Yes," I said.

She looked away from me for a moment, remembering. It was spring, just a few days after David died. We went to the cemetery with the priest, and my mother told him that she wanted three grave sites—one for David, one for herself, and one for my father. I looked at her and thought, What about me? but I didn't say anything. Later that day she asked me if I understood. "No," I said, because I didn't. "You will have another life," she said. "You will have a family and children, and you will have your own place, with them." "I want to be with you," I told her. "You will have a family, and your place will be with them," she said. "How do you know?" I asked. "It is something I know," she said. She was right, of course. I married a wonderful woman, who my parents loved as their daughter, and we had children, as my mother had foretold.

Now, so many years later, I looked at my mother's pale face against the white sheets of the hospital bed, and I felt something shift inside me, the deepest kind of sigh.

"You understand now, don't you?" she asked.

"Yes, I understand," I said.

"That's good," she said softly. "Now tell me, what about Erica?" And we talked then about one-year-old Erica, who had been very ill and was facing another surgery.

"She will be all right," she said, a question without a question mark.

"Yes," I said, "she will be all right, we will make sure she is all right."

"And what about you?" she asked me.

"I will be fine." She fixed me with that look—*You're not getting it, Arthur*—and I said, "I promise. I will take care of myself."

"You will take care of everyone else, Arthur, all these patients will need your help, all the family will be calling you with their problems when your father and I are gone," she said, her forehead creased with concern. "Who will take care of you?"

"We will take care of each other," I said. She was silent, and then she nodded, and I knew she understood.

And so, in these conversations, my mother asked for something to sustain her in her journey, something to hold on to and believe in, something to give her hope. And I knew, in a place that is deeper than memory, deeper than truth, that the future would be as bright for my children as the past had been for me.

My mother smiled, and I know she believed it, too.

EMPATHY'S DEFINITION OF HOPE

Hope inspired by empathy is invariably realistic. Hope is not the belief that everything will turn out all right, rather it is the conviction that even when things go wrong, as they inevitably will, somehow we will find our way through. "Somehow," in empathy's vernacular, always involves relationships. Through our relationships with the world, with each other, and with ourselves, empathy assures us that we will make it through.

Empathy's hope is resilient and tenacious. No matter how many times hope gets knocked down, it keeps getting back up again. Hope is conveyed in both our attitudes ("I *can* do it") and our actions ("I *will* do it"). Hope is a way of "taking heart"—it means finding something to believe in and then resolutely working to make it happen. More than a dreamy way of looking at the future, empathy's hope works to make things better day by day. The attitude of hope is full of purpose and direction; the action of hope keeps us moving.

Hope is created through great effort, diligence, patience, and concentration. We *earn* hope by our commitment to keep putting one foot in front of the other. But to develop a hopeful attitude—to learn how to believe in ourselves—we need others to believe in us, too. When my high school guidance counselor told me I should give up the idea of college because my grades reflected a lack of ambition and academic talent, I was shaken up. Maybe, I thought, he's right. Maybe I should join the Army or the Marines. Maybe that's where I belong.

I turned to my father for help, and he gave me hope. But here's the critical point—he gave me *reason* to hope. He didn't just say, "Arthur, that man is a fool who doesn't know what he's talking about." He let the guidance counselor talk, he listened carefully to his arguments, he tried to understand his perspective, and only then did he tell me why he believed the counselor's assessment of my talent was incorrect. I felt hopeful about my future after that encounter not because my father handed me hope on a platter but because he took the trouble to carve hope out of real-life experience.

Empathy leads to understanding, which always generates hope. Once we enter into a situation with empathy, working hard to understand all the complexities involved, we come to the realization that there is not just one pathway through life. "Every exit is an entrance somewhere," wrote the playwright Tom Stoppard, and that is precisely the point—when a door shuts, look for the open window. When you leave something behind, think about what you are taking with you. Or as Oscar Wilde once said, "Whenever you fall, pick up something."

A few months after my encounter with the guidance counselor, my father drove me to Maine for an interview at Bridgton Academy, a college preparatory institution that catered to high school athletes. In my initial interview at Bridgton, my father and I sat down with Mr. Goldsmith, the headmaster. He thanked us both for coming, and after a few minutes he asked my father to leave the room so the two of us could talk.

We talked about my hometown and the reasons I had decided to apply to Bridgton. "I was wondering why you didn't interview with our admissions people when they visited your high school," Mr. Goldsmith said at one point.

"My guidance counselor didn't think Bridgton would work for me," I said.

"Why is that?"

"He thinks I should join the Army. He doesn't think I can make it academically. I haven't exactly been studious," I admitted.

"Do you think you could make it here?"

"My father thinks I need a school like this to teach me how to study," I said.

"Do you agree?"

"I think so, but I'm still not exactly sure."

At that point Mr. Goldsmith asked me what I liked to read. I told him I didn't read.

"You don't read at all?"

"That's right," I said, not with any pride. In fact, with that answer I figured I'd be working in the local foundry, where my father and his brothers and their father had worked.

"What about the sports page?" Mr. Goldsmith asked.

"Sure, yeah, I read the sports page every day."

We talked about sports for a long time. I told him my favorite player was Jimmy Brown of the Cleveland Browns. "Do you know what his average yard per carry was last year?" Mr. Goldsmith asked. I did. He asked if I knew the score of the NFL championship game. I told him. Only later did I realize that he was giving me a test of sorts, analyzing my ability to remember details in an area that was not threatening to me.

At the end of our conversation, I told Mr. Goldsmith how much I wanted to go to Bridgton. "I want to prove to my parents and myself that I can perform as well in school as I do on the football field," I said.

Mr. Goldsmith shook my hand and told me he would be happy to have me at Bridgton. "I'm convinced you have a great future ahead of you," he said. "You have a good memory, you're passionate about subjects you're interested in, you remember details, you're courteous and thoughtful, and you're a good listener—and, most important of all, I can hear how much it means to you to do well and how much you will appreciate getting a second chance in school."

I left Bridgton that day feeling optimistic about my future because Mr. Goldsmith took the time and energy to find out what I cared about and to offer me a realistic assessment of my potential. Focusing on my memory, my attentiveness, and my willingness to learn—qualities that I had never before associated with academic success—he gave me a sense of my power and potential. Using empathy, Mr. Goldsmith gave me hope.

HOW EMPATHY LEADS TO HOPE

Researchers have confirmed through numerous studies that hope has a deep and lasting impact on our minds, bodies, and spirits. Hope, according to these studies:

- Creates needed energy during adversity
- Enhances creativity, giving us more options and pathways to follow
- Helps us deal with trauma and grief
- Protects us against depression
- Improves school performance
- Increases our immune response

A recent study by the psychologists Vicki Helgeson and Heidi Fritz offers proof that a hopeful attitude can have a dramatic impact on physical health. The researchers gave questionnaires to 298 patients hospitalized for angioplasty, a procedure used to relieve blockage in major arteries. The patients were asked about their general outlook on life and the support they received from family, friends, and doctors as well as more specific questions about how much they exercised and whether or not they felt they could control behaviors that affected their health, like smoking and overeating. After six months the patients were interviewed again; those who had scored high on pessimism were nearly three times as likely to have more arterial blockage as those who had felt confident and hopeful about their situation. Furthermore, patients with a positive mental attitude, high self-esteem, and a strong sense of self-control were less likely to suffer a heart attack, undergo bypass surgery, or require a second angioplasty.

In another fascinating study designed to measure the effect of optimism on performance, the psychologist Martin Seligman gave insurance salespeople a questionnaire to test their optimism. When he matched their test scores with actual sales records, he found that the sales agents who scored high on optimism sold 37 percent more insurance on average than pessimistic salesmen. The salespeople who scored in the top 10 percent for optimism sold 88 percent more insurance than the agents who ranked in the top 10 percent for pessimism.

Optimistic salespeople had a much more empathic way of relating to their potential clients. When a prospect said no, pessimists would consider themselves failures, using such statements as "I'm no good" or "I can't even get to first base." Optimistic salespeople, by contrast, would adopt the other person's perspective, making statements like, "She was too busy when I called" or "The family already has insurance." Rejections were not taken personally, and therefore the optimistic agents remained hopeful about future prospects.

In relationships empathy creates a hopeful attitude by helping us to develop a broader perspective, in which misfortunes and disappointments are seen as temporary, specific to the situation, and ultimately surmountable. If we imagine that the cause is permanent—"I'm stupid," "He's insensitive," "She's thoughtless"—we set the stage for despair and depression. If we think of the situation as unique and confined to the moment—"I just said something really stupid" or "He's usually understanding, but he's not being very responsive right now"—we limit our disappointment to the specific interaction and avoid generalizing to the past and the future.

When the University of Kansas psychologist C. R. Snyder studied the academic achievement of college students, he discovered that hope has a powerful influence on success. Snyder defines hope as "believing you have both the will and the way to accomplish your goals." High-hope students work harder in general, Snyder found, but they also develop an everexpanding repertoire of hope-based skills. Refusing to give in to anxiety or depression, they look for ways to motivate themselves, reassure themselves when they get stuck, creatively search for alternative routes to their goal (or switch goals if necessary), and remain flexible no matter how frustrating things get.

Empathy calms us down, strengthening our relationships with others and helping to create an attitude that allows us to bend rather than break. Empathy turns down the heat of fear and soothes the anxiety that says, "I can't do it!" Working together, reminding ourselves that no one is perfect, slowing things down, we find hope in our relationships.

Empathy-inspired hope creates the connection between people that generates the energy needed to keep putting one foot in front of the other. A story is told about Winston Churchill, who in his schooldays had to repeat English three times while the "cleverer" boys in his class, as he put it, went on to learn Greek and Latin. In 1941, after he was elected prime minister of England and in the early days of World War II, Churchill returned to his school for a visit. In a short speech to the students, he offered a few words of wisdom.

"Never give in!" Churchill bellowed, banging his walking stick against the wood floor. "Never, never, never, never! Never yield in any way, great or small, large or petty, except to convictions of honor and good sense. Never yield to force and the apparently overwhelming might of the enemy."

Never give in—three words that convey the fighting spirit of both empathy and hope.

PRACTICING HOPE

Argue with Yourself

Most of us are fairly versatile when it comes to debating others, but when we're faced with our own self-assessments, we rarely offer any dissenting opinion. "You're so stupid," we say to ourselves. "You always get yourself into messes like this." "Why don't you grow up?" And then we walk around feeling defeated and hopeless.

Start disputing those statements. Who says you're stupid? And why should you believe that assessment? Where's the evidence for your stupidity? Spend your time learning how to assess your capabilities based on today's performance rather than dredging up past failures. If you make a mistake or fail to meet a goal, that doesn't mean you're inadequate or somehow deficient—it only means you're human. Errors are part of the game.

Look for Solutions

Hope is based on the belief that somewhere an answer exists to every question. It may not be the answer we want or expect, but every answer points in a certain direction. We can choose to walk in that direction, or we can head off in a completely different direction. Here's the point—hope is never just one solution to a problem. Keep your options open. Or, as my mother used to say, "Close your books and open your eyes."

Listen to Music

At the end of the day, when my energy is flagging and I still have hours of work to do, I listen to the music of Andrea Bocelli, the blind Italian opera singer. His voice never fails to lift my spirits. What music inspires you? What lyrics soothe your troubled spirit? I know many people who are immediately lifted up by the words of the song "Amazing Grace" or "Bridge over Troubled Water," for example.

In her book *Meditations for Health*, Nancy Burke talks about the music that helped her find the energy and the courage to face her cancer treatments:

> Every week, for two winters and two summers, as I drove to and from the cancer clinic for treatments, I played [Patti LaBelle's] renditions of "Somewhere over the Rainbow" and "There's a Winner in You" over and over. When I was frightened and thought I couldn't make one more trip, I played those songs to get me there. Afterward, when I was tired and afraid I couldn't make the drive home, I played them again. My spirits never failed to recover, and the miles just flew by. I found such courage and hope in her passionate music. In the midst of the darkest time of my life, that voice made me feel grateful to be alive.

Like Nancy Burke, I believe there's a song for all of us, "one incalculable mix of melody and magic that so neatly wraps the heart that we are lifted out of the here and now." What is your song? Why do you find it healing? How does it lift your spirits? How has your song changed over time and with circumstances? Where does it take you? When will you listen to it?

Watch the Movie *It's a Wonderful Life*

Many years ago I worked with a forty-three-year-old high school teacher who attempted suicide after her husband left her. Several weeks before Christmas she asked me for a favor.

"I know you don't like to tell people what to do," she said, "but I wonder if you could give me something that would help me put my life in perspective, something that would help me find some meaning in my life right now. I just don't know if I can keep going, because I don't feel as if I have had any lasting impact on other people's lives."

"You are a teacher who has given so much to so many, Jan," I said. "I know you don't often get to hear how your work affects others. Most of us don't go back and tell our wonderful teachers how deeply they affected our lives. I know I never did. But sitting here right now I can remember certain teachers' words like it was yesterday. You asked me to give you something, but I'd like to ask you for something instead. I'd like to ask you to watch the movie *It's a Wonderful Life* and listen to what Clarence, the angel who is trying to earn his wings, says to George Bailey. Then I want you to think as objectively as you can about what your life has meant to so many people."

On Christmas Day I opened the front door to find a wrapped gift on the porch. It was the video of *It's a Wonderful Life* with this note attached: "You are my Clarence. Merry Christmas. Jan."

I watch the video every Christmas Eve with my family, and every time I watch it, I think about the people I have been privileged to work with who have lost hope and, through courage, hard work, and the healing power of empathy, have rediscovered their fighting spirit. We all "earn our wings" in life by helping others when they are in despair and can see no way out. We earn our wings through the insights and the guiding wisdom of empathy.

Avoid the Word *Always*

"Things like this are *always* happening to me." "I'm *always* overreacting like this." "I *always* make stupid mistakes." "I'm *always* rushing around and forgetting things." "He's *always* late." "She *always* blames everything on me."

Where is the hope in those statements? Where is the "out" in the word *always*? *Always* is an expression with no past, present, or future, a word that stops time dead, a coffin of a word. Even when you use the word *always* in a positive way—"I'm *always* a fast runner," "I *always* do well in school," "I *always* work hard"—you set the stage for disappointment. What if you pull a muscle during an important race? What if you get three hours of sleep before a test and earn a B instead of your usual A? What if you are sick and tired and don't feel like working hard today?

The word *always* slams the door on possibilities and alternative explanations. Honoring life's ever-changing nature, empathy recognizes the threat in the word *always* and substitutes phrases like "sometimes" or "now and then" or "every once in a while." "*Sometimes* I strike out, and *sometimes* I hit the ball over the fence." "*Now and then* I say things I shouldn't." "*Every once in a while* I start searching around for someone to blame instead of taking the responsibility on myself."

These phrases emphasize that the situation is temporary and changing all the time. With this simple variation in language, you will feel less helpless and more hopeful.

Use Your Memory

Memory is a powerful generator of hope; it can also be the cause of much despair. One pathway to hope is to choose your memories very carefully. When something good or pleasant happens—a stranger smiles at you, a friend gives you a compliment, a relative offers you a hug, a child turns to you for solace—put a "frame" around it. Remove that moment from its place in time, put a band of gold around its edges, and "place" it in your memory gallery. So many hopeful things happen day in and day out, but we lose them if we don't stop for a moment, think about them, and consciously frame them.

Be Willing to Change

Hope, like all experiences powered by empathy, is not a passive state of waiting for something good to happen but an active pursuit of goodness. How can you put action into hope? What can you do to create hope, to be hopeful, to engender hope in others?

One of the most fertile grounds for hope can be discovered in the willingness to change. When we are inflexible, rigid, unbending, and unyielding, we create a thick, muddy swamp for hope to slog its way through. But when we bend, flex, yield, and surrender—hope finds its wings.

The mind is its own place, and in itself can make a heaven of hell, and a hell of heaven.

—JOHN MILTON

Chapter 15

Forgiveness

"Since nothing we intend is ever faultless, and nothing we attempt ever without error, and nothing we achieve without some measure of finitude and fallibility we call humanness, we are saved by forgiveness."

—DAVID AUGSBURGER

When we think about forgiveness, we imagine it as something that we confer on others—*I forgive you*. But the heart of forgiveness is the act and the process of forgiving ourselves.

When my brother killed himself thirty years ago, I lost my way. For more than two years I lived in a place of darkness and despair. The only color I wore was brown—all my shirts, pants, socks, and shoes, everything I owned was beige or brown. Every day I went to classes and studied, but I found no joy in the work. Every night I ran for miles, pushing myself to run farther and faster, hearing David's voice ahead of me, behind me, calling me forward, pushing me, giving me strength for miles, only to leave me, suddenly, exhausted and alone.

Three months after David died, I gave up a college teaching position and moved back in with my parents. My thoughts and my emotions were with my parents; I needed to be with them as much as they needed to be with me. Waking up in the house I grew up in, eating in the kitchen where I ate so many meals with my brother, walking down the streets we used to walk down together, I struggled with my grief and my anger. How could David have left us like this? What anguish, what fear drove him to take his own life? What went through his mind that night when he locked his door and put the needle in his arm? I lay awake night after night, trying to imagine David's despair, and I could not enter it—I could not find my way into his heart and his soul.

Why? That was the question that haunted me, and there was no answer I could find that offered any solace. Should I have spent more time with him, cared for him more, talked to him more? Was I so absorbed in my own life that I didn't notice what he might have needed from me? Was it my parents' fault? Did my father expect too much of David? Did my mother cling to him, making it difficult for him to separate from her?

I found myself agonizing over the actions I should have taken, the words I should have said. I wondered, with that weariness of soul that accepts the futility of asking unanswerable questions, what I could have done to save him. Where did I go wrong? Where did I fail?

I never once thought about forgiveness. Forgive what? Forgive who? Forgiveness seemed beside the point. For who could I forgive, and how would forgiveness change anything? Forgiveness wouldn't bring David back to life. I equated forgiveness with the living world. I couldn't see what relevance it had in my life or in my relationship to my brother, who I would never see again.

Week after week, month after month, I went through the motions. I was finished with my coursework for my doctorate and had only the dissertation left to write; as I wrote each page, my mother (the only person in the world who could decipher my handwriting) typed. On weekends I helped my father at his furniture store. I talked to friends and smiled at strangers on the street. I sat on the front steps with my parents, chatted with the neighbors, celebrated holidays with my aunts, uncles, and cousins. I lived. I breathed. I put one foot in front of the other.

And, slowly, I felt a loosening inside. It was almost a physical release, like a muscle cramp unknotting itself. Forgiveness came as a gradual awakening to the truth. David was gone, and nothing I could do would save him. When I looked back I knew I had done what I could. I was not perfect, I made mistakes, I said things I wish I had not said and did things I regretted—but I loved him. I could not have loved him more. So there was one truth—I loved him, and my love could not save him.

If I knew then what I know now about the power of empathy, could I have saved my brother? I believe the answer to that question is yes. When I called David in Amsterdam and he said, "I will kill myself if I have to go to prison," I would have asked him directly about the suicide threat. "Do you have a plan to harm yourself?" I would have said. "How close are you?" With my questions I would have tried to determine how vulnerable he was and how likely he was to hurt himself. When David said, "I love you," I would have said, "I love you, too." I would have listened to his words rather than focusing on my own responses. I would have empathized with him rather than assuming, guessing, letting emotions govern my reactions.

How do I live with the knowledge that I could have said or done something that might have saved David's life? I live with it. That's the only answer I can give—I live with it. I understand who I was and where I was in my own life, and I know I did everything I could have done based on the knowledge and experience I had at the time. I know my parents did everything they could. And David . . . David did everything he could.

Have I discovered forgiveness? Not in the sense of a complete release from grief and pain and unanswered questions. But I no longer torment myself with thoughts of what I could have done or should have said. I focus on today, doing what I can for the living. I remember David—I will never forget him—and I know that my answer to his death is my involvement with people like him who feel lost, alone, and adrift. I keep reminding myself: You are alive. You have work to do. In that work I continue to seek forgiveness for myself, for David, day after day after day.

And every day offers a new opportunity. Last summer I arrived in Maine, exhausted and sleep deprived, for a two-week vacation. I couldn't wait to take naps, walk on the beach with my family, chat with my neighbors, and lose myself in the rhythm of unscheduled days. I arrived on a Friday night, and Tuesday morning I was leaving the house to take a run when Karen, who was talking on the phone, signaled for me to wait. She covered the phone with her hand. "It's John's wife," she told me. John was the electrician who worked on our Maine house. "He's in a deep depression. His best friend was killed in a car wreck two months ago, and he's lost almost fifty pounds. She's afraid he might start drinking again."

Less than an hour later John and I sat down to talk. We spent three hours together that day. He told me he had been treated by a psychiatrist who prescribed Xanax, an addictive, sedative drug, and Zoloft, an antidepressant. The psychiatrist then referred John to a psychotherapist, who told him he was having a midlife crisis.

"I hear this therapist specializes in 'midlife crisis events,' " he said with the first smile of the day.

"How old is he?" I asked.

"About fifty."

We looked at each other, and we burst out laughing. The same thought occurred to both of us—who is having the midlife crisis here? But simmering beneath the laughter I was experiencing a sense of outrage—how could anyone take John's serious life problems and lump them together under the label "midlife crisis"? Both his parents died before his tenth birthday. His brother died in his forties. His best friend was killed in a car accident. For two decades he struggled with an alcohol addiction and only recently got sober. Overwhelmed with grief and fear, he searched for someone to help him, but no one seemed to be listening to the underlying pain causing his depression. A psychiatrist told him he was depressed and offered to dull his pain with sedatives and antidepressants. A social worker told him he was going through a midlife crisis. His AA sponsor warned him to get his act together or he would end up in the drunk tank. His wife feared he might kill himself.

All these individuals were well intentioned, but they were listening from a biased position, unable to empathize with John's experiences because of their own concerns or fears.

And so John talked, and I listened, and we both felt much better. "No one told me that it might be normal for me to feel overwhelmed by my friend's death," John said when he left my house that day. "No one talked to me about my parents or my brother or the strain on my marriage. Why is that? Why didn't anyone ask me about my relationships? Why did they automatically assume they knew what I was thinking and feeling? Why didn't they help me understand?"

And with those questions I find the answer to my own questions, which go back so many years. Sometimes we don't understand. We make mistakes. We misdiagnose, mislabel, falsely categorize, and head off in the wrong direction. I remember talking to David after he visited the priest, who assured him that prayer would solve his problems. I remember David's stories about the doctors who gave him refillable prescriptions for sedatives and tranquilizers, hoping to make his pain go away. I remember spending hours with him in bookstores, looking through the self-help sections, and in health food stores, searching for over-the-counter remedies that might ease his symptoms. And I remember the times when David turned to me for advice, and I offered him sympathy rather than empathy, thinking I understood what he was going through (when, in truth, I did not understand the depth of his feelings) or, even worse, when I counseled him to take responsibility for himself, to be the person I knew he could be. With these misguided responses, I left him alone with his pain.

Empathy takes me back to the past to understand my brother's anguish. I know that all those accumulated years of trying and failing to get help for his problems created the deepest despair. I know that alcohol and heroin pulled him away from the world of the living. When David entered into a full-time relationship with drugs, his flesh-and-blood relationships faded in importance. Filled with shame and guilt, he avoided interacting with his family and friends. Separated by his addiction from those who loved him, he lived in a world with no meaning or purpose. That's when he lost hope and faith. That's when he could not forgive himself for what he had done, for the shame he believed he had brought to our family, for the grief he had caused, for all the heartache he had created in his young life. His world narrowed down until eventually he saw no way out, and he ended his life.

He could not forgive himself. That was the real reason my brother died. He could not live with the idea of what he had become—a college dropout, a heroin addict, a felon, a fugitive from the law, an outcast. Those labels destroyed him, and death became a release from the unbearable pain of his life.

Empathy leads me to understand my brother, and in that understanding I find my own forgiveness. Not once and for all, but day by day, as I work with people who struggle to find a way to live with themselves. I talk to them about forgiveness. I talk to them about the possibility of change, and the fact that every day we start over again. I talk about learning how to live with our imperfections, changing what we can change and discovering how to put up with the rest. Most important of all, I listen as people put words to their despair and search for ways to keep moving. I try to respond with care and respect, honoring their unique experiences. I celebrate their successes, and I participate in their sorrows.

Guided by the power of empathy, I know that I am doing what I can, and I believe it will make a difference. I promise that as long as they keep putting one foot in front of the other, I will never give up on them. And I never do.

EMPATHY'S DEFINITION OF FORGIVENESS

Empathy widens our view of the world and from that expanded perspective, we discover forgiveness for ourselves and others. Empathy reveals forgiveness as an unfolding process rather than an act that is completed and then set aside. Forgiveness comes slowly, as we continue to learn from the tragedies and traumas of the past in the ongoing effort to transcend them. But with time and effort, we are able to move forward, building on the past rather than endlessly repeating it.

In her book *Dead Man Walking* Helen Prejean tells the story of a senseless death and its aftermath. In one early passage the father of the young man who was murdered looks down at his son's body and says, "Whoever did this, I forgive them." As the father would discover, however, that statement was just the first step in a very long journey. For every day, he was forced to travel the way of forgiveness. Prejean writes:

> He acknowledges that it's a struggle to overcome the feelings of bitterness and revenge that well up, especially as he remembers David's birthday year by year and loses him all over again: David at twenty, David at twenty-five, David getting married, David standing at the back door with his little ones clustered around his knees, grownup David, a man like himself, whom he will never know. Forgiveness is never going to be easy. Each day it must be prayed for and struggled and won.

Forgiveness comes with experience; it arrives on the heels of empathy. Empathy allows us to understand on a deeper level where we belong, and through that understanding we come to realize why forgiveness is essential. Forgiveness is not something we can command or control but an experience that arises through the hard work of empathy. Seeking to understand, opening our minds and our hearts to what was once hidden from view, we see what we could not see before, and in that widened perspective forgiveness comes to us unbidden, like a sudden bend in the trail that opens up to reveal a view of the world we have never seen before.

HOW EMPATHY LEADS TO FORGIVENESS

How does empathy teach us to forgive ourselves and others? That is the ultimate question, of course—for even if we know what forgiveness is, what we really want to understand is how to do it. How do we find forgiveness, and what do we do with it when we discover it? How does forgiveness lead us from the past to the present, guiding us to expand our self-awareness and strengthen our relationships?

In the Jewish religion forgiveness is considered a four-stage process: First, you acknowledge that you did something wrong. Second, you apologize to the person you harmed. Third, you compensate that person whenever possible. And fourth, you try not to repeat your error. That fourth step, of course, takes a lifetime.

Empathy offers a similar approach to forgiveness, but one that places the greatest emphasis on our ongoing, developing relationships with each other.

EMPATHY'S FIVE STAGES OF FORGIVENESS

Stage 1: Awareness

Every experience inspired by empathy necessarily begins with the reminder that our perceptions are limited by our experiences and our interpretations of those experiences. The world is infinitely complex, and at any given moment we can comprehend only part of it. "We can only see half of anything," reminds the Jungian psychologist Alice O. Howell. "The other half is the meaning we give to what we see."

Stage 2: Seeking

Acknowledging our limitations, we seek to know more. In the process of forgiveness, empathy asks us to keep searching, sorting, sifting: What more can I learn? Where am I blinded? What are my biases? What prevents me from understanding?

Stage 3: Moving Outward

In the process of seeking we begin to move outward from the self toward others. Empathy allows us to participate in the lives of others, feeling as they feel, thinking as they think. In the active effort to borrow the other person's perspective, we let ourselves go and surrender our worldview (with the acknowledgment that it is necessarily limited).

Stage 4: Change

Having entered the other's world, borrowing his or her thoughts and feelings, we come back to ourselves transformed. After each empathic interaction we change and stretch beyond ourselves. With this expanded perspective we see what we could not see before; contained in that new vision is the experience of forgiveness.

Stage 5: Commitment

Understanding that our state of mind is linked inextricably with the experiences of others, we commit ourselves to the community at large. In Africa, this process of commitment to the whole is called *ubuntu* and signifies a sense of oneness with the world. South African Archbishop Desmond Tutu explains:

> Ubuntu . . . speaks about the essence of being human . . . my humanity is caught up in your humanity because we say a person is a person through other persons. In our African understanding, we set great store by communal peace and harmony. Anything that subverts this harmony is injurious, not just to the community, but to all of us, and therefore forgiveness is an absolute necessity for continued human existence.

Forgiveness is the ultimate act of connectedness. I forgive you because I am you. In forgiving you, I forgive myself. In forgiving myself, I forgive the world.

PRACTICING FORGIVENESS

Wipe the Slate Clean

Forgiveness signifies freedom—releasing ourselves from pride, resentment, and bitterness. We start over again, in a sense, we wipe the slate clean. A wonderful story conveys this idea of forgiveness as renewal.

An old innkeeper kept two ledgers. In the first he listed all the sins he had committed during the year, and in the second he listed all the bad things that had befallen him and his loved ones in that same year. Then, on the last day of the year, he read first from the book detailing his flaws and errors. When he was finished, he picked up the second book and read through all the misfortunes that had befallen him that year.

After the reading, the innkeeper closed the books, folded his hands together in prayer, and lifted his eyes to heaven. "Dear God," he prayed, "I have many sins to confess to you. But you have done many distressful things to me, too. So now we are beginning a new year, and I ask that we wipe the slate clean. I will forgive you, and you forgive me."

In every interaction you have, try to keep in mind that there are always two ledgers—one filled with your mistakes and imperfections and the other containing all the trials and tribulations that were thrown in your pathway. When you feel resentful, remember both sides, but put your energy into wiping your own slate clean. It is not the memory itself you want to erase but the bitter emotions of guilt, resentment, and anger that are attached to the memory.

Write to Yourself

When you take the time to write down your thoughts and feelings, amazing events occur. In a series of studies the Southern Methodist University psychologist James Pennebaker demonstrated that journal writing enhances immune function, reduces days missed from work, improves liver enzyme function, and cuts down on doctor visits. These impressive physiological changes appear to be directly related to the emotional release that comes from unburdening yourself.

Pennebaker's method is straightforward. He asks people to write for fifteen to twenty minutes a day, concentrating on a traumatic event or pressing concern. Then he asks his subjects to create a narrative story and consciously search within the story for meaning. Finding meaning in our troubles gives us a new way to approach them—not as calamities that threaten to crush us but as experiences that offer to enlighten us.

Burn Your Bitterness

In the Hindu tradition resentments are handled in a simple but unusual way. First, you write down the offenses or indignities that trouble your mind and spirit. Then you burn the paper. Watching the paper burn serves as a reminder that everything, even resentments, eventually perishes.

Sit Still

Resentments seem to pile up when we rush from one moment to the next. Find a place and a time in your day to be still with your thoughts and emotions. If you are feeling angry or hostile, don't assume that a few deep breaths will calm you down. Meditation experts believe that we need fifteen or twenty minutes in order to recover from a state of high physiological arousal (say, after a close call on the highway, a nerve-wracking presentation at work, or a hostile interaction with a friend or family member).

Few of us have the privilege of whole days to whittle away, but Henry David Thoreau's meditations on Walden Pond are certainly soothing to consider. Empathy's influence on Thoreau is evident in the first sentence of this reflection:

> I love a broad margin to my life. Sometimes in a summer morning, having taken my accustomed bath, I sat in my sunny doorway from sunrise till noon, rapt in a revery, amidst the pines and hickories and sumachs, in undisturbed solitude and stillness, while the birds sang around or flitted noiseless through the house, until by the sun falling in at my west window, or the noise of some traveller's wagon on the distant highway, I was reminded of the lapse of time. I grew in those seasons like corn in the night, and they were far better than any work of the hands would have been. They were not time subtracted from my life, but so much over and above my usual allowance. I realized what the Orientals mean by contemplation and the forsaking of works. For the most part, I minded not how the hours went.

The day advanced as if to light some work of mine; it was morning, and lo, now it is evening, and nothing memorable is accomplished. Instead of singing, like the birds, I silently smiled at my incessant good fortune. As the sparrow had its trill, sitting on the hickory before my door, so I had my chuckle or suppressed warble which he might hear out of my nest.

Solitude is difficult to bear for the unforgiving, who find in each silent moment another opportunity to revisit the pain of the past. Forgiveness cleanses and releases, allowing us to grow "like corn in the night," moving into ourselves and beyond ourselves to become all that we were meant to be.

There are two ways of spreading light; to be the candle or the mirror that reflects it.

—EDITH WHARTON

Final Thoughts

Every Wednesday night, in a tiny Lutheran church, I lead a group therapy session consisting of eight men and women. On a recent winter night, forty-eight-year-old Sarah walked into the meeting room, sat down on one of the aging, overstuffed chairs, and began to cry. We were all taken aback, for Sarah is the quintessential New Englander, reserved, cautious, and stiff-lipped, with a tenacious spirit that announces to the world, *Hey, I'm struggling—who isn't?—but I'm going to make it come hell or high water.* Sarah has been through the fire, as she would put it. Her alcoholic father committed suicide when she was seven years old, her sister attempted suicide when she was thirty-four years old, and for twenty years Sarah was married to an alcoholic who physically and emotionally abused her. She started drinking "to kill the pain," took Xanax to "soothe" herself, and smoked two packs of cigarettes a day "just for the hell of it." When she began therapy two years earlier, after divorcing her husband, she told me she had cut herself off from half the world. "How is that?" I asked. "Because I hate men," she answered.

Witnessing her distress that night, I wondered what had happened to break through her sturdy defenses. "Can you tell us why you're upset, Sarah?" I asked.

Struggling to control her emotions, Sarah described a meeting with her doctor, who told her he suspected she had lung cancer and had scheduled a biopsy operation later in the week. "He was so cold and unfeeling," she said, clearly as disturbed at that moment by her doctor's behavior as she was by the threat of cancer. For the next hour Sarah tried to put words to her rage and her fear, while the other men and women in the room offered what solace they could. When Sarah left that night, she seemed comforted by the group's support.

The next Wednesday, Sarah walked into the church, shaking snow off her thick rubber boots, and took a seat on the couch next to Matthew. Matthew is a recovering alcoholic who stands six feet, seven inches tall and looks like a modern-day Paul Bunyan, with arms as big around as small trees and deeply chiseled lines cutting through his handsome but weathered face. Cynical and often judgmental, Matthew has been nicknamed Mr. Intolerance by several group members because he has so little patience with people who are different from him. In the past he had been especially critical of Sarah, calling her "ultrasensitive" and "meddling," while she referred to him as "egocentric," "callous," and "aggressive." After many months together in group, they had developed a grudging respect for each other, but the connection was tenuous; whenever they interacted the rest of the group sat back, waiting for the sparks to fly.

Gently, taking care not to upset Sarah, fifty-four-year-old Miriam asked if she had any news about the biopsy. Miriam has been struggling with depression since her daughter died of a drug overdose at age twenty-eight.

"I'll know in another week," Sarah said with a peaceful smile. "But to tell you the truth, I'm not as worried as I thought I would be."

"I'm just wondering what happened between this week and last week when you were so angry and upset," said Gary. Gary, thirty-two, is in the middle of a divorce and custody battle for his five-year-old child.

"Something amazing happened," Sarah said, leaning forward as if to bring the circle even closer together. "When I checked into the hospital for the biopsy, I was terrified. I just couldn't calm myself down. A male nurse was taking my blood pressure, and suddenly I felt faint. I panicked and told the nurse he was losing me. He took my hand, looked in my eyes, and said, 'Sarah, you are not going anywhere without me. I am right here with you, I am holding on to you, and I will not let you go.'

"That's when I thought about you," Sarah said, turning to Matthew.

"You thought about me?" Matthew said in disbelief.

"I remembered all the times you said you felt like you didn't belong in this group," Sarah said. "You said you felt like we were all so different from you and none of us could really understand your feelings."

"Yeah," Matthew said, shifting his weight on the sofa and smiling sheepishly, "that sounds like me."

"I know you don't believe in a higher power, Matthew, but I guarantee you there is one," Sarah said in her deep, gravelly voice. "When the nurse held on to me and told me I wasn't going anywhere as long as he was with me, I knew that I was not alone. And I realized that's what we do for each other in this group—we hold on to each other, we let each other know that we'll walk through it together, and we'll never, ever leave each other alone."

Sarah took a few deep breaths to steady herself; she was near tears. "I need to tell you all that if this cancer scare had happened a year ago, before I had your support, they would have had to lock me up in the loony bin. I wouldn't have made it without you. That includes you, Matthew. We've had our problems, that's for sure. You used to drive me crazy with your intolerant comments and your refusal to trust people. But we're both changing, we're both learning how to trust people and reveal our feelings. And I want you to know—I'm telling you here in front of everyone—that no matter what happens, I will always stick with you. I won't ever give up on you."

Now Matthew had tears in his eyes. For a moment no one said a word, and then we watched in stunned silence as this massively built man, who prides himself on his self-control, put his head in his hands, shoulders shaking, and began to cry. After a moment I asked Matthew if he could tell the group what had happened to create the intense emotion.

"When someone really cares about me," he said, wiping the tears from his face, "and I really feel it, deep inside me, like I just did with Sarah, something happens to me. I just can't hold back."

That night, sitting on musty old furniture in a darkened church, the coffee perking, the snow gently falling outside, we all felt the presence of empathy. Two people who once insisted they had nothing in common had discovered a deep and abiding connection. The bond between them expanded, encompassing the rest of us and eventually extending beyond our small circle into the outside world. For when we said our goodbyes that night, every one of us felt the power of empathy, remembering how a nurse's sensitive response calmed a woman's fear, how she took his caring and concern and passed it on gratefully, almost prayerfully, to another struggling soul, and how all of us who witnessed that interaction felt something shift inside our own hearts.

I imagined Sarah going home that night, fixing her tea and watching the snow falling outside her kitchen window as she thought about Matthew and the group; she's a night owl and likes to do her thinking when the rest of the world is getting ready for bed. I thought about Matthew walking upstairs to tuck his two little boys into bed, reminding them that he loves them; that was one of the great joys of sobriety, he told me once, kissing his boys good night and waking up in the morning to remember it. I thought about all the men and women in the group, recalling their struggles, their triumphs, and their ongoing efforts to find meaning and purpose in their lives. I thought about my parents, my brother, and all the relatives, friends, and teachers who have been part of my journey through life. That night I went home and listened to my wife's and my daughters' stories about their day, feeling a sense of peace and an even deeper gratitude for these, the gifts of my life.

This is how empathy works, not in sudden, spectacular ways but slowly, like the sun rising over distant hills, creating a gradual dawning of awareness, a spreading warmth of understanding and insight. Empathy shines its light on our deepest needs, never allowing us to forget that our very survival depends on our ability to accurately understand and sensitively respond to each other. Empathy is our common language, giving voice to the heart's most profound yearnings, eloquently articulating the soul's most anguished questions.

Through its thoughtful actions and interactions, empathy creates the invisible connections that hold us together, one human to another, neighborhood to village, community to country, nation to planet. With the connectedness that empathy engenders, the world itself becomes a less frightening place. A sense of belonging replaces loneliness, strangers appear less strange, defenses seem less necessary, and hope replaces hopelessness. Doubts give way to faith, resentments fade, and our hearts, once closed by fear and pain, open up to the possibility of forgiveness.

This is the power—and the promise—of empathy.

NOTES

Introduction

Page ix **"I would not exchange"** From Kahlil Gibran, *Tear and a Smile* (New York: Knopf, 1950, translated by H. M. Nahmad). In this wonderful book of parables, stories and poems, Gibran explores the idea that a meaningful life necessarily includes both joy and sorrow.

Chapter 1: Empathy's Paradox

Page 7 Heinz Kohut, M.D., has had a powerful, enduring influence on my approach to therapy and life. In 1976 I was supervised by a classical psychoanalyst from the Boston Psychoanalytic Institute as a requirement for my post-doctorate internship. My supervisor, responding to my frustration with the classic analytic view emphasizing the effects of sexual and aggressive instincts on behavior, suggested I read Kohut's work. Fascinated by Kohut's detailed theory of empathy and his conviction that empathy is fundamental to human life and survival, I read everything he had ever written.

The reference to Hitler's manipulative use of empathy is in Arnold Goldberg, M.D., editor, *Advances in Self Psychology* (New York: International Universities Press, 1978), page 459. In Kohut's last public address in October 1981, he again discusses the Nazis' use of "fiendish empathy" to manipulate their victims. This paper is published in Paul H. Ornstein, editor, *The Search for the Self: Selected Writings of Heinz Kohut 1978–1981* (New York: International Universities Press, 1991), volume 4, pp. 525–535.

Other books by Kohut that profoundly influenced my work include: *The Restoration of the Self* (New York: International Universities Press, 1977), and *How Does Analysis Cure?* (Chicago: University of Chicago Press, 1984), which was edited after Kohut's death by long-time colleagues Arnold Goldberg and Paul Stepansky.

Interested readers might also look at the following works: *The Kohut Seminars on Self Psychology and Psychotherapy with Adolescents and Young Adults* (New York: W.W. Norton, 1987), edited by Miriam Elson. In this fascinating book Kohut responds to clinicians' requests for help in using self psychology methods with college students struggling to make the transition from adolescence to adulthood.

Self Psychology and the Humanities (New York: W.W. Norton, 1985), edited by Charles B. Strozier, contains some of Kohut's most interesting papers on courage, leadership, creativity, charisma, religion, ethics, and values.

The Psychology of the Self: A Casebook (New York: International Universities Press, 1978) written with the collaboration of Heinz Kohut and edited by Arnold Goldberg helps to clarify how empathic techniques differ from conventional psychoanalytic methods.

The Theory and Practice of Self Psychology (New York: Brunner/Mazel, 1986) by Marjorie Taggart White and Marcella Bakur Weiner. Self psychology comes to life in this book, which is unusually readable for an analytic text and filled with fascinating clinical examples. The authors address the critical concepts of aggression, grandiosity, idealization, and empathy and discuss how special populations like child abusers and the elderly can be aided by self psychology.

Page 10 William Ickes, a psychologist at the University of Texas in Arlington, is the researcher most responsible for making empathy—and specifically empathic accuracy—a major focus of psychological research. Ickes edited *Empathic Accuracy* (New York: Guilford Press, 1997), a collection of scholarly articles on the evolutionary origins and physiological aspects of empathy, gender differences in empathic abilities, empathy's role in creating and maintaining intimate relationships, and the difference between "automatic" and "controlled" empathy.

Ickes defines empathic accuracy as "a form of complex psychological inference in which observation, memory, knowledge, and reasoning are combined to yield insights into the thougths and feelings of others." Empathy, he argues, is critical to our success in social and business relationships:

> Empathically accurate perceivers are those who are consistently good at "reading" other people's thoughts and feelings. All else being equal, they are likely to be the most tactful advisors, the most diplomatic officials, the most effective negotiators, the most electable politicians, the most productive salespersons, the most successful teachers, and the most insightful therapists. [p. 2, *Empathic Accuracy*]

"Empathic inference" In Ickes, p. 2.

Page 13 My first book, written primarily for a professional audience, is *Treatment of Abuse and Addiction: A Holistic Approach* (Northvale, NJ: Jason Aronson, 1997).

Chapter 3: Wired for Empathy

Pages 24–25 The slime mold and ant-loving caterpillar examples are used in R. Buck and B. Ginsburg, "Communicative Genes and the Evolution of Empathy" in *Empathic Accuracy*, pp. 17–43.

Page 26 Jonathan Weiner, *The Beak of the Finch: A Story of Evolution in Our Time* (New York: Vintage, 1994), p. 239.

Page 27 Jeffrey Masson, *When Elephants Weep: The Emotional Lives of Animals* (New York: Delta, 1995) is the source of the stories on these pages. The elephant and rhino story appears on page 155, and the sparrow in the chimp cage on page 117. Toto the chimp story appears on page 161. Masson cites the original source of the Toto story as C. Kearton, 1925, cited in *The Great Apes: A Study of Anthropoid Life* (New Haven, CT: Yale University Press, 1929) by Robert Yerkes and Ada Yerkes, p. 298.

Page 29 *Empathic Accuracy*, edited by William Ickes, contains several interesting sections about nonverbal communication and decoding skills; see R. Buck and B. Ginsburg, "Communicative Genes and the Evolution of Empathy" (chapter 1) and N. Eisenberg, B. Murphy, and S. Shepard, "The Development of Empathic Accuracy" (chapter 3).

Page 31 The experiment with monkeys is described on pp. 103–104 of Daniel Goleman's groundbreaking book *Emotional Intelligence: Why It Can Matter More than IQ* (New York: Bantam, 1995). See also L. Brothers, "A Biological Perspective on Empathy," *American Journal of Psychiatry* (1989) 146, 1.

Pages 31–33 For insights into the development of empathy in children the following books may be especially helpful: Bruno Bettelheim, *The Uses of Enchantment: The Meaning and Importance of Fairy Tales* (New York: Vintage, 1977); Robert Coles, *The Spiritual Life of Children* (Boston: Houghton Mifflin, 1990); Erik H. Erikson, *Childhood and Society* (New York: W.W. Norton, 1993); Alice Miller, *Prisoners of Childhood* (New York: Basic Books, 1981); William Pollack, *Real Boys* (New York: Henry Holt, 1998); Daniel Stern, *The Interpersonal World of the Infant* (New York: Basic Books, 1987).

Chapter 4: Expressing Empathy

Page 40 **"Climbing mountains and pursuing empathy"** in S. Hodges and D. Wegner, "Automatic and Controlled Empathy" (chapter 11), *Empathic Accuracy*, p. 320.

Page 45 **The strenuous mood**   William James, "The Sentiment of Rationality," in John J. McDermott, ed., *The Writings of William James: A Comprehensive Edition* (Chicago: University of Chicago Press, 1977), p. 337.

Page 50 **"It is generally thought"**   In Robert W. Levenson and Anna M. Ruef, "Physiological aspects of emotional knowledge and rapport," in Ickes, *Empathic Accuracy*, p. 65

Page 50 **Negative emotions create intense physiological arousal**   See *Anger Kills: Seventeen Strategies for Controlling the Hostility That Can Harm Your Health* (New York: HarperPerennial, 1994 or Harper Paperbacks, 1993) by Redford Williams, M.D. and Virginia Williams, Ph.D. This practical guide to understanding how anger affects physical and emotional health lists empathy as one of seventeen "survival skills" recommended to control hostility. See pages 141–146.

Dean Ornish also discusses the effects of hostility on premature death and disease in *Love and Survival: The Scientific Basis for the Healing Power of Intimacy* (New York: HarperCollins, 1998), pages 58–61. Ornish reviews current research on the influence of emotions, both positive and negative, on emotional and physical well-being.

Page 53 Physiological synchrony is discussed in R. W. Levenson and A. M. Ruef, "Physiological Aspects of Emotional Knowledge and Rapport" (chapter 2) in *Empathic Accuracy*, pp. 44–69.

Page 53 **"an autonomic nervous system response"**   In Levenson and Ruef, p. 48.

Pages 55–56 **Facial mimicry**   See Levenson and Ruef, pp. 56–59.

Page 55 Edgar Allan Poe quote is cited in R. W. Levenson, Page Ekman and W. V. Friesen, "Voluntary facial action generates emotional-specific autonomic nervous system activity," *Psychophysiology* (1990):45, 363–384.

Psychologist Paul Ekman of U.C. San Francisco has conducted many studies on facial expression; see Paul Ekman and Wallace Friesen, *Unmasking the Face* (Englewood Cliffs, NJ: Prentice Hall, 1975). See also Daniel McNeill, *The Face* (Boston: Little Brown, 1998).

Page 55 The golf tee experiment is described in R. J. Larsen, M. Kasimatis, and K. Frey (1992), "Facilitating the furrowed brow: An unobtrusive test of the facial feedback hypothesis applied to unpleasant affect," *Cognition and Emotion*, 6, pp. 321–338.

The pen between the teeth experiment is described in F. Strack, L. Martin and W. Stepper (1988), "Inhibiting and facilitating condition of the human smile: A nonobtrusive test of the facial feedback hypothesis," *Journal of Personality and Social Psychology*, 54, pp. 768–777.

Page 56 **Smiling and facial mimicry**   In *Empathic Accuracy*, editor William Ickes comments on p. 57:

While almost all facial expressions have the capacity to induce mimicry, it seems that some are particularly powerful. In the emotional realm, for example, smiles seem to be especially potent, having the capacity to induce smiles in others directly and almost irresistibly, without any appreciable cognitive mediation.

Page 59 **"Psychologists who study the origins of male anger"** See Robin Fivush, "Exploring sex differences in the emotional content of mother-child conversations about the past," *Sex Roles*, 20 (1989):675–91; Greif, E., Alvarez, M., and Ulman, K., "Recognizing emotions in other people: Sex differences in socialization," Paper presented at the biomedical meeting of the Society for Research in Child Development, Boston (April 1981), p. 44.

"It is very challenging . . ." in William Pollack, *Real Boys: Rescuing Our Sons From the Myth of Boyhood* (New York: Henry Holt, 1999), p. 44.

"A boy who is cared about . . ." in Pollack, *Real Boys*, p. 350; end of quote in italics appears on p. 356.

For additional reading on violence and aggression, I recommend psychiatrist Jim Gilligan's recent book *Violence: Reflections on a National Epidemic* (New York: Vintage, 1997). A psychiatrist at a hospital for the criminally insane, Gilligan tells the stories of the rapists and convicted murderers he treated over a period of twenty-five years. He concludes that shame and humiliation are the common denominators underlying violent crimes, and he specifically targets poverty and the humiliations that accompany lack of financial security.

Page 63 For the Mahatma Gandhi story we thank Manfred B. Steger, Ph.D., Associate Professor of Political Science at Illinois State University and author of the forthcoming book *Gandhi's Dilemma: Nonviolent Principles or Nationist Power* (St. Martin's, 2000). Perle Besserman, Ph.D., author of *Kabbalah: The Way of the Jewish Mystics* and numerous other books, first brought this story to our attention.

Chapter 5: Empathic Listening

For a general reference on the art of listening see Lawrence E. Hedges, *Listening Perspectives* (Northvale, NJ: Jason Aronson, 1983).

Page 65 The two ears and one mouth phrase is attributed to the fifth century B.C. Greek philosopher Zeno, who said: "The reason why we have two ears and only one mouth is that we may listen the more and talk the less."

Pages 65–66 Quaker writer Douglas Steere is quoted in *Spiritual Literacy: Reading the Sacred in Everyday Life* (New York: Scribners, 1996) by Frederic and Mary Ann Brussat, p. 283.

Page 78 **"By learning to tune out"** In T. Graham and W. Ickes, "When Women's Intuition Isn't Greater Than Men's," *Empathic Accuracy*, p. 140. The Hancock/Ickes article referred to in this quotation is M. Hancock and W. Ickes (1996), "Empathic accuracy: When does the perceiver-target relationship make a difference?" *Journal of Social and Personal Relationships* 13, 179–199.

Page 78 Heinz Kohut distinguishes empathy from both sympathy and intuition in his long, erudite paper "Reflections on Advances in Self Psychology" in Goldberg, ed., *Advances in Self Psychology*, pages 473–552.

See also L. Wispé, "The distinction between sympathy and empathy: To call forth a concept, a word is needed," *Journal of Personality and Social Psychology*, 50 (1986): 314–321.

Pages 79–80 **The difference between empathy and sympathy**   "Pathos" is the Greek root of both words. According to Dana Burgess, associate professor of classics at Whitman College, "pathos" has several meanings relevant to our discussion of empathy:

> At its most root level in Greek "pathos" means "that which happens to someone," from which it can mean an "incident" or an "accident." The meaning closest to this is "experience," so "pathos" can mean simply what you experience, either for good or bad. It is often used in the negative sense as "the bad things one experiences" or "misfortune."
>
> A second meaning is "emotion" or "passion." This is the sense in which Aristotle used the term and it is this sense which was so important for European aesthetic theory as in "the pathos of the drama."
>
> The first meaning is about what happens to us and the second meaning is about how we feel about what happens to us.

Page 85 **"The next time you get in an argument"**   In *On Becoming a Person: A Therapist's View of Psychotherapy* (Boston, New York: Houghton Mifflin, 1961) by Carl Rogers, pp. 332–333.

In this classic work, Rogers explores human growth and potential, offering fascinating insights into the therapeutic process in general and "client-centered therapy" in particular. I have always been impressed by Rogers' empathic ability to see the underlying hurt in others and bring it forth with great tact and sensitivity. Interested readers might also look at Rogers' *Becoming Partners: Marriage and Its Alternatives* (New York: Delacorte, 1972).

Rogers explains his view of empathy in C. R. Rogers (1975), "Empathic: An unappreciated way of being," *The Counseling Psychologist*, 5, 2–10.

Chapter 6: Sex, Intimacy, and Empathy

Page 86 **"the most powerful enactment"**   In Rollo May, *Love and Will* (New York: W.W. Norton, 1969), p. 113. This book describes with poignant insight how meaning can be obtained through intimacy.

Page 92 **"Falling in love"**   Elvin Semrad, *The Heart of a Therapist* (Northvale, NJ: Jason Aronson, 1980), p. 33.

Page 93 **"I have to know"**   In Erich Fromm, *The Art of Loving* (New York: Harper-Perennial, 1989), p. 29. This classic work examines love in all its varied aspects including romantic love, parental love, brotherly love, erotic love, self-love, and love of God.

Page 93 For thoughts on the relationship between narcissism and objectivity, see Fromm, *The Art of Loving*, p. 109. For a more scholarly treatment of narcissism (and particularly the power of empathy to help people emerge from narcissism) see Ernest S. Wolf, M.D., *Treating the Self: Elements of Clinical Self Psychology* (New York: Guilford Press, 1999).

Pages 99–100 Ann Landers column in the *Walla Walla Union Bulletin*, December 20, 1998.

Page 102 V. S. Helgeson (1993), "Implications of agency and communion for patients and spouse adjustment to a first coronary event," *Journal of Personality and Social Psychology* 64/5: 807–816.

Pages 102–103 For inspiring many of the ideas contained in these pages, we acknowledge the work of Ernest Kurtz, Ph.D., coauthor with Katherine Ketcham of *The Spirituality of Imperfection* (New York: Bantam, 1992).

Page 104 **"To empathize with a person"**   In S. D. Hodges and D. M. Wegner, "Automatic and Controlled Empathy," *Empathic Accuracy* (chapter 11), p. 312.

Hodges and Wegner cite several references in this quotation: J. Piaget and B. Inhelder, *The Child's Conception of Space* (London: Routledge & Kegan Paul, 1956), F.J. Landon and J. L. Lunzer (trans.); D. T. Regan and J. Totten, "Empathy and attribution: Turning observers into actors," *Journal of Personality and Social Psychology*, 32 (1975):850–856; G. H. Bower, "Experiments in story comprehension and recall," *Discourse Processes*, 1 (1978):211–231; D. M. Wegner and T. Giuliano, "Social awareness in story comprehension," *Social Cognition*, 2, 1983:1–17; E. Stotland, "Exploratory investigations in empathy," in L. Berkowitz (ed.), *Advances in Experimental Social Psychology* (New York: Academic Press, 1969), vol. 4, pp. 271–314; C. Hoffman, W. Mischel, and K. Mazze, "The role of purpose in the organization of information about behavior: Trait-based versus goal-based categories in person cognition," *Journal of Personality and Social Psychology*, 40 (1981):211–225; M. W. Baldwin and J. G. Holmes, "Salient private audiences and awareness of the self," *Journal of Personality and Social Psychology*, 52 (1987):1087–1098.

Page 104 Many psychologists and psychiatrists have written on the phenomenon of projection. For readers who would like more information on projection, I recommend the following books: Richard Chessick, *Intensive Psychotherapy of the Borderline Patient* (Northvale, NJ: Jason Aronson, 1977); Althea Horner, *Object Relations and the Developing Ego in Therapy* (Northvale, NJ: Jason Aronson, 1979); Otto Kernberg, *Borderline Conditions and Pathological Narcissism* (Northvale, NJ: Jason Aronson, 1975); Joel Latner, *The Gestalt Therapy Book* (New York: Bantam, 1974); Frederick Perls, *Gestalt Therapy Verbatim* (New York: Bantam, 1991); Marjorie White and Marcella Weiner, *The Theory and Practice of Self Psychology* (New York: Brunner/Mazel, 1986).

Page 106 **"The individual increasingly comes to feel"**   In Rogers, *On Becoming a Person*, p. 119.

Pages 106–107 **"You're so sure you're right"**   In *Lonesome Dove* (New York: Simon & Schuster, 1985), p. 625.

Pages 107–108 **"Because each person"**   In *The Healing Connection: How Women Form Relationships in Therapy and in Life* (Boston: Beacon, 1997) by Jean Baker Miller, M.D. and Irene Pierce Stiver, Ph.D., p. 29.
Miller and Stiver highlight the central role of mutual empathy in creating and maintaining intimacy. This important book, which features the authors' work at the Wellesley College Stone Center in Wellesley, Massachusetts, also explores "relational therapy" and the moments of "connection" that help to foster individual development.

Page 111 **"The primary word I-Thou"**   In *I and Thou* (New York: Charles Scribner's Sons, 1958) by Martin Buber, trans. by Ronald Gregor Smith, page 11.

Page 112   The Rabbe Moshe Leib story is often told; this version is from *A Dialogue with Hasidic Tales: Hallowing the Everydays* (New York: Insight Books, 1988) by Maurice S. Friedman, p. 86.

Chapter 7: The Dark Side of Empathy

Pages 113–114   In *The Gift of Fear* (New York: Dell, 1997) and its sequel, *Protecting the Gift: Keeping Children and Teenagers Safe (and Parents Sane)* (New York: Dial Press, 1999), violence expert Gavin de Becker argues persuasively that intuition (i.e., empathy) is a powerful defense against violence and victimhood.

Pages 116–117   The Hitler quotations appear in Ian Kershaw's superb 845-page biography, *Hitler: 1889–1936 Hubris* (New York: W.W. Norton, 1998). "I can't free myself . . ." (p. 454); "They spring, yelling . . ." (p. 588); "Not every one of you . . ." (p. 591).

Page 118 **"If anything motivated me"**   In *All Rivers Run to the Sea: Memoirs* (New York: Knopf, 1995) by Elie Wiesel, pp. 80–81.

Pages 131–132   Story told by Bernard Lown, M.D., of Harvard University School of Public Health appears in the introduction to *The Healing Heart: Antidotes to Panic and Helplessness* (New York: Avon, 1983) by Norman Cousins, pp. 13–14.

Page 134 Story appears in *Protecting the Gift*, pp. 210–212.

Page 136 Exit, neglect, voice and loyalty behaviors are discussed in V. L. Bisson-nette, C. E. Rusbult, and S. D. Kilpatrick, "Empathic Accuracy and Marital Conflict Resolution," *Empathic Accuracy* (chapter 9), pp. 252–254. See also W. Ickes and J. A. Simpson, "Managing Empathic Accuracy in Close Relationships," in *Empathic Accuracy* (chapter 8).

University of Washington psychologist John Gottman has analyzed the crucial role of empathy and emotional intelligence in intimate relationships in *Why Marriages Succeed or Fail* (New York: Simon and Schuster, 1994) and *What Predicts Divorce: The Relationship Between Marital Processes and Marital Outcomes* (Hillsdale, NJ: Lawrence Erlbaum Associates, Inc., 1993).

For gender differences in emotional expressions, see Leslie R. Brody and Judith A. Hall, "Gender and Emotion," in Michael Lewis and Jeannette Haviland, eds., *Handbook of Emotions* (New York: Guilford, 1993).

Page 140 "Hate Rock" by Achy Obejas in the *Chicago Tribune*, March 16, 1999, Section 2, p. 1.

Chapter 8: Honesty

Page 155 **"A group of students"** This story is adapted from a story that appears in *Cutting Through Spiritual Materialism* (Boston: Shambhala, 1987) by Chögyam Trungpa, edited by John Baker and Marvin Casper, p. 41.

Page 160 **"At her first summer job."** In *Respect: An Exploration* (Reading, MA: Perseus, 1999) by Sara Lawrence-Lightfoot, pp. 6–7.

Page 161 The importance of empathy in the present moment is explained in G. Thomas and G.J.O. Fletcher, "Empathic Accuracy in Close Relationships," in *Empathic Accuracy*, p. 195. Thomas and Fletcher comment:

> Empathic accuracy requires an awareness of a target's internal states on a moment-by-moment basis, rather than simply a knowledge of more stable and enduring characteristics, such as target's personality, traits, and opinions.

Page 161 The influence of stereotypes and biases on empathic accuracy is discussed in Thomas and Fletcher article in Ickes, *Empathic Accuracy*, pp. 203–207.

Page 161 Cathy Spatz Widom's research was featured in a *Boston Globe* article, "Stress early in life may leave imprint for violence," *Boston Globe*, October 16, 1995, pp. 29–32.

Page 161 Misinterpreting positive behaviors: see the following scholarly articles: J. M. Gottman et al., "Behavior exchange theory and marital decision making," *Journal of Personality and Social Psychology*, 34 (1976): 14–23; D. M. Guthrie and P. Noller,

"Married couples' perceptions of one another in emotional situations," in P. Noller and M. A. Fitzpatrick (eds.), *Perspectives on Marital Interaction* (Cleveland, OH: Multilingual Matters), pp. 153–181; P. Noller, "Misunderstandings in marital communication: A study of couples' nonverbal communication," *Journal of Personality and Social Psychology* 39 (1980) : 1135–1148; P. Noller and C. Venardos, "Communication awareness in married couples," *Journal of Social and Personal Relationships* 3 (1986): 31–42.

Page 162 **Importance of passion and romance** See Thomas and Fletcher article in Ickes, *Empathic Accuracy*, page 206:

> . . . a strong belief in the importance of passion and romance was related to higher levels of empathic accuracy . . . emphasizing the importance of passion and romance would predispose couples to focus on the internal dynamics of their own relationships, therefore facilitating superior empathic inferences.

Page 162 **"Faith creates its own verification"** (William James) see note in chapter 4, p. 59.

Complacency and familiarity in relationships See W. Ickes and J. A. Simpson, "Managing Empathic Accuracy in Close Relationships," in *Empathic Accuracy* (chapter 8). Ickes and Simpson argue that perceptual biases can arise from knowing each other too well, citing research by A. L. Sillars, "Attributions and interpersonal conflict resolution," in J. H. Harvey, W. J. Ickes, and R. F. Kidd (eds.), *New Directions in Attribution Research* (Hillsdale, NJ: Erlbaum, 1981), vol. 3, pp. 279–305.

Ickes and Simpson believe that familiarity can result in less understanding because:

> . . . partners who know each other well may be less motivated to seek out new and potentially diagnostic information about the other that could improve empathic understanding. Excessive familiarity can also reduce empathic understanding by solidifying old impressions that partners have of each other that are no longer valid. [p. 232]

In G. Thomas and G. J. O. Fletcher, "Empathic Accuracy in Close Relationships," p. 212:

> Empathic accuracy may peak during the earlier years of marriage when couples are expending considerable cognitive effort to understand their partners and negotiate their relationships. As relationships stabilize over a very long period of time, however, partners become complacent and extremely familiar with one another, and therefore become less motivated to actively assess their partners' thoughts and feelings.

Chapter 9: Humility

Pages 167–168 Mitch Albom, *Tuesdays with Morrie: An Old Man, a Young Man, and Life's Greatest Lesson* (New York: Doubleday, 1997).

Page 167 The "interesting question" conversation takes place on pp. 133–134.

Page 168 Morrie's version of the little wave story is told on pp. 179–180.

Page 169 **"Well, Oren"** Oren Lyons story is told in Huston Smith, in *The World's Religions* (New York: HarperCollins, 1991), p. 371.

Page 170 The stork story is adapted from one told by Martin Buber in *Tales of the Hasidim: The Later Masters* (New York: Schocken, 1948), pp. 231–232.

Page 171 **"Humility is just as much"** In *Markings* (London: Faber and Faber Ltd.), p. 147.

Page 172 **"To have humility"** Ibid., p. 148.

Page 173 **Egocentrism** See N. Eisenberg, B. C. Murphy, and S. Shepard, "The Development of Empathic Accuracy," in *Empathic Accuracy*, pp. 73–116; see also E. T. Higgins, "Role taking and social judgment: Alternative perspectives and processes," in J. H. Flavell and L. Ross (eds.) *Social Cognitive Development* (New York: Cambridge University Press, 1981), pp. 119–153.

Page 173 **Perspective taking** See S. Hodges and D. Wegner, "Automatic and Controlled Empathy" in Ickes, *Empathic Accuracy*, chap. 11, pp. 323–327. The references at the end of the chapter on pp. 334–339 will guide interested readers to further studies.

Page 174 Daniel Goleman discusses empathy throughout his book *Emotional Intelligence*; see especially chapter 7, "The Roots of Empathy," pp. 96–110.

Page 174 **Empathy can be taught** See W. Ickes, C. Marangoni, and S. Garcia, "Studying Empathic Accuracy in a Clinically Relevant Context," in *Empathic Accuracy*, pp. 282–310.

See also Part 4 of Daniel Goleman's *Emotional Intelligence*, particularly chapter 16, "Schooling the Emotions." In this chapter Goleman discusses various curriculums like "Self Science" designed to teach children how to manage and express their feelings, practice empathic listening, take others' perspectives, communicate effectively, and resolve disagreements.

Page 175 **"If you want to save your soul"** In *Soul Friend* (San Francisco: Harper & Row, 1977), by Kenneth Leech, p. 43. *The Wisdom of the Desert* (Boston: Shambhala, 1994), trans. by Thomas Merton, contains many stories about the value of silence. "There is nothing better than to keep silent" (p. 128). One of the desert monks, it is said, carried a stone in his mouth for three years until he learned to be silent.

Page 176 **"You'll come to my grave?"** In *Tuesdays with Morrie*, p. 170.

Page 176 **"Prayer arises"** In *Ways of Imperfection: An Exploration of Christian Spirituality* (Springfield, IL: Templegate, 1985) by Simon Tugwell, p. 229.

Page 176 Harvard experiments by Herbert Benson are described in his book *Beyond the Relaxation Response* (New York: Times Books, 1984).

Page 176 *Healing Words* (San Francisco: HarperSanFrancisco, 1993) by Larry Dossey. For a review of the relevant research see chapter 11, pp. 169–195. The effects of prayer on fungi, yeast, and bacteria are described on pp. 190–192.

Chapter 10: Acceptance

Page 178 The John F. Kennedy, Jr., story was told many times on television and in print media. Syndicated columnist Ellen Goodman of the *Boston Globe* mentioned this story in her July 22, 1999, column.

Page 179 **"By acceptance I mean"** In *On Becoming a Person: A Therapist's View of Psychotherapy* (Boston: Houghton Mifflin, 1961), p. 34.

Page 180 **"The theory of I'm O.K., You're O.K. is deadly teaching"** In *Mastering Sadhana: On Retreat with Anthony de Mello* (New York: Doubleday, 1988) by Carlos G. Valles, p. 24–25.

Page 181 **William James on surrender** *The Varieties of Religious Experience* (New York: Touchstone, 1997) by William James, p. 101.

Page 181 **"When I accept myself as I am"** In *On Becoming a Person* by Rogers, p. 17.

Page 183 **"Let go your hold"** *Varieties of Religious Experience*, p. 101. James tells the story on page 102.

Page 184 **"They will say"** Antonio Porchia, trans. W. S. Merwin, *Voices* (Chicago: Big Table, 1969), p. 24.

Page 186 **"If I am attached to another person"** In *The Art of Loving*, p. 101.

Page 186 **"Self-love establishes"** In *By Way of the Heart: Toward a Holistic Christian Spirituality* (Mahwah, NJ: Paulist Press, 1989) by Wilkie Au, p. 31.

Chapter 11: Tolerance

Page 191 **"Judge not"** In *The Holy Bible* (New York: Thomas Nelson and Sons, 1952), Matthew 7:1–5.

Pages 191–192 My father's O.S.S. unit is featured in Also Icardi, *American Master Spy* (New York: University Books, Inc., 1954). See also R. Harris Smith, *OSS: The Secret History of America's First Central Intelligence Agency* (Berkeley, CA: University of California Press, 1972).

Page 193 Zillman's research on rage is described in "Mental Control of Angry Aggression," in *Handbook of Mental Control* (Englewood Cliffs, NJ: Prentice Hall, 1993), edited by Daniel Wegner and James Pennebaker.

For further thoughts on anger, rage, aggression, and violence, see Williams and Williams, *Anger Kills; Anger: The Misunderstood Emotion* (New York: Touchstone, 1989) and James Gilligan, *Violence.*

Goleman notes on page 60: "A universal trigger for anger is the sense of being endangered."

Page 194 Empathy weakened by biases   See S. Hodges and D. Wegman, "Automatic and Controlled Empathy," in Ickes, ed., *Empathic Accuracy.* "The tendency to adopt another person's perspective . . ." quotation appears on page 319 of this article.

Page 194 "If I want to learn the art of loving"   In Fromm, *The Art of Loving,* p. 109.

Page 195   This old Hasidic tale has been told and retold in many versions; in our retelling of this story we drew on *Peacemaking Day by Day* (Pax Christi, 348 East Tenth St., Erie, PA 26503).

Page 197 "A woman complained"   Story in de Mello, *Heart of the Enlightened* (New York: Doubleday, 1989), p. 122.

Page 198 "When we are intolerant"   In Williams and Williams, *Anger Kills,* p. 147.

Page 198 Experiments on anger and death   See John C. Barefoot, W. Grant Dahlstrom, and Redford B. Williams, "Hostility, CHD incidence, and total mortality: A 25-year follow-up study of 255 physicians," 45 *Psychosomatic Medicine* (1983), pp. 59–63.

Effects of isolation and loneliness on heart disease   See Redford B. Williams et al., "Prognostic importance of social and economic resources among medically treated patients with angiographically documented coronary artery disease," *Journal of the American Medical Association* 267 (1992), 520–524; see also Redford Williams, *The Trusting Heart* (New York: New York Times Books/Random House, 1989).

Page 199   Williams' key points are elaborated in *Anger Kills,* p. 60.

Chapter 12: Gratitude

Page 200 "A blind man was begging"   Our version of this favorite story is taken from Gabriel Daly, "Widening Horizons," *The Tablet* 244:7811 (March 31, 1990), pp. 419–420.

Pages 204–205   Heinz Kohut, "On Empathy," in *The Search for the Self;* the story we include here ("About fifteen years ago . . .") is told in vol. 4, pp. 534–535.

Page 206   Hoffer is quoted without specific citation by James Hillman in Sy Safransky, "The Myth of Therapy: An Interview with James Hillman," *The Sun*; Issue 185 (April 1991): 2–19.

Page 207 **"Drink your tomato juice"**   In Joseph Campbell, *The Power of Myth* (New York: Doubleday, 1988), pp. 117–118.

Pages 207–208 The marshmallow challenge experiment is described in Yuichi Shoda, Walter Mischel, and Philip K. Peake, "Predicting adolescent cognitive and self-regulatory competencies from preschool delay of gratification," *Developmental Psychology*, 26, 6 (1990): 978–986.

Chapter 13: Faith

Pages 211–212 Tolstoy's struggle with depression and rediscovery of faith appear in William James, *The Varieties of Religious Experience*, pp. 130–135 and 156–157.

Page 215 Breast cancer study is described in David Spiegel, *Living Beyond Limits: New Hope and Help for Facing Life-Threatening Illness* (New York: Ballantine, 1993). See also, D.J. Spiegel, et al., "Effect of psychosocial treatment on survival of patients with metastatic breast cancer," *The Lancet*, 1989, ii: 888–891.

Page 216 **"I had to sit down"**   In Spiegel, *Living Beyond Limits*, p. 78.

Page 218 **"You love too indiscriminately"**   This excerpt is from Melannie Svoboda, *Everyday Epiphanies: Seeing the Sacred in Everything* (Mystic, CT: Twenty-Third Publications, 1998) p. 54.

Chapter 14: Hope

Page 223 Dozens of studies on hope and optimism are presented in Martin E. Seligman, *Learned Optimism* (New York: Knopf, 1991).

Page 223–224 Vicki Helgeson and Heidi Fritz, "Cognitive adaptation as a predictor of new coronary events after percutaneous transluminal coronary angioplasty," *Psychosomatic Medicine* 61 (1999): 488–495.

Page 224 **The effect of optimism on sales**   Experiment is described in Seligman, *Learned Optimism*, pp. 97–107.

Page 224 **Hope and academic success**   C. R. Snyder et al., "The will and the ways: Development and validation of an individual-differences measure of hope," *Journal of Personality and Social Psychology* 60, 4 (1991): 579; see also Daniel Goleman's interview with Snyder in *The New York Times* (Dec. 24, 1991).

Page 225 Winston Churchill story is told in Robert Lewis Taylor, *Winston Churchill: The Biography of a Great Man 1874–1965* (New York: Pocket Books, 1965), pp. 74–75.

Page 226 **"Every week, for two winters and two summers"**   Nancy Burke is quoted in Brussat and Brussat, *Spiritual Literacy*, p. 303, who cite Burke's book *Meditations for Health* (New York: Wings Books, 1995).

Chapter 15: Forgiveness

Page 235 **"He acknowledges that it's a struggle"**   Sister Helen Prejean, *Dead Man Walking: An Eyewitness Account of the Death Penalty in the U.S.* (New York: Random House, 1994), pp. 244–245.

Page 237 **"Ubuntu . . . speaks about the essence"**   Desmond Tutu is quoted in *Spirituality & Health*, Winter 1999, p. 29; this passage appears in Tutu's foreword to Robert Enright and Joanna North (eds.) *Exploring Forgiveness* (University of Wisconsin Press).

Page 238 **"An old innkeeper kept two ledgers"**   This story has been told in many versions. Our adaptation is drawn from Abraham J. Twerski, *Living Each Day* (Brooklyn, NY: Mesorah, 1988), p. 342.

Pages 238–239 Pennebaker's journal writing exercises are described in James Pennebaker, "Putting stress into words: Health, linguistic and therapeutic implications," paper presented at the American Psychological Association meeting, Washington, DC (1992). See also: James W. Pennebaker, *Opening Up: The Healing Power of Confiding in Others* (New York: William Morrow, 1990).

Pages 239–240 **"I love a broad margin to my life"**   Henry David Thoreau, *Walden and Other Writings* (New York: Bantam, 1971), p. 188.

RECOMMENDED READINGS

Albom, Mitch. *Tuesdays with Morrie: An Old Man, a Young Man, and Life's Greatest Lesson*. New York: Doubleday, 1997.

Benson, Herbert. *Timeless Healing*. New York: Scribners, 1996.

Cooper, Kenneth. *It's Better to Believe*. Nashville: Thomas Nelson, 1995.

Dossey, Larry. *Healing Words*. San Francisco: HarperSanFrancisco, 1993.

Frankl, Victor. *The Will to Meaning*. New York: Plume, 1969.

Fromm, Erich. *The Art of Loving*. New York: Harper and Row, 1956.

Gibran, Kahlil, *Tear and a Smile* (translated by H. M. Nahmad). New York: Knopf, 1950.

Gibran, Kahlil, *Broken Wings* (translated by Juan Cole). New York: Penguin USA, 1998.

Gilligan, James, *Violence: Reflections on a National Epidemic*. New York: Putnam, 1996.

Goleman, Daniel. *Emotional Intelligence: Why It Can Matter More Than IQ*. New York: Bantam, 1995.

Grollman, Earl. *Living When a Loved One Has Died*. Boston: Beacon, 1997.

Hallowell, Edward. *Connect: Twelve Vital Ties That Open Your Heart*. New York: Pantheon, 1999.

Kabat-Zinn, Jon. *Wherever You Go There You Are*. New York: Hyperion, 1994.

Keen, Sam. *To Love and Be Loved*. New York: Bantam, 1997.

Kurtz, Ernest and Katherine Ketcham. *The Spirituality of Imperfection*. New York: Bantam, 1992.

Lynch, James J. *The Broken Heart*. New York: Basic Books, 1977; Baltimore: Bancroft, 1998.

Maslow, Abraham. *The Farther Reaches of Human Nature*. New York: Viking, 1971.

Miller, Alice. *The Drama of the Gifted Child: The Search for the True Self*. New York: Basic Books, 1994.

Miller, Alice. *The Untouched Key: Tracing Childhood Trauma in Creativity and Destructiveness*. New York: Doubleday, 1990.

Miller, Jean Baker and Stiver, Irene Pierce. *The Healing Connection: How Women Form Relationships in Therapy and Life*. Boston: Beacon, 1997.

Parker, Beulah. *My Language Is Me*. New York: Ballantine, 1962.

Pelletier, Kenneth. *Sound Mind—Sound Body*. New York: Simon & Schuster, 1994.

Pert, Candace. *Molecules of Emotion: Why We Feel the Way We Feel*. New York: Scribner Books/Simon & Schuster, 1997.

Pipher, Mary. *Reviving Ophelia: Saving the Selves of Adolescent Girls*. New York: Ballantine, 1995.

Pollack, William. *Real Boys: Rescuing Our Sons from the Myths of Boyhood*. New York: Random House, 1998.

Rogers, Carl. *On Becoming a Person: A Therapist's View of Psychotherapy*. New York: Houghton Mifflin, 1961.

Wolpe, Rabbi David. *Making Loss Matter: Creating Meaning in Difficult Times*. New York: Riverhead, 1999.

ACKNOWLEDGMENTS

It seems that I have been working on this book in one form or another for the last twenty-five years. So many wonderful people have helped directly and indirectly.

Everyone needs anchors in their lives and my wife Karen has been mine. We met at a difficult time in my life and almost instantly I felt my spirit return. Your love of life and most important your love for meaningful relationships is melted into these pages. Your idea to "write another book for the public" was all I needed to dig in again. Thank you for reading every word and for offering your honest, insightful comments on each and every draft of the manuscript. It takes such courage to be honest, and that is your gift. Your heart seems to have endless possibilities.

The delights of my life are our children. No experience teaches more about the profound importance of empathy than parenting. To our daughter Erica, your courage and engaging social presence have always been an inspiration to me. Your energy to explore and "try new things" and meet "different kinds of people" reveals your openness to the world and brings fresh air to your family. To our daughter Alaina (Miss Congeniality), your warmth and loving way make you a delight to be with daily. Every "I love you, Dad" made the next page easier to write, the next story more meaningful to relate.

To my greatest teachers, my mother Camie and my father Arthur, Sr. (Tudor). I am eternally grateful for your teaching me the true meaning of empathy and unwavering love.

To my dear friend Kathy Ketcham, the master of the written word. Your insight, creativity, tenaciousness, and above all uncanny ability to take the spoken word and make it come to life on paper will be forever appreciated. Your empathy is woven throughout this book. You gave my private thoughts and, most important, the teachings of my family a clarity I could have never attained without your collaboration. Thank you for your patience, your unfailing belief in my work and, most important, your faith in the power of empathy. I will always be indebted.

To my agent Jane Dystel, your unmistakable candor, energy, dedication, and perseverance are most appreciated. To Jane's partner Miriam Goderich, my thanks for improving the proposal and final manuscript with your insightful comments.

To Brian Tart, editor-in-chief at Dutton Plume publishers. From our very first conversation I had a good feeling about our collaboration, and that feeling has grown to deep appreciation for your energy, enthusiasm, organizational skills, and your commitment to bring this book to the widest possible audience. I thank Lisa Johnson, publicity director at Dutton, for her prompt responses and publicity acumen, and I am grateful to Kara Howland, editorial assistant, and Susan Brown, copy editor, for their most competent efforts.

I have been most fortunate in having an extended family of relatives who are unfailing in their support of my work. For the love and kindness I have received over so many years I offer my very deep gratitude to Mary and Phil Ciaramicoli, Ann and Doc DiVittorio, Olga and Frank DiVittorio, Jeanne and Mark Fitzpatrick, Gerry and Richard Tessicini, and Donna and Philip Wood.

To my colleague Andrea Waldstein, LICSW. I know of no psychotherapist who has devoted more time or energy to understanding and implementing the power of empathy than you. We have had hundreds of conversations about the value of the empathic way. I thank you for your friendship and for helping me reach needed clarity in my thinking.

A note of appreciation to my friend, colleague, and exercise buddy, Bob Cherney, Ph.D., and his wife, Mary Ellen, for their supportive comments during the writing of this book, to my colleagues and long-time friends Valerie Sawyer-Smith, Ed.D., and Peter Smith, Ed.D., and to our dearest friends Diane and Richard Werner for proving that distance never separates hearts. A special thank you to Reverend Richard Fleck for his spiritual guidance over so many years, and to nurse specialist Frieda Albertini-Duffy and her affable husband, Dennis.

To Frankie Boyer of Langer Broadcasting's *Healthy Living* radio show in Boston. Thank you for your support, friendship, and belief in the value of talking about empathy on air. I learn and have fun on our weekly broadcasts—a great combination. Thanks also to John Marable, production manager, for teaching me "the radio ropes" early on.

To the Italian tenor Andrea Bocelli: "Romanza" released the passion that let the words flow. Your voice reminds me every day how music enlivens the soul.

A special thanks to my colleagues at MetroWest Wellness Center, MetroWest Medical Center, and Harvard Medical School for providing an empathic milieu to work within.

And most important, underlined a thousand times in red, I thank the individuals who have come to me for help. You have given me the enormous privilege of learning how broken hearts can be mended. You have deepened my understanding of human nature and given me the magnificent gift of faith. I am forever indebted.

—ARTHUR P. CIARAMICOLI
October 1999

One of empathy's most profound experiences is the realization that we are nothing without each other. I owe so much to so many. I am deeply grateful to Arthur Ciaramicoli, a man of passion and principles, whose willingness to open his life and his heart to me allowed this book to come into being. I am inspired by his courage, his wisdom, and his humility. For the laughter and the tears, I am forever indebted.

Literary agent Jane Dystel suggested my name to Arthur; for her role in creating and nurturing this collaboration, I am very grateful. I also thank Miriam Goderich, vice president of Jane Dystel Literary Management, for her help with the manuscript.

Kathleen Anderson, my literary agent, has an uncommonly generous spirit. I am grateful for her unwavering support, her love of the written word, and her calming presence.

Brian Tart at Dutton Plume never failed to offer his energy, enthusiasm, and support for this project. Kara Howland, editorial assistant, was a great help in the final stages of preparing the manuscript for publication and copy editor Susan Brown offered many helpful suggestions and sensitive revisions.

I learned about empathy first from my parents, Frank and Joan Ketcham, and my brothers and sisters, Mike Ketcham, John Ketcham, Billy Ketcham Heath, and Debbie Ketcham Goodeve. My mother and father would have loved this book; I only wish they could have seen it.

To my wonderful friends—Melinda Burgess, Sharon Kaufman-Osborn, Laurie Becker, Marilyn Dickinson, Tracee Simon, and the poker group—who listen to me, laugh and cry with me, and for some reason continue to seek my company, I am more than grateful. Special thanks to Melinda, who read the manuscript and offered the wisdom of her insight and experience.

To my buddies Perle Besserman and Manfred Steger, who give me so much and ask for so little in return—someday I will find a way to return the bounty you have bestowed upon me.

To Ruthanne, who allowed me to include her story in this book, I want to say that I will never forget you. Your spirit shines on.

I am indebted to Ernie Kurtz, who taught me about the connection between storytelling and spirituality; William F. Asbury, whose stories led to my very first book twenty years ago; Mel Schulstad, whose bigness of heart never fails to inspire me; and Dana Burgess, associate professor of classics at Whitman College, for his insights into the literal meaning of the word *empathy*.

To my children—Robyn, Alison, and Benjamin Spencer—whose patience, laughter, and consoling words have helped me through so many days and nights, I want to say that the work never came first. You are the sun, moon, and stars of my life, and there would be no light without you.

And, finally, I thank my husband, Patrick Spencer, whose kindness and compassion continue to expand the boundaries of the world I am so deeply privileged to inhabit. For all the gifts you have bestowed upon me, I owe more than gratitude.

—KATHY KETCHAM
October 1999

INDEX

None